T0319650

BETWEEN MONOPOLY AND FREE TRADE

PRINCETON ANALYTICAL SOCIOLOGY SERIES

# BETWEEN MONOPOLY AND FREE TRADE

The English East India Company, 1600–1757

*Emily Erikson*

PRINCETON UNIVERSITY PRESS

Princeton and Oxford

Published by Princeton University Press, 41 William Street, Princeton, New Jersey 08540
In the United Kingdom: Princeton University Press, 6 Oxford Street, Woodstock,
    Oxfordshire OX20 1TW

This book was published with the assistance of the Frederick W. Hilles Publication Fund
    of Yale University

press.princeton.edu

ISBN 978-0-691-15906-5
Library of Congress Control Number: 2014933831

British Library Cataloging-in-Publication Data is available

This book has been composed in Janson Text

Printed on acid-free paper ∞

Printed in the United States of America

10 9 8 7 6 5 4 3 2 1

# CONTENTS

———

# PREFACE

Although companies are relatively new to history—and are now so common as to be taken largely for granted—they have been an important social, economic, and political force since their first appearance. The English East India Company was one of the earliest companies and very possibly one of the most important to understanding the evolution of the modern world. It played a central role in Britain's rise to commercial prominence, the creation of the British Empire, and the integration of global commercial markets. Initially titled the Governor and Company of Merchants of London trading into the East Indies, the English Company was formed in the last years of the reign of Queen Elizabeth I. On December 31, 1600, Queen Elizabeth issued a charter granting the Company monopoly privileges to all overseas trade with the extensive area then called the East Indies, indicating the entire area east of the Cape of Good Hope and west of Cape Horn. It was not within the power of Queen Elizabeth to award a true monopoly, as English law was unable to legislate the rights of other nations to engage in trade, but the Crown charter granted the Company the enforceable right to exclude other English, and eventually British, citizens from overseas trade with the East.

Over the course of the next two centuries, the English Company significantly increased the overseas trade between Asia and Europe. It was not, however, responsible for introducing intercontinental trade or a market ethos to Asia. Prior to its incorporation, a long history of overseas commerce linked the regions of Africa, Asia, the Indonesian Archipelago, and the Middle East. England participated in this trade, but indirectly and as a marginal figure. The trade routes that linked it to the thriving commercial worlds of Asia stretched through the Mediterranean and Baltic Seas, past the opulent cities of Bukhara and Samarkand, as well as the Himalayan towns of Srinagar and Leh, to India and the Yellow River Valley in China. Many of the same goods that the English Company carried aboard their ships in the seventeenth century were carried along these routes, at times by boat, but also by horse, camel, steer, and even people, over long overland trails. Silk was traded for gold and silver; jade, exotic animals, ostriches, lions, and bears for fur and timber; resins, dyes, ceramics, and frankincense for pepper, cardamom, and nutmeg.

Beginning approximately with the voyage of Bartolomeu Dias around the Cape of Good Hope in 1488, elites of the northwestern European states sought to circumvent existing trade routes and establish direct links to the thriving commercial circuits of Islamic Eurasia and the Far East by way of the passage around Africa. Dias's voyage ushered in what has variously been called the Commercial Revolution, the Age of Commerce, the Age of Sail, and less appropriately the Age of Exploration and Discovery (as only remotely placed Europeans experienced it in this fashion). In this era, which lasted for roughly the next three centuries, there was a vast increase in overseas trade, new financial and commercial institutions were created to facilitate the ongoing process of market expansion, and a remarkable number of Europeans migrated to other areas of the world, bringing European institutions and practices along with them. The era ended with the onset of the Industrial Revolution, the invention of the steam engine, a largely integrated global commercial market, and a stable pattern of British world hegemony.

Soon after Dias's voyage, and only seven short years after Vasco da Gama was first able to successfully navigate the journey to Calicut, India (now Kozhikode) by way of the Cape route, the Portuguese Estado da Índia was established (1505). The Estado was a viceroyalty created to govern and extend Portuguese territorial possessions in India. King Manuel I of Portugal hoped to outflank the Ottomans and Mamluks and redirect the spice trade from their lands to the Cape route. He did not achieve great success in either endeavor, although the Portuguese did become a lasting presence in Asia. Perhaps because of the difficulties experienced by the Estado in achieving its goals, other European countries did not follow this model of direct state intervention. Instead, nearly all other regular European contact with the East was conducted under the auspices of state-sponsored companies holding domestic monopolies in their country of origin. Indeed by the seventeenth century, the chartered company seemed to be the favored instrument of European merchants and rulers for establishing trading links and extending political dominion—in the Americas as well as in Asia.

Though most chartered companies were commercial in nature, this did not indicate that they were not tied to the state or unwilling to engage in militaristic territorial acquisition—as we might assume with the multinational organizations of the contemporary world. Often the company form provided only a thin buffer for the state. In significant cases, European East India companies were formed with the specific intent to further state interests by aggressively colonizing and settling areas of Asia. This was true, for example, of the Dutch East India Company and early iterations of the French East India Company.

Unlike these competitors, the English Company was largely commercial at its inception. The group of merchants behind its creation included many of the leading merchants of London. A large proportion of them had previously been active in the Levant Company, which dealt in the overland trade to the East (Brenner 2003: 48). The Company's first voyage, commanded by Sir James Lancaster and composed of four ships (the *Dragon*, *Hector*, *Ascension*, and *Susan*), set out in February 1601. After the return of the ships in 1603, the venture was considered a success, and the English East India Company began to accumulate the rights and privileges that came to define its trade over the course of many years.

On August 9, 1606, the Company was granted permission to sell spices for reexport to other European nations. On May 31, 1609, their East Indies monopoly was made "perpetual." On December 14, 1615, they were granted permission to transport silver bullion to the East. On February 4, 1623, they were given the right to rule of law over all English persons residing in the East (East India Company, Birdwood, and Foster 1893: xvi). These powers were granted in addition to the authority held by the Company over all English subjects employed on the trade voyages.

The organizational form of the Company evolved along with its legally defined rights. A governor, deputy, and Court of Committees, consisting of twenty-four elected shareholders, were elected to manage the administration of Company affairs on a weekly basis. A general court, composed of all shareholders, met less regularly. Initially, capital was raised to finance operations on a voyage-by-voyage basis. After the tenth voyage, the Company had amassed enough financial support to fund a series of voyages. A somewhat haphazard process of raising capital continued for several years. After surviving both the English Civil War (1642–51) and the first Anglo-Dutch War (1652–54), provisions were finally made for the creation of a pool of permanent capital in 1657. This act made the Company one of the first joint-stock organizations in history. In 1709 the Court of Committees was renamed the Court of Directors. As trade matters grew more complex and Company affairs increased in scope and complexity, special committees were formed to oversee particular aspects of trade. The Committee for Private Trade was created in 1660. Over time the members of the Court of Directors met more frequently and began to accumulate a significant staff of full-time employees to assist them with the business of running the Company (Furber 1976: 18, Anderson, McCormick, and Tollison 1983).

The directors in London oversaw and guided the general direction of operational decisions made in Asia. Day-to-day operations in Asia were supervised by presidencies, which were regional subunits in Asia, led by a president and their council. In the eighteenth century, presidencies were located in Bombay (Mumbai), Madras (Chennai), and Calcutta (Kolkata). Each president and council retained a staff, organized their affairs through subcommittees established to oversee specific aspects of operations, and held ultimate authority over the factors (lead merchants) stationed in the other ports in their region (Chaudhuri 1978: 25–28). One exception was the absence of a presidency to oversee the China trade, due to restrictions on permanent residency imposed on English citizens by the Chinese government. In this case, the Council of Supercargoes was the local Company authority.

Initially the merchants who founded the Company did so in order to enter the existing and immensely profitable trade in pepper, cinnamon, cardamom, nutmeg, and mace. Over time the Company expanded its range of goods, finding particular success in importing cotton textiles, silks, tea, coffee, and indigo. By the end of the seventeenth century the Company's Asian trade was beginning to have a large impact on English society. The affordability of imported cotton textiles from India engaged new portions of the larger population into status-driven consumption cycles, ultimately creating a demand that was to encourage the development of the English textile industry (Lemire 2011: 223, Findlay and O'Rourke 2007: 339). Coffeehouses sprang up across Britain, creating new centers for intellectual, commercial, and civic activity (Pincus 1995).

As the Company's trade transformed consumer culture, its domestic political influence grew. By 1699–1701, trade with the East Indies constituted 13 percent of England overseas imports.[1] England's tax base had traditionally rested largely upon overseas trade, thus the increase in state revenues directly provided by the business of the Company was far from negligible. The Company also made direct loans to the monarchs of England prior to the Glorious Revolution (1688). Perhaps most important, the Company was a central actor in establishing a modern system of public debt for the British nation—after the control of funds had come into the hands of the British Parliament (Carruthers 1996: 137–59). This step was crucial to the emergence of a modern bureaucratic nation-state in England.

A more dramatic shift in the political fortunes of the Company occurred in 1757. In the seventeenth and early eighteenth centuries, the English Company had acquired control over small pieces of land, but did not possess much actual territory in the East. And although there were distinctly sovereign aspects to the Company's conduct in its limited settlements (Stern 2011), military conquest and colonization were not an integral part of the English Company's business strategy (Chaudhuri 1978: 16). This pattern changed with the 1757 Battle of Plassey. This conflict deeply involved Company officials in a complicated contest with political and commercial dimensions that extended well past the boundaries of Asia and directly into the heart of European colonial ambitions and continental politics.

The Battle of Plassey was fought over the fate of Bengal (now West Bengal and the nation of Bangladesh), which was at that time a rich textile- and opium-producing region. By the late 1750s the region was a flash point in the heightened political tensions among the French, the English, and the Mughal Empire. The French had been making large inroads into the trade of Bengal, often through forging political alliances with local rulers. The English Company was both troubled by the increased French presence and worried that the sitting *nawab* (Mughal governor) of Bengal, Siraj ud-Daulah, was aligning with the French. The nawab was in fact unhappy with the English Company's increasing influence in the region. The English employee's private trade had been particularly problematic as English private traders evaded paying taxes to the Mughal ruler by illicitly using privileges granted to the Company for its official trade. These tensions ultimately culminated in the nawab's decision to attack the Company's base of operations at Calcutta.

The nawab's forces took Calcutta, looted the treasury, and by one account imprisoned 146 English citizens—many of whom died. This incident, known as the Black Hole of Calcutta, quickly became highly politicized. The English moved to retaliate by authorizing the young Robert Clive to seek a local political alliance that would aid him in overthrowing the nawab. Clive was able to recruit Mir Jafar, a general of the nawab Siraj ud-Daulah, as his collaborator. With Mir Jafar's help, British troops won a decisive victory at the Battle of Plassey, thereby defeating Siraj ud-Daulah. Mir Jafar then became the new nawab. In 1765, the Company was declared the *diwan* of Bengal, the court-appointed tax collector for the Mughal Empire (Marshall 1987, chap. 3, 70–92). These convoluted events were of tremendous importance because they established the Company as a significant political power in India. After assuming formal control over Bengal, the Company began to expand its territorial possessions into a colonial empire that would eventually span the Indian Subcontinent.

The accession to political power in India further entangled the Company in the affairs of the British state. Without the assistance of the British Crown, Calcutta could not have been retaken and the Battle of Plassey might never have been fought. In recognition of this, the British government was directly involved in the distribution of power and resources that followed. Even without its direct involvement, there is good reason to believe that the British government would have taken a strong interest in the process by which its citizens were beginning to acquire a sizable territorial empire overseas.

In the immediate aftermath of Plassey, the Company was able to retain a degree of autonomy from the British state, purchased at a rate of £400,000 a year (Stern 2011: 209). This attempt to buy off the government merely delayed the more active engagement of the British government in what had truly become an affair of state. Soon ad hoc parliamentary committees were being formed to investigate the Company's affairs in Bengal. In 1784, the Board of Control, chaired by the British secretary of foreign affairs, was created to oversee the political affairs of the Company. Although the creation of the board was in a sense a victory for the Company—as it had been able to resist outright incorporation—it was now under the direct supervision of the British government. The autonomy of the Company was further curtailed by the Act of 1786, which strengthened the control of the governor-general of Bengal, whose appointment was made subject to the approval of a government committee.

On the other hand, individuals within the Company were becoming increasingly well represented in state politics. In the period from 1768 to 1774, thirteen Company directors were simultaneously serving in Parliament. By 1784, thirty-six members of Parliament were current or former directors or employees of the Company (Barber 1975: 101). By the end of the eighteenth century, the political and economic importance of the Company was felt so keenly that Company issues appeared at times to overshadow domestic policy decisions (Philips 1937: 83). This is the same period in which Edmund Burke was quoted as saying, "[T]o say the Company was in a state of distress was neither more nor less their saying the Country was in a state of distress" (Greenberg 1951: 213).

In the post-Plassey phase of colonial expansion, commercial interests were quickly subordinated to imperial aggrandizement as the Company went from a dynamic economic force to an extractive rentier. After the Company's monopoly privileges in India were revoked in 1813, the Company largely withdrew from trade and devoted itself to military expansion and tax collection. The last vestiges of the monopoly disappeared when the Act of 1833 opened trade to China. By this time, the Company was no longer a business in any real sense. Within a few decades, the rest of the Indian Subcontinent, as well as much of Southeast Asia, had been incorporated into the Company empire, which in turn had become the cornerstone of British Imperial rule. In 1858, after the Sepoy Rebellion, the colonial empire created by the Company was converted into the British Raj. Thus the commercial empire built up by the Company over two centuries had largely integrated the economies of England and Asia while ultimately serving as the foundation of British overseas empire and world hegemony. The effects of the Company's long history were particularly profound for the societies of the Indian Peninsula, British society, and global economic and political relations.

My research into the Company began as a dissertation project. I had a truly incredible advisor, Peter Bearman, and a truly incredible committee, Harrison White and Duncan Watts. If I attempted to adequately express my gratitude to these three for their impact on my intellectual trajectory, I would have to write another book—this is particularly true of Peter Bearman.

Chapter 4 is based on a coauthored paper with Peter Bearman published in the *American Journal of Sociology*, "Malfeasance and the Foundations for

Global Trade: The Structure of English Trade in the East Indies, 1601–1833" ©2006 by the University of Chicago. I thank Peter and the *American Journal of Sociology* for permission to include that chapter here. Chapter 3 benefited immensely from collaborative work with Sampsa Samila as we developed a related research project on information transfer within organizations and network activation. Sampsa helped refine the data, introduced an important control variable, and produced figures 3 and 7. Our discussions and work together have been very significant in improving both the analysis and exposition in this chapter.

While still in the dissertation stage I benefited from multiple conversations with my colleagues Philip Stern, Jessica Goldberg, Joseph Parent, Delia Baldassarri, Henning Hillmann, Damon Centola, Matthew Salganik, Tammy Smith, and Paolo Parigi. Gueorgi Kossinets was just about the only other person I could find who was doing work with large, continuous longitudinal network data during my graduate years. I modeled my initial dissertation chapter on network dynamics on his work. I eventually abandoned this for an event-based model of information diffusion, but he was an inspiration in those dark ages of network dynamics (2004–6). Ivy Washington and Zachary Luck assisted with data collection. I gratefully acknowledge financial support from the Institute for Social and Economic Research at Columbia University, the Center for International Business Education and Research at Columbia University, and the Center for Spatially Integrated Social Science at UCSB.

I received invaluable comments from Yally Avrahampour, Richard Lachmann, Peter Dodds, Rebecca Emigh, Donald Tomaskovic-Devey, Robert Faulkner, Enobong Hannah Branch, Julia Adams, Scott Boorman, and Nicholas Hoover Wilson. At different points I received extremely helpful advice from Heather Haveman, Neil Fligstein, Karen Barkey, Charles Tilly, Craig Calhoun, Josh Whitford, Tom Diprete, Nicole Marwell, Amy Schalet, and Sanjiv Gupta. Douglas Miller helped me with Python code for an early version of ArcGIS. Christopher Wildeman helped me with a recalcitrant R-script late in the game. Also in a later stage, Steven Pincus and William Bullman organized a helpful conference on new institutionalism in economic history. My mother, Anne Todd Erikson, helped me proof the manuscript. And just as the entire process was wrapping up, I was extremely pleased to be introduced to the work of Maxine Berg, Hanna Hodacs, Mieke Fellinger, Tim Davis, Felicia Gottman, and Chris Nierstrasz, all of whom are engaged in an exciting collaborative comparative project on the East India Companies, as well as all the participants in a 2013 conference, "The Companies: Continuity, Transition, or Disjuncture." I also thank my husband, Joseph Ligman, for his support, and daughter, Gabriella Ligman.

# BETWEEN MONOPOLY AND FREE TRADE

*Chapter 1*

# INTRODUCTION

---

The English East India Company has long sat at the center of debates on the relative virtues of monopoly forms of organization and free trade. The Company figures prominently in the work of Adam Smith, Thomas Mun, James Steuart, James Mill, David Ricardo, and John Stuart Mill, among others, and was a significant influence on the development of economic thought in Britain (Barber 1975, Khan 1975, Muchmore 1970: 498–503). Supporters of the Company argued that monopoly rights were necessary to create and maintain the expensive infrastructure that made long-distance trade with Asia both possible and profitable. Free trade advocates attacked the Company as a boundary to the expansion of commerce. Arguments over the efficacy of the Company's monopoly continue to this day (Carlos and Nicholas 1988, Jones and Ville 1996a, 1996b, Carlos and Nicholas 1996, Irwin 1992, Anderson and Tollison 1982). These debates have largely glossed over the fact that the Company was never a true monopoly.

The English Company had monopoly rights in England, but had always competed against other European organizations in Asia—and happily traded with them.[1] The Company was known as a monopoly because it had exclusive rights to the East Indies overseas trade in England. However, all the East India Company's respective governments granted that privilege. The European companies competed both in Asia and in the European re-export market. The companies were attempting to capture a market long dominated by numerous, successful, and well-provisioned Asian merchants, better versed in the vagaries of their local trade. In England itself, the East India Company faced competition from the Levant Company, which held a charter awarding exclusive privileges to the overland trade of Asia.

Even within its own purview, the Company ceded several of its monopoly privileges to its own employees. These employees engaged in what was called the private trade, trade upon their own account and in their own interest, while in the employ of the Company. The private trade allowances both contributed to and were a part of a larger pattern of decentralized decision making in the English Company. This book investigates how organizational decentralization and the intertwining of private and Company interests aboard the voyages of the East Indiamen ships both encouraged exploration of new market opportunities and created a powerful internal network of communication that effectively integrated Company operations across the East. Monopoly rights were not the key to Company success; it was the partial abrogation of those rights that sustained England's commercial success in Asia.

Some idea of the importance of the private trade has been apparent since the days of the Company itself; however it has not been considered as an intrinsic component of the distinctly decentralized organizational form the Company took on early in its existence, except by those that saw that decentralization as a negative (Moreland 1923: 314, Arasaratnam 1986: 37, 329, Lawson 1993: 73). Instead, the private trade of the employees has been mainly conceptualized as a distinct alternative to the monopolistic strategy of the firm—although in practice the two worked in concert.

Contemporaries of the Company took the success of the English private trade as evidence of the superiority of free markets. Influential actors, such as David Scott (friend of Henry Dundas and chair of the East India Company from 1778 to 1800) cited their experience with private trade in the East as the source of their support for the ideal of free trade (Philips 1951: xiv). When requesting the renewal of monopoly privileges, Company officials argued that the failure of the private trade to take up more than a quarter of the tonnage offered by the Company demonstrated the efficacy of the existing system of monopoly (Hansard 1812: 47). The relationship linking the private and Company trade was ignored in increasingly polarized arguments about the merits of free markets.

In the end, the 1813 and 1833 acts rescinding the Company's monopoly privileges, first to India and next to Asia, were seen as ideological breaks from the mercantilist system of monopoly privilege that put the nation on a path toward economic rationalism and free trade practices. The English Company came to represent the evil and conservatism of the monopoly form. The decentralized, networked organizational form it had actually possessed during its years of expansion was largely ignored. The argument I make here, which builds upon the work of historians of the private trade, is that the East India Company is miscast as a simple monopoly—and the private trade is misunderstood as a version of free trade. The Company provided essential infrastructure and coordinative capacity that unaffiliated traders would have lacked. Private traders working out of that infrastructure sought out opportunities that would have been overlooked by the corporation itself. The private trade that existed within the monopoly form of the Company effectively decentralized the corporation and spurred the creation of networks of informal information exchange within the otherwise hierarchical organization. In spirit and conception, the East India Company was meant to be a monopoly firm that accumulated profits by controlling market opportunities and restricting competition. In practice, it benefited from the then unique organizational structure produced by the combination of its hierarchical corporate form and what was often perceived as a challenge to the monopoly privileges of the firm: the private trade.

I argue that this decentralized organizational structure—constructed through the combination of private and Company trade—was the central pillar of the English East India Company's continued expansion and adaptability over nearly two centuries as a predominantly commercial operation. By fostering the use of social networks as well as a cohesive internal structure of connections between ships and ports, the decentralized structure of the firm simultaneously expanded and integrated Company operations in the East. Social networks within the Company transferred valuable information between employees, leading to the incorporation of more and new ports into the larger network of Company trade. Additional ports brought new opportunities, new markets, and new types of commodities into the Company trade. Decentralization in the form of private trade allowances encouraged employees to stay longer in the East, exploring new ports and linking existing English settlements into a tighter network of communications—feeding back into and encouraging the process of lateral information transfer that was also a product of putting significant autonomy into the hands of local agents of the Company.

The importance of this degree of decentralization, and its systematic effects on the conduct of the English Company trade, implies that the remarkable expansion and growth of the English East India Company was not a product of imperialism or the centralization of administrative forms. Instead decentralization and profit sharing within a larger organizational framework, that is, the company form, introduced an innovative capacity that was essential to the long-term success of the firm. That innovative capacity was sustained by the willingness of Asian merchants to trade with both the Company and its servants. In the end, the long-term commercial success of the Company depended upon the existence of open societies in the East just as much as its employee's private trade.

## THE RISE TO COMMERCIAL PROMINENCE

The English East India Company was formed December 31, 1600. Queen Elizabeth I granted the small group of merchants a monopoly of trade to lands east of the Cape of Good Hope and west of Cape Horn. Initially, the Company was funded on a voyage-by-voyage basis. A total of £68,373 (£6,843,520 or $10,951,685 in 2011) worth of shares sold to roughly two hundred investors provided the initial capital for the Company's first voyage (Clough 1968: 162). These funds provided for four large ships and one small supply ship, manned by nearly five hundred men. At its peak in 1796, the Company sent out eighty-four ships in one year, by which time it also employed over 350 home office administrators (Carlos and Nicholas 1988: 403).

The Company grew to be a huge political and economic power in both England and Asia. K. N. Chaudhuri described its trajectory in the eighteenth century in glowing terms: "The East India Company went from strength to strength. Its trading capital amounting to £3.5 million was held in the form of government securities and its bonds bearing fixed-rate interest linked to the yield on the gilts were regarded as ideal short-term investment by the financiers of the City and Amsterdam. The Company continued to make huge profits on its Asia trade" (Chaudhuri 1986: 117). Throughout most of the eighteenth century the Company returned 8 percent in dividends to investors (a healthy return), falling only occasionally to 6 percent (Bowen 1989: 191).

According to K. N. Chaudhuri, the preeminent Company historian, the Company's most rapid development occurred from 1660 to 1700. In this period import and export quantities grew significantly in both absolute and relative terms (Chaudhuri 1978: 82). The number of ports included in the trade network of the English East Indiamen ships also increased most appreciably in this period. Despite this expansion, in the late seventeenth century the English Company's trade was still overshadowed by that of its largest competitor, the Dutch East India Company (Vereenigde Oost-Indische Compagnie). The Dutch Company was another powerful European overseas trade monopoly. For the first half of the seventeenth century, the Dutch Company was much larger than the English Company. The initial capitalization of the Dutch Company was 6.5 million guilders, ten times the amount of the English Company's capitalization (De Vries 1976, 130). Still the Dutch Company was dissolved more than a half century before its English counterpart and had grown stagnant long before that time.

There is moderate disagreement over the exact moment at which the English Company overtook the Dutch. In terms of the sheer number of outward-bound ships, the English Company did not come to rival the Dutch until the 1780s. In the 1600s, the Dutch Company frequently sent out more than double the number of English Company ships; however, Dutch investment in terms of ships peaked by the 1730s (Vermeulen 1996: 144). Despite this, it was still a large presence for some time to come. By 1770, the English Company was just on the verge of catching up, with 233 recorded official voyages as compared to 290 Dutch Company voyages. It was not until the 1780s that the English Company finally sprang ahead with 318 versus 297 Dutch Company ships (Bruijn and Gaastra 1993: 179).[2]

These numbers, however, do not capture the English country trade. The country trade was trade confined to Asia. For the Dutch, this was official Company trade (until the 1740s). For the English, beginning in the mid- to late seventeenth century, the country trade belonged to the employees. In the 1720s and 1730s, English country trade grew tremendously. In his study of Bombay and Surat, Holden Furber finds that it doubled in the period from 1724 to 1742 (Furber 1965: 44). By the 1730s it was clear from port records that the English were supplanting the Dutch (Furber 1965: 45).

Based on his evaluation of import/export growth rates in the English Company, Chaudhuri believes it came to rival the Dutch enterprise during the English Company's most rapid phase of growth, from 1660 to 1700 (Chaudhuri 1978: 82). Bal Krishna also believes that the rising fortunes of the English Company were surpassing the Dutch prior to the eighteenth century, noting that the English were investing £26,000,000 in trade, whereas the Dutch invested significantly less, £19,000,000 (Krishna 1924: 177). By 1720–31 the average annual value of the English Company's imports from Asia was exceeding the value of Dutch imports (Steensgaard 1990: 110).

In a meticulous study of the stock prices of the two firms, Larry Neal found the English Company stock valuation making large gains on the Dutch in the 1730s and 1740s. When reacting to general market conditions, both Companies' shares moved in the same direction. The gains made by the English Company stock in the 1730s and 1740s were marked by significant losses in the Dutch price, indicating that capital was moving from one firm to the other as investors realized greater growth potential in the English firm (Neal 1990: 218–20). Kristof Glamann's work corroborates this view, as he found that contemporaries of the firms were aware of the decline in the relative position of the Dutch Company by the 1730s and 1740s (Glamann 1981: 2). In fact, at this time the Dutch Company began to implement significant reform efforts, one of which was imitating the English Company by opening the country trade to its employees.

The 1720s marked the beginning of a long tumble for the stock of the Dutch Company—during which time English Company prices fared much better (Neal 1990: 198). Gaastra explained this sustained decline in terms of a series of events occurring over the eighteenth century (Gaastra 2003: 59). A definitive end to the Dutch Company came in 1799 when it was formally dissolved. The gradual pattern of decline over the 1700s indicates that, rather than suffering one definitive external shock, the Dutch firm suffered from a gradual erosion of its commercial position, leading Neal and Glamann to believe that the firm's difficulties lay in the inability to successfully adjust to increased competition and changing market conditions (Neal 1990: 220, Glamann 1981: 2). Thus any theories regarding the expansion and eventual triumph of the East India Company in the commercial world of the East should focus at least on the period from 1660 to 1740, which begins with the rapid expansion of the English Company and ends with their supplanting the Dutch as the major European commercial power in the East.

The period of 1660 to 1740 is also a time when English East India Company employees enjoyed especially high levels of legitimate autonomy in the form of the official acceptance of the private trade. I focus my research in this book on this period, although I extend the time frame to include 1760, which marks a natural break in the organization of the East India Company in the aftermath of the Battle of Plassey and the beginning of the Company's transition to colonial rule. The analysis also includes other periods in the Company's history—in order to construct comparisons with the crucial private trading period. Since the focus here is on the means by which the English Company achieved commercial prosperity, I do not address the period after it lost its last claim on monopoly privileges and was directed to end its commercial business in 1833.

## ALTERNATIVE EXPLANATIONS FOR THE SUCCESS OF THE COMPANY

### Domestic Conditions

There are several existing explanations for the East India Company's rise to prominence. It is perhaps most commonly believed that the rising fortunes of England led to the success of the English East India Company. This argument suggests that organizational structure and events in the East are unimportant elements of the story—simply outcomes rather than causal factors—however it falls short of providing an adequate explanation.

There has been a great deal of controversy over exactly when real growth accelerated national economic development in Britain, but little argument that anything other than the structural preconditions were in place before the beginning of the eighteenth century. Phyllis Deane and W. A. Cole identify a turning point in British economic growth in 1745, but find that real acceleration occurred after 1780 (Deane and Cole 1967: 80). Crafts later amended this to argue that growth did not really begin a marked upward movement until after 1820 (Crafts 1985: 2), also arguing that even the gradual structural shifts leading up the change were not in evidence until the beginning of the eighteenth century (Crafts 1985: 7). R. V. Jackson has since suggested amendments to Crafts's work that push growth estimates from 1700 to 1760 downward and upward in the period from 1760 to 1800, bringing them back closer in line with Deane and

Cole's original research (Jackson 1990: 225). More recently there has been an emphasis on the existence of long-term slow growth in England as well as other areas in Europe and Asia, followed by only a very slight increase in the pace of England's development in the latter half of the eighteenth century (O'Brien 2000: 127, Goldstone 2000, 2002). This research indicates that real change occurred after 1830 (Mokyr 1999: 1). The same researchers have pointed out that although industrialization occurred in Britain prior to 1830, it was confined to a few localities that accounted for a small proportion of the total economy—reinforcing the point that the national economy did not experience a strong acceleration until after 1830 (Mokyr 2003) Although disagreements about the causes of development will undoubtedly continue into the future, they are very unlikely to challenge the view that the rapid development of the East India Company preceded the rapid development of the British economy by several decades. Indeed the fact that commerce grew significantly well before the Industrial Revolution has led many to argue that it was a cause of economic development.

In contrast, the English Civil War occurred before the expansion of the East India Company. Therefore the installation of bourgeois interests at the head of the government could have affected the future of the firm. The war's outcome did not initially seem to favor the English Company, as it had been a Crown supporter (Brenner 2003: 324). However, the Company was able to renew its charter under Oliver Cromwell and had, in fact, experienced periodic difficulties with the monarchy. For example Charles I had directly threatened the East India Company's monopoly by supporting a rival company, the Courteen Association (Furber 1976: 69).

A comparative perspective, however, makes the state-led argument less compelling. A merchant elite had dominated the Dutch government since the mid-sixteenth century (Adams 1994b: 327), so this does little to explain why the English Company would have fared better than the Dutch in the eighteenth. In addition, neither the political nor economic conditions in England can explain why the East India Company succeeded, where other British joint-stock organizations failed. The Royal African Company, formed in 1660 when it was known as the Company of Royal Adventurers Trading to Africa, had lost its monopoly by 1690 and all but failed by 1730 (Carlos and Kruse 1996: 291). Similarly, the South Seas Company has become infamous over the years for its spectacular collapse, which nearly brought the British economy down with it (Anderson and Tollison 1982: 1241). Indeed, Gary Anderson and Robert Tollison argue that Adam Smith's well-known dislike of the joint-stock form was based on the poor performance of such firms in his lifetime (Anderson and Tollison 1982: 1240). A prominent exception (not to Smith's criticism) was the East India Company.

## War and Seapower

The first three Anglo-Dutch Wars have been cited as a cause of the decline of Dutch overseas trade (De Vries 1976: 122), and therefore should be considered a possible cause of Dutch East India Company decline. The first Anglo-Dutch War took place from 1652 to 1654, the second from 1665 to 1667, and the third from 1672 to 1674. Although domestic and international political considerations played a role in instigating these wars, the commercial aspects are most relevant, so I confine my discussion to these elements.

In the beginning of the seventeenth century, the Netherlands dominated not only the Eastern trade, but also trade throughout Europe (De Vries 1976: 116). Particularly because the Dutch also controlled the herring trade conducted off the shores of England, English merchants resented Dutch predominance. It is clear that this commercial rivalry fed into the hostilities between nations; however their impact on the fates of the East India Companies is less obvious.

There is significant evidence that the Dutch and English Companies sidestepped formal animosities in the East Indies in order to continue to pursue trade with as little interruption as possible, particularly in the second and third Anglo-Dutch Wars (Boxer 1974: 59, Pincus 1992). In addition, the outcome of the three wars did not clearly favor the English. The English seemed to gain the advantage in the first war (Boxer 1974: 19), but the second favored the Dutch. At the conclusion of the second war, the Treaty of Breda (1667) altered the Acts of Navigation in favor of the Dutch. These acts had been the central point of contention in the tensions leading up to the war, so this was a strong sign that the Dutch had gained the upper hand in the conflict. The terms of the treaty also dictated that the English Company renounce their claim to Pulo Run (while Britain gained Manhattan) (Boxer 1974: 39). The direct result for the English Company was therefore the loss of ground in the East Indies. The third Anglo-Dutch War, in which England was allied with France, was very hard on Dutch trade, but ended inconclusively. The battles between the English and Dutch were generally fought to the advantage of the Dutch and ended with the English paying out an indemnity of two million guilders (Boxer 1974: 58). Although Jan De Vries seems to disagree, Charles Boxer believed that the Dutch Republic recovered more quickly than England from the financial difficulties of the wars (Boxer 1974: 63). Jonathan Israel concluded that, although the French and English intended to end the Dutch trade supremacy in the Third War, they simply failed to do so (Israel 1998: 297). Dutch trade supremacy resumed again at the war's end, although it did mark the beginning of a long and gradual decline.

Finally, the timing of the rise and fall of the East India Companies does not support the centrality of the first three Anglo-Dutch Wars. If these conflicts had created the English Company's success through the suppression of a Dutch trade advantage in the East, there should be clearer evidence of Dutch decline after the war. Instead the Dutch Company continued to expand until at least the 1730s. Kristof Glamann discusses the 1700 to 1730 period as the culmination of the Dutch Company's power and an apparent golden age (Glamann 1981: 2).[3]

The English and French were also at war several times during the English Company's history. In contrast to the conflicts between the Dutch and English states, these were hostilities between the English and the French Companies and were fought in the Indian Subcontinent. These battles mark an exciting chapter of the history of the East India Company history, filled with strategic machinations, shifting alliances, complex court intrigues, and the oversized figures of Robert Clive and Joseph François Dupleix. However the timing again does not support their importance in determining the success of the English Company. The first Carnatic War was fought from 1746 to 1748, the second from 1749 to 1754, and the third from 1757 to 1763. The English were victorious in these conflicts, which played a central role in establishing Britain as a strong colonial power in the Indian Subcontinent. They also came nearly a century after the period of accelerated growth of the Company identified by Chaudhuri and well after the erosion of the Dutch position in the East. Even if the continued commercial success of the English Company was predicated on English victory in these wars, which is not entirely clear, it is very unlikely that the Company would have succeeded militarily without access to the resources which its commercial success had provided.

Over the same period the British Royal Navy was built up into a formidable force; however again there is little reason to believe that it played a direct role in the expansion of the English Company. The Royal Navy did not have a sustained advantage over the naval forces of other nations until the eighteenth century (Modelski and Thompson 1988), and it was not until the Carnatic Wars that the capacity of the Royal Navy played a direct role in the operations of the Company. In this period, both English and French companies drew upon state resources to pursue their goals. By contrast the Dutch Company was unable to successfully secure additional naval or military support from the government. Lack of naval and military support from the state made direct participation in the territorial competition between the French and English an impossibility for the Dutch and has been considered a central factor in the ultimate decline of the Vereenigde Oost-Indische Compagnie (Nierstrasz 2012). These factors, however, only came into play after the commercial ascendance of the English Company had already been established.

Prior to this period, the Royal Navy had minimal impact on trade in the East. The ships of the Royal Navy were rarely to be seen in the waters of the East Indies before the 1740s. The only brief exceptions to this rule were scattered forays pursuing European pirates in the area around Madagascar (Rodger 2004, Stern 2011: 141). Beginning in 1690 the British Royal Navy provided assistance to the Company by escorting ships through the Atlantic as a safeguard against pirates and hostile combatants in times of war (Stern 2011: 153). The convoy protection offered by the Royal Navy should be considered a potentially essential but not sufficient factor for the continued success of the Company. It was necessary, but did not provide a competitive advantage for any of the East India Companies, all of which were able to provide relatively safe passage for ships through the Atlantic waters. In any case, this date falls after the English Company had already begun its trajectory of rapid growth. It was, in fact, unlikely that the British state would have offered these protections if the English Company had not already proved itself to be a vital and expanding source of state revenue, a situation that in turn depended upon the already expanding profitability of the Company trade.


## Protection Costs

A related line of research has argued that the internalization of protection costs created a competitive advantage for the European companies that ensured their success in the Eastern trade (Lane 1966, 1979, Steensgaard 1974). It is important to note that the object of explanation is different in this research than in my argument. Niels Steensgaard focused on the Company's success as a type, including both the Dutch and English Companies, whereas I am focusing on the greater relative success of the English over the long term. Still, Steensgaard's research was an important contribution to understanding the East India Companies and should be addressed.

The internalization of protection costs has at least two possible meanings. In one, a detailed accounting procedure is used to take the cost of protection rents into consideration when calculating business prospects. In the second, a commercial organization internalizes activities associated with protecting the organization from theft or violence, for example by hiring security guards. Steensgaard's argument indicates that both types both played an important role.

Steensgaard provides detailed and convincing evidence that the greatest costs to merchants traveling the overland route through the Middle East came from customs duties, bribes to local officials, and protection costs paid out to other smaller communities along the caravan trail. According to Steensgaard, these expenses significantly overshadowed transport costs. Therefore the European companies saved a great deal by taking the Cape route, despite the higher transportation costs involved. In keeping with the protection costs argument, the savings must have been part of the decision to take the Cape route. This explanation however does not provide an answer as to why the Portuguese Estado da Índia, which also took the Cape route, was a commercial failure, particularly in comparison with the Dutch and English Companies.

It is also true that the European companies integrated protection functions into their operations. The benefit of integration assumes that there is in fact a real threat; otherwise investment in defense would simply cut profits. Somewhat problematically, many historians of the Indian Ocean assert that, in comparison with the Atlantic Ocean, it was a *Mare Liberum*, a free sea. In this case protection functions would simply be an additional and unnecessary expense. There were, however, Asian merchants who also combined military force and profit seeking into organized commercial operations. For example, the Omani state was mercantile and willing to defend territory through military action (Cole 1987: 195), and the Mappila of Malabar and Western Ceylon (now Sri Lanka) was an armed and aggressive merchant group (Subrahmanyam 1995: 769). These groups existed, but did not dominate the East, which, in itself, provides some grounds for skepticism.

The European East Indiamen, however, were armed with superior weaponry, and each of the companies engaged in at least sporadic military action. We can consider the importance of investing in armaments by comparing the Portuguese Estado da Índia, the Dutch East India Company, and the English East India Company in the seventeenth and early eighteenth centuries. The Portuguese were the most militarized, followed closely by the Dutch, who were trailed by the English, a distant third. The English Company did not have any significant armed land forces until 1660 (Bowen 1996: 351). By contrast, half of Dutch Company employees were military personnel (Knaap 2003: 116). The Portuguese Estado simply was a militarized arm of the government. They did not create a commercial apparatus, that is, a company, until 1628, and even then, the Company's existence was short-lived. In 1615 the Portuguese assault force that attacked Goa included 6,000 Indians and 2,600 Europeans (Desphande 1995: 262). In 1626, a single Dutch fleet sent to protect Amboina included 1,200 soldiers (Van Veen 2001: 88). It was not until 1740 that English forces came close to rivaling these numbers. Total English forces numbered fewer than 2,000. Only one hundred men defended Madras when French forces attacked and took the site (Parker 1991: 182). Similarly, by 1623 the Dutch had a large naval force in place in the East, with roughly sixty-six ships actively engaged in various military actions across ports (Van Veen 2001: 92).

In contrast, the Bombay Council requested three small vessels to protect coastal English trade in 1669. They received two (Deshpande 1995: 283). This requisition made for the very modest beginning of the Bombay Marine, the Company's first naval force.

These differences reflected the strategies of the three organizations. The Dutch and Portuguese actively pursued conflict as a means to acquire territory in the East (Subrahmanyam 1990a: 252–97), whereas, prior to Plassey, the English did not. The English instead pursued a largely peaceful trade, following the advice of Sir Thomas Roe, the Company's ambassador to the court of the Mughal Emperor: "Lett this bee received as a rule that if you will Profitt, seeke it at Sea, and in quiett trade; for without controversy it is an error to affect Garrisons and Land warrs in India." Roe argued specifically that war "is the beggering of the Portugall" and "hath also been the error of the Dutch" (Foster 1899: xxxiv). In contrast, Jan Pieterszoon Coen, the famous governor-general of the Dutch Company, went by the phrase, "Trade without war, and war without trade cannot be maintained" (Parthesius 2010: 38).

Philip Stern and Bruce Watson have shown that there was military buildup in the English Company related to and following Child's War with the Mughals (Watson 1980b, Stern 2011).[4] However the Company used their fortifications to defend existing settlements—not too engage in aggressive acts. Instead they continued to avoid conflict whenever possible (Stern 2011: 122), again, unlike the Dutch and Portuguese. Of course this pattern changed after the Battle of Plassey which was also after the Company had established itself as the dominant European commercial power in the East.

If militarization was the only or most important factor in producing commercial success for European organizations in the East, we should see Portuguese and Dutch commercial ascendancy. Instead, the Portuguese were markedly less commercially successful than the Dutch or English, and the English became more commercially successful than the more militaristic Dutch.[5] Indeed, by the eighteenth century, the Dutch seem to have regretted the high costs of their aggressions and pulled back into a more pacific mode (Winius and Vink 1994: 40). And evidence indicates that the English Company's finances suffered substantially with the onset of their post-Plassey policy of aggressive territorialization (Tripathi 1956: 3).

It is undeniable that there was an element of aggression and force to the trade of all European companies trading in the East. Even the English East Indiamen were armed. That things happened this way does not mean that it necessarily had to be so. The fact that the English Company, which was the weakest and least militaristic of the organizations, was also the most successful over the long term suggests that the internalization of protection costs was not as profitable as many have believed. In the end, large-scale militarized organizations, that is, states and empires, were nothing new; however successful commercial firms with global reach were unique. The real innovation was the commercial side of the organization, not the incorporation of violence.

## THEORIES OF THE PRIVATE TRADE

In addition to being less militaristic than the other European companies, the English firm was also more permissive of the private trade of its employees. The private trade was any trade not undertaken by one of the large chartered organizations of the early modern period. In many of the early overseas companies employees participated in the private trade while in the service of these monopolies. The degree to which the private trade was tolerated varied across the different organizations. The Muscovy Company, formed much earlier in 1555, did not allow private trade within or without the company when it was organized as a joint-stock corporation (Scott 1910: 47 and 52, Willan 1953: 405). The Hudson Bay Company, formed in 1670, outlawed employee private trade in 1672 (Carlos and Nicholas 1990: 863). The second iteration of the Royal African Company, established in 1672, did not allow private trade among employees and put considerable effort into controlling it (Carlos and Kruse 1996: 298). At roughly the same time, the English East India Company was loosening its private trade regulations to allow employees more leeway.

A similar situation prevailed among the European East India Companies. Holden Furber, who pioneered work on the private trade, summarily states, "The English East India Company placed less restrictions than any other on the private concerns of its servants" (Furber 1965: 25).[6] Some researchers have portrayed the private trade in a negative light. For K. N. Chaudhuri, it was a minor source of disruption to the otherwise well-oiled logistical machinery of the Company (Chaudhuri 1978: 74–77). W. H. Moreland and Sinnappah Arasaratnam had more negative opinions, arguing that it harmed the Company trade (Moreland 1923: 314, Arasaratnam 1986: 258–63). There were certainly some negative consequences. Smuggling goods into England cut into Company profits by creating an alternative supply in England. The country trade of the employees hurt the Company in different ways. Some embezzled Company monies to fund their own trade (Furber 1965: 29). Private trade buyers were also usually in competition with the Company in Asian ports—with the private traders representing both parties. This situation usually led to higher prices and lower quality goods for the Company.

Nevertheless most historians now agree that England's fortunes in the East were closely tied to the rise of the private trade. Holden Furber has influentially argued that the development of the English country trade (trade confined to the East) of the employees was responsible for the events leading to the creation of the British Empire in the Indian Subcontinent (Furber 1965: 69). P. J. Marshall and Ian Bruce Watson have documented the paths by which British private traders entangled the English Company—and eventually the British government—into political conflicts that led to colonial rule (Marshall 1976, 1993, Watson 1980b).[7] Others have further developed some of the implications of Furber's original argument by saying that the British private trade squeezed the Dutch Company out of the country trade, leading to its downfall (Emmer and Gaastra 1996: xx), and that the failure of the French to expand their country trade led to their lack of commercial success (Lombard 1981: 186). Many of these arguments explicitly state that the private trade allowed English traders to penetrate into local markets and commercial networks, and that this penetration and partnership with Asian merchants was the foundation of British commercial success (Furber 1965: 46, 1976, Asaratnam 1995: 16, Tripathi 1956: viii).

Despite a general sense that there was a positive synergy between the private and official Company trade, the mechanisms that have been identified by researchers are negative benefits, meaning they are ways in which the Company reduced costs—not improved its trading position. Furber emphasized how private country trade helped the Company streamline its operations—in particular by removing the considerable expense of creating and maintaining a country trade fleet (Furber 1976: 201). Others have stressed the reduction in monitoring and enforcement costs (Watson 1980b: 75), closely related to the resolution of principal-agent dilemmas (Hejeebu 2005), as well as the positive, though indirect, benefit to the Company of taxes paid by private traders, their dependents, and any secondary support services created to serve the increasing population in Company held ports (Watson 1980a: 77). This advantage grew in later years as the English Company's territorial possessions expanded.

Private trade also became increasingly important as a source of capital for the Company itself. In its overseas ports, the Company frequently fell short of the necessary funds to supply return voyages and turned to its own employees for infusions of capital. The country trade of the factors served as an additional source of overseas capital that was used to cover the purchase of return goods in Asia (Cheong 1979: 9). There is also evidence that the private trade attracted employees, encouraging individuals to work for the Company and lowering the wages necessary to induce appropriate behavior (Anderson, McCormick, and Tollison 1983: 228–29). While all of these mechanisms may have played a role, they miss a crucial facet of the private trade.

When the Company acknowledged the private trade as a legitimate pursuit for its employees, it was a signal that the Company recognized and even supported a high degree of autonomy for its employees. This was not merely a matter of allowing employees greater freedoms during their leisure time. The private trade practices affected the operations of the firm itself. In some cases, the legitimate private trading practices of factors grew so large that they helped shape the pattern of Company settlements in the East. For years overseas factors refused orders to abandon the troublesome fort at Bencoolen (now Bengkulu, Indonesia) because they found it advantageous for their own private trade (Sutton 2010: 83). And, as I discuss in more detail in chapters 4 and 5, captains regularly diverted the routes of their ships in order to pursue their own private trade in amenable ports. Thus decisions about the paths of its ships and the location of its forts devolved into the hands of lower-level employees. The private trade allowances were not just a means of accommodating employees; the legitimacy of private trade pursuits radically decentralized the firm and placed operational decisions into the purview of locally informed employees. The English East India Company in the private trading period is therefore an early example of a decentralized firm.

My central contribution to the historical literature on the private trade of the English East India Company is one that stresses the positive and systematic impact of decentralized decision making on the functions of the Company as a whole. Most studies of the private trade concentrate on one port or period. Søren Mentz explored the private trade of Madras (2005). P. J. Marshall described employee trade in Bengal (1976). Even Furber looked most intensely at Bombay (1965). The detailed nature of archival study often drives researchers to a narrow focus. The research here instead addresses the range of Company operation across all ports visited by East Indiamen through the commercial history of the firm. The broader perspective reveals systemic network effects that could not have been pieced out or observed at the level of individual ports of call.

### THEORETICAL FRAMEWORK

There were two novel aspects to the English East India Company. It was one of the very first large and bureaucratic commercial organizations. In this sense, the Company was novel in that it was more centralized than previous forms of early modern commercial organization, such as partnerships or joint ventures. However, it also had extremely high levels of employee autonomy, indicating that it was more decentralized than other similar joint-stock companies. Given that the trajectory of the modern firm is understood currently as going from centralized administrative behemoths to decentralized multidivisional firms to the increasingly networked, global firms of the twenty-first century (Chandler [1962] 2003, DiMaggio 2009), the East India Company is also novel in a contemporary sense, because of the way it incorporated decentralized elements into the larger administrative hierarchy.

Economic historians have often emphasized the importance of centralization and the joint-stock form, both in terms of an advance in the sophistication and efficiency of organizations more generally and with respect to the advantages this form conferred on the English East India Company more particularly. K. N. Chaudhuri was the Company historian arguably the most influenced by organizational theory and focused on the logistical capacity of the board of managers in explaining the Company's success. He argued "the reason for its commercial success is perhaps to be found in the creation of a system which rested on a logical application of theoretical principles to the solution of business problems" (Chaudhuri 1978: 21). Shepard Clough noted the general benefits associated with the joint-stock form for raising capital (Clough 1968: 161). Robert Ekelund and Robert Tollison argued that its efficiencies derived instead from increases in business owners' ability to easily transfer property (Ekelund and Tollison 1980: 717).[8] Ann Carlos and Stephen Nicholas singled out the decrease in costs associated with vertical integration when firms are faced with high transaction costs and a large volume of transactions (Carlos and Nicholas 1996: 916). Clearly these are all important benefits linked to the organizational innovations of the joint-stock form, which benefited the East India Company, but just as plainly they do not explain variation in performance across joint-stock firms. Therefore attempts to explain the specific success of the English Company have had to consider other elements of its organizational structure.

Over the past thirty years, decentralization has become increasingly recognized as a powerful means by which organizations may successfully navigate the complex and dynamic environments encountered by today's global firms (Bartlett and Ghoshal 1989, Bower and Christensen 1995, Birkinshaw 1997, Benner and Tushman 2003, Almeida and Phene 1994, O'Reilly and Tushman 2004, among many others). This research has not been ignored by historians of the English Company. Without identifying the mechanisms at work, Kenneth McPherson has suggested that the "flexible organization" of the Company and its lenience with regard to the private trade were two of the reasons for its success (McPherson 1993: 202). Søren Mentz has advanced similar views, concentrating most on the way in which private trade allowances increased the capital flow between London and Madras (2005: 275).

The importance of decentralization has been most centrally explored in investigations of the multidivisional nature of the English Company. K. N. Chaudhuri first hinted that the East India Company's success was related to its divisional organization (Chaudhuri 1981: 29–46),[9] but the argument was fully developed by Gary Anderson, Robert McCormick, and Robert

Tollison two years later (1983). Based on the work of Alfred Chandler and Oliver Williamson, Anderson, McCormick, and Tollison persuasively argued that the English Company was indeed a multidivisional firm, which cannot be taken for granted as the M-form is commonly understood to be a twentieth-century phenomenon (Chandler [1962] 2003). It had the equivalent of a chief executive officer (the governor), board of directors (the Court of Directors), special committees, and overseas managers (factors) (Anderson, McCormick, and Tollison 1983: 224–26). They argued the advantage of this decentralized structure was twofold. Following Chandler, dividing operational and strategic decision making between managers (factors) and directors reduced the information load on directors, which allowed for an expansion of operations and subsequent gains from increases in scale and specialization. Following Williamson, the expansion made possible by decentralization reduced transaction costs (such as locating and evaluating potential exchange partners), thereby increasing the overall efficiency of the firm.[10]

The argument I present does not dismiss the importance of a multidivisional structure to the sustained commercial success of the Company. It adds a new dimension to understanding the viability of this complex organizational form, particularly in an era when modern methods of communication and transportation did not exist. Anderson, McCormick, and Tollison's account, while compelling, largely ignores (1) the impact of the private trade on the firm, (2) the extent of the autonomy of Company employees—which penetrated past divisional presidents to captains and factors, and (3) the social conditions within the firm that made successful decentralization possible. In my explanation of the competitive advantage held by the English Company, these three elements are closely linked.

In decentralization, the communication flow between center and periphery is reduced (the reduction of information load on the center is considered one of the advantages of decentralization). However, this implies that if the center remains the hub of an information transmission system, the information content available to others in the firm will be significantly reduced. Integration and communication remain important to firm operations, so another decentralized means of information transmission must take the place of a centralized system. Successful decentralization therefore depends upon the existence some type of horizontal communication between employees. Thus the use of social networks, by which I mean informal and decentralized relations facilitating communication, to transmit commercial information within a decentralized firm should contribute to its success. This observation has been borne out in research conducted since at least the early 1980s on social networks, demonstrating that they are a crucial component of economic organization with large positive impacts on firms (for overviews, see Powell 1990 and Brass et al. 2004).

I trace the use of social networks within the East India Company and find that the private trade is associated with the use of social networks in directing Company operations and the exploration of new commercial opportunities. Social networks linked employees to a system of communication that integrated firm operations without threatening the productive autonomy of employees. High levels of employee autonomy and cohesive networks of peer communication fed into each other, increasing the overall flow of commercially valuable information within the Company.

Thus, rather than ignoring the private trade, or treating it as a problem to be solved, I incorporate it as an element that effectively decentralized the organizational structure of the English Company beyond a multidivisional form. Decentralization, understood largely through the legitimation of the private trade, affected the flow of information between employees, the rate at which new ports were incorporated into the trade of the Company, and the pattern by which overseas operations were integrated into a larger network of communication and transportation. Previous research on the Company and the evolution of the joint-stock business form has missed how networks and employee autonomy contributed to the sustained viability and success of the English Company. Considering these positive effects of organizational decentralization suggests, in turn, a new way of looking at the early modern corporation.

## Neither Monopoly nor Free Trade

The English East India Company has always had vocal critics. Many of those critics have argued that the success of the private trade demonstrated that the Company's monopoly was a hindrance to trade. If interlopers could successfully engage in the Eastern trade, the Company was not shipping enough goods to satisfy the full demand of the market: consumers, who wanted to buy Eastern goods, could not buy as much as they desired. Therefore, by inhibiting new entrants to the market, who could otherwise have put goods into the hand of those consumers, the Company was standing in the way of trade expansion (Anderson and Tollison 1982: 1245–48). Thus the private trade was turned into a powerful argument in support of free trade.

Opponents of this view suggest that it overlooks costly investments in infrastructure made by the Company that were necessary to the overseas trade of the East. From this perspective, the interlopers were instead free riders illegitimately profiting from the warehouses, forts, and diplomatic accords built, maintained, and negotiated by the Company (Carlos and Nicholas 1988: 414–15, 1996: 917–18). The argument over the private trader as either free rider or free market champion does not capture the dynamic possibilities for innovation and within-firm communication, that is, knowledge transfer, that come with increased employee autonomy.

By emphasizing the importance of networks in the English East India Company, many readers will immediately recognize an implicit debt to the work of Harrison White. White has long been a champion of networks in many different forms. In this case, I have particularly benefited from his work on the interstitial, generative nature of connections that have not yet been crystallized into hardwired institutionalized role sets (White 2008: 20–62). Readers may also be reminded of Walter Powell's related argument that the organization of the economic sphere cannot be adequately explained by the categories of market and hierarchy—and that networks and networked forms of organization constitute a distinct third type (Powell 1990). I am not, however, describing an autonomous third form in Powell's sense, such as interorganizational networks, but instead the not uncommon combination of hierarchy and networks that characterized the organizational patterns of the Company.

Reframing the English Company as a networked firm, one that combines hierarchy with horizontal network structures, links the historical importance of the Company to more recent developments in organizational theory. We can better understand its impact by drawing upon the work of White and Powell, as well as that of organizational theorists of the decentralized multinational (Bartlett and Ghoshal 1989). Embedding the English Company in organizational theory also allows its example to reflect back upon our modern conception of the essential characteristics of successful firms. In this case the organization was an instrument of change not because autonomy was suppressed within it—as might be advanced by theory following Max Weber's work on organizations—but because it embodied one of those rare moments when coordinated action by decentralized actors has taken center stage (Udy 1959).

Here the work intersects and complements research on the limitations of patrimonialism. Patrimonialism is an ideal type of political power developed by Max Weber in which ties of kinship, patronage, and personal allegiance constitute the foundation for governing power (see Charrad and Adams 2011 for a recent and fuller description). Prior to the consolidation of centralized state power in Europe, patrimonial political power was the norm. The Netherlands had risen in political and economic power in the seventeenth century in part through creating a particularly entrenched form of state patrimonialism (Adams 1994a, 2005). As Julia Adams shows, although initially the basis for Dutch efflorescence and prominence, the patrimonial networks eventually became a heavy mesh, holding Dutch society in a static pattern of traditionalism, resistant to innovation and transformation.[11] The Dutch East India Company was firmly integrated into these patrimonial networks of power, which had a similar dampening effect in the context of the East Indies. Indeed, patrimonial networks of control were more effective at circumscribing employees' activities in the larger, more centralized, and better-equipped firm (Adams 1996). What was initially a Dutch advantage, made private trade concessions unnecessary for the larger firm, setting the stage for the commercial stagnation evident by the early eighteenth century. Adams's work presents a negative case, in which we see how principles of exclusivity, patronage, and subordination eventually stifled the overseas expansion of the Dutch chartered company. The English Company was also a patrimonial organization; however, the private trade allowances—which reduced exclusivity and broadened privileges within the firm—introduced avenues through which agents could introduce local information encountered in the field into the larger patterns of organizational behavior. A crucial difference was the structure of principal-agent relations, where the adoption of private trade allowances in the English Company institutionalized a pattern in which agents and principals interests were independent but aligned.

By bringing network analysis to bear on the historical question of British expansion into the East, I am also contributing to a well-defined line of comparative-historical network analysis. In many instances, the goal of this research has been to show how the reconfiguration of social relations between different groups is often the basis for the creation of new and important institutions, such as a centralized state (Padgett and Ansell 1993) or commercial partnership (Padgett and McLean 2006). Historical network analysis has also shown how emergent relational patterns shaped important historical events, such as English Civil War (Bearman 1993), the Paris Commune of 1871 (Gould 1995), and the installation of a merchant oligarchy in medieval Genoa (Van Doosselaere 2009). My goal is actually more modest than this—to explain economic growth through patterns of social interaction.

Thus, though the theory and methods belong to historical network analysis, the goal and the setting bring my work into conversation with the new institutionalism of economic history. The new institutionalism in economics (which is significantly different from the new institutionalism in sociology) has been concerned with explaining economic growth through specific social institutions, such as property rights, courts of law, and impersonal exchange (North 1973, 1981, 1990, Landa 1981, Acemoglu and Johnson 2005, Acemoglu, Johnson, and Robinson 2005, Greif 2006b). This interest has also naturally led to research on the origin of these institutions (Knight and Sened 1995, Greif 2006), all of which has led to a focus on economic history. Britain in the eighteenth and nineteenth centuries has been of particular interest to economic historians because it was during that period when Britain's economy markedly diverged from more modest growth patterns in premodern, medieval, and ancient economies, as well as development patterns in Africa and Asia. I see three points of contact between my research on the English East India Company and the new institutionalism of economics.

First, the success of the English Company was a part of the larger process whereby England experienced significant economic growth. Research on the Company is therefore research on a theoretically privileged period, which has been used to understand the roots of modern economic development. There is no question that the English East India Company was only one part of the larger process, but improving our understanding of one of the many commercial successes experienced by England in this transitional period contributes to our comprehension of the overall picture.

Second, although my goals are similar to those of the new institutionalists in economics, important differences remain. The new institutionalists explore the emergence of institutions through individual behavior via rational choice or game theory. Jack Knight describes this mode of explanation as the "'invisible hand' mechanism: social institutions are the unintended consequences of individual action" (Knight and Sened 1995: 3). I hope that my focus on the role of social networks in this large organization emphasizes the importance of *social* action in institutional formation and call attention more generally to its role (i.e., through forming and dissolving relations that spread influence and information) in economic development.

Finally, and more similarly, the networks of information and innovation that emerged within the English Company were the result of the distribution of rights and privileges across different groups—on the one hand owners/managers versus employees of the firms and on the other elites versus nonelites within the ports. In both cases, the economic growth of the firm depended upon a more equitable distribution of the right to participate in and profit from market exchange—not simply the invention and implementation of more effective coordinating mechanisms. Participation and profit do not always go hand in hand as many employees of large organizations participate in market exchange, but do not share in the profits—or receive a negligible share. Most recently Douglass North, John Wallis, and Barry Weingast (2009) have argued that open societies, which do not impose minimum restrictions on individuals' right to participate in or create organizations, experience the greatest economic growth. The distribution of rights and rewards within the organizations is not given much attention. My research on the English Company suggests that it may also be of value to consider whether open organizations, meaning those that embrace decentralization and some form of profit sharing, are also necessary components of economic growth.

## ANALYTICAL SOCIOLOGY AND THE HISTORY
## OF THE EAST INDIA COMPANY

Throughout this book my approach is to consider the micro-level behavioral patterns and opportunity structures that allowed for the development and transformation of the English Company and, through it, larger patterns of global trade. Networks take a central role in my explanatory strategy exactly because they may be used to link individual behavior to larger macro-level social and organizational outcomes. In this sense the research is intended to contribute to a growing subfield that has embraced many of the same larger theoretical goals found in the earlier historical-comparative network research: analytical sociology (Hedström and Swedberg 1998, Hedström 2005, Hedström and Bearman 2009, Demeulenaere 2011).

The existence of analytical sociology as a well-defined approach is relatively new. Beyond an emphasis on precision, rigor, and clarity (desirable in all analysis), its most pronounced features are a focus on building links between micro and macro levels of analysis and the use of mechanisms as a central component of any explanatory strategy. The notoriously large number of definitions that have been generated to describe the idea of a social mechanism has created some uncertainty about the term, but the definition adopted within analytical sociology itself is derived from Peter Machamer, Lindley Darden, and Carl Craver's article "Thinking about Mechanisms" (2000). "Mechanisms can be said to consist of entities (with their properties) and the activities that these entities engage in, either by themselves or in concert with other entities. These activities bring about change, and the type of change brought about depends upon the properties and activities of the entities and the relations between them" (Hedström and Bearman 2009: 5). Although this definition is agnostic as to the identity of the activity-engaging entities, it is clear in analytic sociology that because the outcomes of interest are at the social or group level (as determined by the boundaries of the field of sociology), micro-level explanations should be based in or near the level of individuals. Thus the beliefs and behaviors of individuals are central to explanation in analytic sociology.

Although I am ready to admit that readers may find themselves slip-sliding around the bathtub model of micro and macro levels of analysis as they read through these chapters, there is a general, if nested and recursive, pattern to the layout of the chapters of the book and the means by which they engage the problem of linking micro and macro levels of analysis. I outline here the way in which they link individual behavior and larger social outcomes. Figure 1 presents a modified version of James Coleman's multilevel bathtub model (Coleman 1990: 8, Hedström and Swedberg

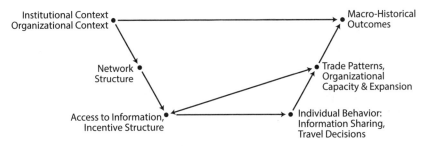

**FIGURE 1**. Modified model of multilevel social transformation.

1998: 22, Hedström and Bearman 2009: 34), also influenced by Karen Bar-key's model of cultural and structural dynamics (Barkey 2009: 724). The modifications I have made to the diagram are intended to illustrate the argument of this book, not as a fundamental intervention or restatement of the relationship between different levels of social observation. In the paragraphs that follow I both summarize the chapters and locate them with respect to the diagram of multilevel social processes.

Chapter 2 sets out the stakes of the argument, situating the Company with respect to some of the larger processes of transition and change in the early modern period and the dawn of modernity in the nineteenth century, which means the arc of the book begins not on the left, but on the right side of the diagram. The issues addressed are large-scale macro-historical outcomes, such as economic development in the West, underdevelopment in Asia, growth in state capacity, the development of economic theory, and the emergence of new organizational forms. All are linked to and inter-twine with the story of the English East India Company. The following chapters build up to the relationship between the Company and these global-historical outcomes.

Chapter 3 undertakes a comparative analysis of the organizational char-acteristics of the Company, highlighting the firm's record of sustained innovation through the incorporation of new markets, and the extent to which this may be explained by the degree of militarization in the Com-pany, relations with the state, and the management of employees' private trade. Over the long term, the English Company was the most successful of the European companies. Like the Dutch Company, it was not owned by the state. Unlike the Dutch Company, the English Company legalized the private country trade of its employees at an early stage. And like many smaller European companies, it was less militaristic than the Dutch. These comparisons suggest, in keeping with the insights of previous historians, that the private trade of the English Company played an important role in English success in the East. While setting up a comparative argument for why individual-level trading decisions (associated with the private trade) are important to understanding the differences between the English and other East India companies, this chapter also provides the organizational background necessary to understanding why employees of the English Company would engage in certain patterns of behavior—thus putting it back on the upper-left-hand corner of the diagram in figure 1.

Chapters 4 and 5 both work to capture the full relationship among organizational context, individual behavior, and group-level outcomes, with chapter 4 focusing more intensely on the process of individual decision making, bottom left, and chapter 5 devoting more attention to the structural outcomes of individual behavior, middle-right of the diagram. Chapter 4 identifies how organizational context affects individual behavior and the propensity to incorporate information from peers into important operational decisions. The identification of this relationship illuminates, in turn, the larger question of how—or the mechanisms by which—decentralization contributed to the pattern of innovation found in the English Company. The analysis focuses on evaluating the relative importance of different types of information in leading captains to choose trade in one port over another, including formal orders given by the Company, a personal history of contact with ports, and information transmitted via social networks from ship to ship. The results show that social networks were an important source of information for captains when deciding which port to travel to next. However, the use of social networks varied over time. In the first century and a half of the Company's life, when private trade flourished and captains possessed considerable autonomy, social networks played an important role in determining patterns of trade. In the colonial period of the Company's history, from 1757 to its dissolution, social networks were depressed (or repressed).

The social networks were an important mediating factor in the structure of the English trade network because they kept smaller ports active in the larger network and sustained the expansion of the English trade to a growing number of ports. In other words they were central to the incorporation of innovation. When captains used these networks they anchored the Company into multiple commercial worlds, embedding it in local economies and opening up new avenues of opportunity for British trade. Thus organizational context channeled individual behavior that cumulated into new patterns of trade at the group level, eventually feeding back into individual behavior through the type of information available to actors. This feedback effect is represented by the double-arrowed line linking "trade patterns, organizational capacity and expansion" to "access to information and incentive structure."

Chapter 5 provides further analysis of organizational incentive structures, linking the behavior of individuals to the larger macro structure of trade, which may also be seen as an intermediate step linking individual behaviors to the largest outcomes described in chapter 2. The analysis here explores the unintended consequences of the private trade allowances. The unique private trade allowances of the English Company created a perverse incentive for the captains and crew. Those who were engaged in the private trade (which was most employees) had an incentive to illegally extend their voyages in the East and seek out new commercial opportunities. Company officials condemned this practice; however it had an unexpected impact on the firm. While "losing the season" to extend their voyages, captains took the risks necessary to directly link distant markets within the Company network. Through opportunistic and malfeasant behavior, they wove the many regions and ports into one multilateral commercial network. The decentralization of control over the conduct of trade in the English Company contributed to the creation of a cohesive network of information well suited to shuttling timely information from all ports between captains and factors, and even to Company officials in Britain. Again, there is a recursive pattern here, represented by the double-arrowed line, within the larger pattern of micro-macro links as changes in network structure affect the information available to individuals traversing the network. In addition, new ports, containing new markets and goods, were discovered along these voyages and incorporated into the larger trade network.

Chapters 6 and 7 return to the upper left side of the diagram, to outline the environmental conditions outside of the organization also necessary to producing the particular pattern of behavior found in employees of the Company. A story that one-sidedly focuses on the Company at the expense of the Asian context is simply incomplete. The innovative structure of the English Company could not have materialized without the sophisticated commercial markets of the East. This is not merely to say that the allure of Eastern riches encouraged English entrepreneurialism. The continued success of the Company lay in the synergy between the Company and the activities of its employees pursing the country trade. It is however not possible to understand the importance of the relationship between the Asian commercial context and the private trade without first investigating the micro-level patterns of behavior in chapters 4 and 5.

The development of the small-scale country trade of captains and factors depended upon the commercial opportunities available in the ports of the East. In chapter 6, I begin a two-chapter argument that the English Company was most successful in ports with a large local merchant class already adept at overseas trade. The captains were able to engage in trade because of preexisting financial and commercial networks that were willing and able to accommodate a large influx of small-scale commercial actors (factors, captains, officers, and seamen), as well as the larger interests of the

Company itself. Overviews of foreign trade institutions, regulations, and practices at eight different ports of call—Batticaloa, Madras, New Guinea, Madagascar, Bantam (Banten), Whampoa (Huangpu, port of Guangzhou), Goa, and Batavia (Jakarta)—demonstrate this point. Each presents a window into the complex social and political structures of eighteenth-century Asian trading ports. These longer port descriptions ground the analysis of ships' data presented in the following chapter.

Chapter 7 presents systematic evidence that decentralized, commercially sophisticated ports were preferred by the English Company. The data on Company trading voyages show that they spent more time in and had longer trading partnerships with ports that were already set up to accommodate the commercial interests of both the Company and employees. These data also cast doubt upon theories that English trade patterns in Asia were driven by the presence of other Europeans. The central finding, however, is that Asian merchants and the commercial institutions they had created before the arrival of the British played a vital role in the expansion of England into the East through their support of decentralized market exchange. Thus the institutional context of the organization in the societies with which it came into contact must also be considered in order to understand the full range of options for individual-level actions.

Because they address different components of the relationship between micro and macro layers of analysis, these chapters are meant to be read in relation to each other, not as separate arguments about different components of the English Company trade. The comparison across firms presented in chapter 3 is merely suggestive without the identification of specific mechanisms that could have improved firm operations, presented in chapters 4 and 5. Similarly the mechanisms outlined in chapters 4 and 5 are meant to relate to the commercial success of the firm documented in chapter 1—they can only indirectly be considered one of several contributing factors for large issues at stake in the history of the Company, outlined in chapter 2. Chapters 6 and 7 are inextricably linked to chapters 4 and 5, since the beneficial mechanisms of information transmission and innovation described in the earlier chapters rest upon decentralization and private trade, which in turn depended upon open, cosmopolitan, and heavily commercialized ports.

As a whole, the research presented in this book investigates the dramatic progress of commercial expansion in the seventeenth and eighteenth centuries by examining how the English Company successfully negotiated complex and dynamic market environments through networks: decentralized patterns of interaction and communication. The East India Company was not simply a monopoly and the private trade was not simply a version of free trade. The Company was a network form of organization created by difficult conditions, inadequate control, and simple opportunism.

## NETWORKS AND ANALYTICAL SOCIOLOGY

A central unifying theme that runs throughout this book is the importance of networks to understanding the trajectory of the Company. Indeed, networks serve more than one function in the analysis and the diagram represented in figure 1. It is the position of analytical sociology that the micro layer of individual behavior is not the cause of macro-level patterns, but instead both are instantiations of each other—a relationship of supervenience (Hedström and Bearman 2009: 11). Actors' behaviors do not cause organizational behavior because they are organizational behavior—what else is an organization other than a group of individuals engaging in routinized patterns of behavior? Thus any causal effects should be understood as traveling from the right to the left of the diagram, not from the top to bottom or bottom to top.

It has frequently been emphasized that this position implies that causal processes work only at the bottom, micro level. I would instead like to draw attention to the implications it has for our perception of the social world as researchers. The relationship of supervenience between micro and macro levels of social existence might also suggest that micro and macro levels of behavior are in effect the same phenomenon, viewed in different ways. This understanding of the relation could further imply that causal processes do run across the macro level, from one macro property to another—it is just that the causal process is being described at different level, as for example one refers to a table stopping the movement of a plate without referring to its molecular properties. The problem, however, is that, although referring to the solidity of a table is more than adequate for most of our purposes, our perception of macro-level social properties is not sufficiently granular to perceive real differences that occur at the micro level. These differences—which are not immediately apparent at the group, organizational, or institutional level—are often important enough to create dissimilar outcomes for individuals and groups. Since different micro-level properties, which produce different social outcomes, are often perceived as similar organizational or institutional forms, adequate social explanations really have to reach down to the micro layer.

This brief excursus helps to explain the dual role of networks in this work. Networks function both as a causal mechanism and also as an aid to the interpretability of the social world. Because of their complexity in aggregate, it is very difficult to observe all the micro-level behaviors, patterns, and links that are instantiated in macro-social processes. Networks help us to make sense of aggregate patterns of behavior at the individual level and to thereby see the link between micro and macro levels. They are an intermediate level of observation that allows the analyst, researcher, or reader to see the relationship between individual and group behavior more clearly—an analytic tool used for understanding and knowledge building. In this book, they serve this purpose most clearly in chapter 5, where structural analysis reveals the connectivity patterns that facilitate information transfer at the organizational level.

Figure 1 also contains a diagonal line running between trade patterns and access to information and incentive structures, indicating networks have an effect at the micro level. This line indicates the second role networks play in this book, which is as a central mechanism of information diffusion operating within the larger narrative of institutional transformation. This aspect of how networks function in the larger argument is most pronounced in chapter 4, where the analysis captures how social interactions between peers affect the behavior of individuals under favorable institutional conditions. In this latter sense, however, networks are only one of a number of mechanisms operating to link the left and right sides of the diagram.

As Diego Gambetta has noted, most satisfactory explanations are composed of concatenations of smaller, simpler mechanisms (Gambetta 1998). Understanding how the employees of the East India Company used social networks involves not only mechanisms of information transfer, but also preference and belief formation (Freese 2009, Rydgren 2009): Do captains prefer riskier or safer commercial opportunities? How do they come to believe that travel to certain port offers a significant investment opportunity? Certainly, these processes have to do with rational imitation (Hedström 1998), where individuals intentionally mimic the behavior of others (in this case past behavior) when faced with uncertainty (lack of direct knowledge about commercial opportunities) in order to make more effective decisions. The timing of individuals' movements across the trade network, or the scheduling of ships, determines rates of information transfer as interactions can take place only when ships come into contact with each other, that is, if they are in the same place at the same time (Winship 2009). Lack of organizational control led individuals to introduce random perturbations into network structure when profit maximizing in a market environment. The randomness introduced into the larger system created a small-world effect (Watts 1999), increasing information flow across ships and within the firm. And all of these individual-level behaviors were based on the opportunities (Petersen 2009) created for individual trade by a subset of commercially open ports of the Indian and Eastern Seas.

Thus the shape of my argument is strongly aligned with the principles laid out in analytical sociology through the incorporation of mechanisms and the analysis of the links between micro and macro levels of social action. Also these mechanisms inevitably have some link to individual actors, whether through shaping their perceptions, providing opportunities for certain types of behavior, or simply influencing them to take a certain course of action. It is this last point where I believe that combining comparative historical work with analytical sociology can contribute to the larger analytical project and illuminate some of the obscured strengths of the perspective.

## ANALYTICAL AND COMPARATIVE HISTORICAL SOCIOLOGY

The two most pervasive criticisms of analytical sociology to date have been that it does not present a sufficiently developed model of social action (Gross 2009, Little 2012, Edling 2012) and that it does not orient researchers to investigate and take into account the context in which actors take action (Little 2012, Sewell 2012, Reed 2012). On the one hand these concerns are tied to lingering fears that analytical sociology is simply rational choice theory dressed in new clothes. I believe this fear is unjustified and the commitment to more complex models of cognition (i.e., beyond rationality) is made clear in the *Oxford Handbook of Analytical Sociology* (Hedström and Bearman 2009). However it is also clear that these criticisms point to an avenue of development, not a finished product.

The problem of culture, understood as a symbolic sign system, has yet to be directly addressed within the framework of analytical sociology. It is a difficult problem because culture has largely been theorized as a collective product that exists outside of individuals and has a logic and dynamism in and unto itself.[12] This book is not the place to dive into this large issue, but it should be clear that for analytical sociology to successfully incorporate a developed conception of culture more research on cognitive models will be necessary to understand how culture is instantiated at the micro level. Exciting progress has been made along these lines within and without analytical sociology (McLean 2007, Mische 2008, Sperber 2011, Martin 2011).

What historical work does is make it perfectly clear that convincingly identifying micro-level mechanisms requires a deep attention to the culture in which individuals operate. The process of trying to understand the motivations, actions, preferences, and opportunities of the individuals— reaching down to the micro layer of social processes in order to identify mechanisms driving social and organizational change—requires nothing so much as thinking very seriously about the social, cultural, and material circumstances of the actors themselves. In historical circumstances, these simply cannot be taken for granted.

Two crucial examples from this work that should serve to illustrate this point include, one, the values placed on the private trade and, two, assumptions about the prevalence of market mentalities. The findings in chapters 4 and 5 are largely driven by the private trade practices of employees, which encouraged both informal mechanisms of information flow and exploratory behavior. The private trade, or the idea of combining the conditions of employment and self-employment into one position, is not commonly found in twenty-first-century labor practices. Even in the early modern world this amalgamation occupied an ambiguous position. The Company simultaneously accepted and rejected the practice (when it could). Cultural factors that contributed to its partial acceptance within the Company were based in both the different value placed on venality and corruption in the early modern world—where such practices were often the means by which the world worked—and the beginnings of the emergence of an appreciation of commercially based self-interest that has become so pronounced in our own time (Hirschman 1997).

Similarly where rational choice theorists might assume all actors are profit maximizers, that is, take as given a certain type of market mentality, chapters 6 and 7 argue that British agents of the Company were channeled into market participation by institutional circumstances. The development of the idea of a right held by individuals to engage in self-interested, long-distance trade outside of a corporate body, that is, a private trade, was facilitated by macro-institutional arrangements found in Asia. Thus, rational profit-maximizing market behavior is far from a baseline assumption in the book. Indeed, I would hope this research makes a small contribution to the much larger problem of understanding the process whereby self-interested commercial behavior became a central component of the emerging capitalist system, whether via the Company's influence on the development of economic theory, discussed in chapter 2, or through the example of its thriving private trade.

To return to the larger point, focusing on micro-level description in historical contexts requires a consideration of the environment of the social actors because their perceptions and interpretations of the world they inhabit are central to understanding their desires, beliefs, and motivations. Thus the orientation of analytical sociology to micro-level mechanistic explanation is, if anything, an invitation for further development of theories relating the actor to their cultural, social, and material contexts—particularly as historical work is one of the few ways by which researchers can compare across radically different cultural systems to draw lessons about potentially generalizable cultural processes. If analytical sociology uses historical contexts to explore how experiences, practices, and events contribute to the larger process of organizational, institutional, and even cultural transformation, it will inevitably enrich our theories of culture.

*Chapter 2*

# MERCHANT CAPITALISM AND
# THE GREAT TRANSITION

---

The period in which the English East India Company grew and expanded is known under several names: the early modern period, the mercantilist period, and the era of merchant capitalism. Stretching roughly from 1500 to somewhere between 1750 and 1800, it can be understood as having begun with the Reformation and ended with the Industrial Revolution. The Industrial Revolution ushered in a new era of industrial capitalism, which has also been referred to as modern capitalism, or simply modernity. During the Industrial Revolution the English Company's commercial interests declined as the organization transitioned into a colonial power and was eventually taken over by the British government. Due to its longevity, the English Company was an important historical actor in both periods, so its relationship to the larger historical currents of each is at stake.

There has been a tremendous amount of work on the causes of the Industrial Revolution. Depending on who is consulted, a great deal of importance occurred in the early modern period of European history or, instead, it was neither an entirely sufficient nor unique prelude to the real transformation, which occurred during the Industrial Revolution. This difference in interpretation revolves around the issues different authors choose to focus on. Generally it is understood that significant transitions even in the earlier period include state centralization, marketization, urbanization, increasing agricultural innovation, overseas trade expansion (i.e., globalization), bureaucratization, rationalization, proto-industrialization, financialization, as well as the rise of consumerism, imperialism, mass politics, and new forms of economic organization and coordination.

The English Company was not directly linked to all of these macro historical processes, but played an important role in a surprisingly large number of them. Its role is a complex one however. The Company was a product of the era of merchant capitalism that survived into the era of modern capitalism. Therefore, it seems to have been both a part of the process whereby the preconditions for a capitalist transition were created and a barrier to the final stages of the transition. To further complicate its role, the Company prefigured organizational forms that were not widely adopted until the twentieth century. Thus, the Company seems to have both contributed to many of the changes we associate with the transition to modernity and at other times impeded that change, as when it sided with James II in the Glorious Revolution, and in addition it offers a vision of a path not taken—in terms of networked organizations, multinational business forms, or sovereign corporations.

All of the different transitions that occurred during the lifetime of the English Company have been linked in some manner to the rapid economic growth experienced by England, and later Europe; however they are also interesting historical developments in and of themselves. They should not be understood solely through the lens of the Industrial Revolution, but also considered as separate streams of historical processes that contributed to the larger pattern by which we eventually came to recognize the contours of the modern world (Emigh 2004: 379). In this chapter I position the Company with respect to the Industrial Revolution, and also explain its role in several other important historical processes: underdevelopment in Asia, the emergence of the modern state, the rise of economic theory, and the emergence of new organizational forms. Although these developments have at times been indirectly linked to the Industrial Revolution, they should also be considered as separate phenomena and important topics in their own right.

## INDUSTRIAL REVOLUTION

The historical period during which the English Company engaged in commercial activity leads up to and encompasses the early stages of the Industrial Revolution and the tremendous increase in economic productivity that set England, and soon Europe, apart from the rest of the world. I have already argued that the Company was well established as the preeminent commercial power in the East before the onset of the Industrial Revolution, and that therefore the commercial success of the Company cannot be explained away by the rapid economic development of England. Indeed, the timing of events indicates that the Company may have played a role in the dynamics leading up to that growth. The most direct approach to this question is to consider the relationship of the expansion of overseas trade to the Industrial Revolution.

Many have linked the Commercial Revolution with the Industrial Revolution because of their close historical proximity. England's overseas trade expanded rapidly beginning in 1600 and was the most dynamic sector of the economy until roughly 1780, when the really spectacular uptick of the Industrial Revolution took place. The growth of the East Indies trade, forged by the East India Company, was a part of this expansion, although only a fraction of the larger total. For example, the annual rate of growth for English exports to Asia from 1600 to 1649 was 2.97, 2.79 from 1650 to 1699, and 1.88 from 1700 to 1749 (O'Rourke and Williamson 2002: 419–20).[1] These increases are at times approaching the phenomenal expansion of the nineteenth century at annual rates of 3.7 to 3.8. However the percentage of England's manufactures being exported to Asia was only 3 percent in 1699–1701, 2.4 percent in 1722–24, and 11.2 percent in 1752–54 (Davis 1962: 291). Indeed, the Asian trade is only a fraction of the overseas trade of England, which even in total is not enough to directly account for the rapid growth of the nineteenth century (O'Brien 1982: 4).

Despite evidence that overseas trade did not directly produce much industrial expansion, there is increasing evidence that overseas trade played an important role in sustaining modern patterns of economic growth (O'Rourke and Williamson 2005, Findlay and O'Rourke 2007: 325–64). However it was the dramatic expansion of the nineteenth century that potentially sustained economic development into the twentieth century—not the expansion prior to 1760–80, which is when the Company itself was expanding operations.[2] The issue at stake in this point is what kind of international trade could disrupt the premodern relationship linking population growth, falling wages, and increasing rents. Modern growth is predicated on breaking the Malthusian cycle that had previously bound these factors into a recurring pattern of growth and stagnation. Prior to 1760, overseas trade was not at levels that indicate it would have had this kind of effect. It did however reach such levels in the nineteenth century.

Global price convergence, which signifies a disruption of local relationships among factor prices, population growth, and land rents, did not take place until the 1800s. Therefore we might conclude that although trade expansion occurred prior to the late 1700s, it was of a qualitatively different kind than that found in the nineteenth century, and could not have been directly responsible for the initial shift in economic productivity associated with the Industrial Revolution. This analysis is consistent with the views of world systems theorists as well as economic historians.

The economists Kevin O'Rourke and Jeffrey Williamson lay stress on the difference between eighteenth- and nineteenth-century international trade volumes, emphasizing the role of free market practices and technological innovation in transportation, such as the invention of the steam engine, in dramatically increasing trade. World systems theorists instead emphasize the rise of colonialism in the nineteenth century and its relationship to changes in international trade. Although Immanuel Wallerstein

is generally associated with the idea that trade caused capitalism, this sim-
plification does not capture his full argument. Wallerstein has long held
that the world system, essential to the growth of modern capitalism was not
fully integrated until at least 1760, when a colonial apparatus was able to
funnel raw materials from Asia and the Americas to the industrial capitalists in Northern Europe (Wallerstein 1986). Similar to O'Rourke and Williamson, Wallerstein points to a qualitative difference in early modern and
modern trade. The importance of the early Asian trade in luxuries, from
1500 to 1800, was to begin the process of building up this system, which
would later sustain capitalist expansion. Thus it was a historical precondition necessary to the creation of a functioning capitalist system—a turning point but not a cause in the sense of a direct and immediate stimulus
(Wallerstein 1976, 1980, 1983, [1989] 2011).

The argument for indirect links between the expansion of trade and the
growth of manufacturing is indeed much stronger than the evidence for a
direct link. Wallerstein argues that global expansion of the early modern
period laid the foundation for the emergence of capitalism by initiating
the process whereby Asia and the Americas were drawn into the European
economic system. Once merged these economies became a world system
that sustained capitalist expansion (Wallerstein 1976, 1980, 1983). Jacob
Price has argued that the expansion in overseas trade helped to lay an institutional groundwork that provided fertile terrain for the innovations that
were to spark so much productivity in the nineteenth century. Trade expansion helped create a transportation and communication infrastructure
that supported further development. In the East India Company case the
contribution to this infrastructure would have been largely focused around
docks and shipping capacity. More crucially, Price argues that trade expansion led to the creation of important institutions, such as banks, clear-
ing houses, insurance companies, and stock exchanges. Furthermore, it
contributed to the development of commercial practices and law, a skilled
commercial class, and a type of generalized trust, which Price refers to as
"good will," that supported the ready extension of credit (Price 1989: 284).
Building upon earlier arguments by Douglass North, Robert Thompson,
Barry Weingast, and others of the new institutionalism in economics,
Daron Acemoglu, Simon Johnson, and James Robinson argued more recently that early trade expansion was essential to later economic growth
because it shifted political power into the hands of merchants who were
able to introduce legal protections for property rights, which then made
rapid economic expansion possible (2005).

All of these approaches suggest that is it worth considering whether
global market integration in the 1800s would have been possible without
the commercial and institutional foundations laid in the 1600 and 1700s—
to which the East India Company was a central contributor. This entails

considering the counterfactual: what would have occurred if England did not already have a well-developed global trade network in the 1800s? For example, the invention of the steamship, and the resulting drastic decrease in transportation costs, might have been enough to call global trade expansion into being at that late date without prior development. However, this hypothesis seems unrealistic for several reasons.

Research on twentieth- and twenty-first-century globalization processes underscores the importance of institution building even in the face of low transportation costs (Fligstein and Mara-Drita 1996, Gotham 2006, Halliday and Carruthers 2007). These findings imply that early modern trade would also have been significantly hindered without the presence of the commercial and financial institutions developed from 1500 to 1780. Furthermore, overseas trade patterns seem to have a significant amount of path dependency built into them, meaning that their trajectory is constrained by the conditions that existed at their founding. In particular, trade with former colonies significantly exceeds trade between other nations (Rauch 1999). If even the drastically reduced transportation costs experienced in the twentieth century do not erase political, cultural, and institutional boundaries, it is unlikely that these would have been immediately overcome in the nineteenth through technological invention alone.

Free trade policies were largely an outgrowth of British imperial policy, implemented because the terms of trade favored manufacturing in England (Semmel 1970). British colonialism, particularly in Asia, was an outgrowth of commercial enterprise, so in the absence of previous trade expansion, there is reason to doubt that Britain would have acquired all of its overseas possessions, and therefore British elites would have significantly less ability to institute free trade policies in those sites. Thus both colonialism and free trade would have had much less impact on encouraging trade in the nineteenth century without prior expansion. It is also true that the commercial position of Britain would have been quite different, potentially making free trade policies less advantageous. Even the invention and adoption of the steamship might have been delayed had not long-distance trade already become an important part of European commerce.

If a preexisting foundation of commercial and institutional development was necessary to the rapid expansion of trade experienced in the nineteenth century, it may still be asked whether the development of the Atlantic trade could have by itself produced the essential infrastructure without the addition of the East Indies trade. This question is more difficult to address; however the increase in trade between 1500 and 1800 involved a three-way interaction among the demand for Asian goods in Europe, the products of the silver mines in the Americas, and increasing manufacture of goods for export to the Americas—in addition to the better known Atlantic triangle

trade in cotton, slaves, and textiles—indicating that the idea of strictly separating the two developments is questionable.

In addition to the East India Company's general contribution to overseas trade expansion, there is also a very specific feature of the East India
trade relevant to understanding the roots of the Industrial Revolution. As
is well known, cotton textiles were a leading growth sector in the Industrial
Revolution. The development of the cotton industry in Britain was really a
classic case of import substitution, where economic development is based
on the replacement of foreign imports, in this case Indian textiles, with
domestically produced goods.

Cotton played a central role in the Industrial Revolution as a site of
technological innovation and growth, but also had an unprecedented ability to stimulate consumer demand. As Beverly Lemire documents, cotton
textiles allowed lower-class consumers to mimic aristocratic fashions, allowing new status pretentions and presentations of self and creating a novel
"visual language" of stylistic distinctions (Lemire 2011: 223). All of this
indicates that cotton textiles had unique characteristics, and that another
type of industry could not have easily taken on the same role in spearhead-
ing the development of manufacturing (Findlay and O'Rourke 2007: 339).

The role of the East India Company was to introduce Indian textiles to
the mass market. The export cotton industry in India had been in existence
since at least the thirteenth century (Subrahmanyam 1990b: 81). Trade between Europe and Asia—by other paths and through other hands—had also
existed for centuries, so it was not that cotton was unknown in England.
Surplus production in Asia and the rise of living standards in England must
have contributed to the boom in textile consumption, but there is little
reason to believe that India would have begun to ship cotton to England.
As I describe in more detail in chapter 3, the Dutch did not recognize
the potential for cotton sales until the English began to focus heavily
on the trade, and even the English Company did not develop it until later
in the seventeenth century. At worst, the English East India Company was
a convenient funnel, linking supply in Asia to demand in England at a time
that intersected neatly with increasing rates of technological innovation in
England. At best, the Company recognized and pioneered the large-scale
import of the good when others did not.

In summary, despite the fact that the expansion of the English East India
Company was far from the most significant causal factor in producing or
sustaining the long-term economic development that began with the Industrial Revolution, it was an important link in a sequence of events that
contributed to that development. It is far from sufficient, but for those who
regard England's transformation as the result of a chain of contingencies
and a congruence of conditions (Wallerstein 1974: 401, Lieberman 1997:
499, Pomeranz 2000: 32, Goldstone 1998, 2000, 2002: 332, O'Brien 2000,
Clark 2001: 5, Jones 2003), it should be viewed as an important component.

## UNDERDEVELOPMENT

The time when England and Europe pulled ahead of the rest of the world in terms of economic development should also to be understood as a moment when other regions fell behind. Since different causes may have been at work in propelling growth in England and Europe and retarding growth in Asia—or the same cause may have had different effects within different contexts—these two processes should be considered separately. Indeed, the degree to which these two phenomena are related is subject to considerable debate.

In this section, I am not addressing the extent to which expropriation of wealth from Asia affected patterns of growth in Europe. The focus here is on the effect that the European presence had on Asia. This effect is, of course, significant in and of itself. England and Europe were intimately involved in other areas of the world, and because of this involvement there is reason to believe that regions that might have otherwise experienced economic growth were held back or depressed because of European interference, and even more specifically colonial expropriation. It is difficult to always tease out the separate effects of each European company on regions where they were all active, so I will first discuss the potential impacts of European involvement in Asia in general and then briefly focus in more specifically on the impact of the English Company.

The question of European impact on Asia has taken on several different formulations. The older, Orientalist literature was built around the assumptions of a static, traditionalist society that absorbed ineffective European attempts to stimulate growth and development. The position taken in this literature was that Asian economies, in particular India, were stable—that is, had never experienced levels of growth similar to even what had occurred in Europe in the early modern period—and that Europeans could do little to change that. This position was never tenable, although it seems to have been accepted in the past as a political expedient. At the other end of the pole, a counterargument emerged asserting that certain regions of Asia had been on the verge of industrialization until European intervention derailed this economic progress. This position has also been widely discredited, although not to the extent of the older Orientalist stance.

The question that remains is whether a more modest pattern of economic growth was negatively or positively affected by the presence of Europeans. The answer has proved to be complex, as many have argued that European commercial involvement initially provided a stimulus to existing growth in certain productive regions of Asia, while colonialism later inhibited that growth. Furthermore, aspects of this position have been cast into doubt by the most recent work comparing wages and GDP across the early modern world.

First, a number of scholars have argued that Europe and Asia experienced roughly comparable levels of development from 1500 to the mid-eighteenth century (Goldstone 2003, Wong 1997, Frank 1998, Pomeranz 2000). Kenneth Pomeranz provides a particularly good overview by considering a range of possible sources of economic advantage. In all cases he finds similar levels across productive regions of Asia and Europe. These factors include transport capital, life expectancy, birth rates, average income, labor productivity, agricultural innovation, and commercialization (Pomeranz 2000: 31–107). David Washbrook observed organized and price-responsive markets, autonomous and powerful merchants, advanced accountancy practices, labor mobility, and long-distance trade in bulk goods in the historical record of the Indian Subcontinent (Washbrook 1988: 62–63, 66). Similar types of development in the north during the eighteenth century have been noted by Christopher Bayly (1983: 30–34).[3]

Second, it has been argued that the presence of European trading companies in regions of Asia stimulated economic growth. Om Prakash found that together the English and Dutch companies supported 8.69 to 11.11 percent of the work force through their trade in Bengal in the early eighteenth century, and that overall the companies increased the output and incomes of the region, as well as employment rates. The exchange of European silver for manufactured goods (i.e., cotton textiles) was particularly beneficial for the Bengal economy (Prakash 1976: 178). Prakash also finds that the cultivation of arable lands increased in Bengal during the 1700s, tax revenues grew, and trade expanded (2005). Frank Perlin argued that the expansion of overseas trade from 1500 to 1800 stimulated an existing trend toward the development of merchant capitalism in the Indian Subcontinent, which included the expansion of peasant settlements, a rising urban population, the development of new financial institutions and taxation techniques, monetization, and a rise in manufacturing (Perlin 1983: 67–70). Sanjay Subrahmanyam, who positions himself as in disagreement with Perlin's central premise, nevertheless finds that European trade stimulated the cotton textile trade of Coromandel in the 1600s, but that cotton production subsequently stagnated in the 1700s for structural reasons having little to do with the European presence (Subrahmanyam 1990b: 110).

Third, the transition to colonialism had significant negative impacts. There is widespread agreement that British Imperial authorities either began or hastened a process of deindustrialization in India. Both structural forces and British colonial rule depressed the cotton trade: technological innovations in textile production made British goods more competitive, political instability and drought conditions in India raised grain prices, and the British government imposed free trade agreements that acted to the detriment of Indian industry (Clingingsmith and Williamson 2008). The result in India was a significant decrease in secondary industry employment rates and a reduction of available capital (Bagchi 1976). In Bengal, the English Company used its newly acquired political power to exclude other European Companies from the region's trade while eroding the autonomy of Indian merchants, thus destroying the foundations for a competitive market (Prakash 2005). Furthermore, once the Company was able to collect bullion through tax revenues in its colonial territory, the influx of foreign bullion ceased. Instead Company operations and related English trade began to drain bullion out of the country, with considerable negative economic consequences (Arasaratnam 1979: 28–29). Sinnappah Arasaratnam showed that the autonomy of the merchant class in Coromandel was diminished as the Company used its political power to establish direct control over weavers (Arasaratnam 1979: 36), and, according to Christopher Bayly, urbanization rates began to decrease across the board under the colonial rule of the Company (2000: 91).

Prasannan Parthasarathi has argued that the endemic poverty, low wages, and low standard of life found in India today were produced during British colonial rule (2001: 2). However this strong thesis has received considerable pushback by researchers who also question the extent of the development experienced by Asia in the eighteenth century. Tirthankar Roy has found evidence that the average income in Bengal was significantly lower than in Europe (one-fifteenth) and that it neither grew nor declined from 1722 to 1881, which encompasses the transition to colonialism, indicating that colonialism had no significant impact on wages (Roy 2010: 188). Stephen Broadberry and Bishnupriya Gupta have found that India's GDP declined steadily from 1600 to 1871 and point to 1650 as the beginning of the divergence with Europe, at which time Indian GDP was 80 percent of England's. By 1871 they find that it had shrunk to 15 percent (Broadberry and Gupta 2010). Since the European influence was still limited across the subcontinent at this time, this indicates that other factors beyond European presence were at work in the decline. Roman Studer has come out very strongly against the claim that India was comparable to Europe in the 1700s and shown that grain markets in India were localized, and therefore inefficient, until the mid-nineteenth century (Studer 2008).

Some of these recent comparisons are not quite fair. The current nation of India is roughly one-third the size of Europe. Pakistan alone is nearly six times the size of England, which is about the same size of the Indian state of Punjab. There could certainly be significant regional differences hidden in the aggregate data. However, Broadberry and Gupta found that wages in the Yangtze valley and northern and southern India were similar to those in Central and Eastern Europe and diverging from the Northern European bases of industrial growth in the early modern period (Broadberry and Gupta 2006). Robert Allen and his coauthors produced similar results in an examination of standards of living in the leading cities of China. They found that these cities had comparable standards of living to Eastern and

Southern European cities, all of which were outpaced by Northern European cities as early as 1738 (Allen et al. 2011).

This recent research provides strong evidence that colonialism alone did not derail an imminent transition to modern growth, vis-à-vis an industrial revolution of some kind, which is something that few would contradict. To many of the authors the research also indicates that market forces account for the relative stagnation of Asia compared to Northern Europe, not European colonialism. However, the research still does not address to what extent colonialism and British imperial policy sustained, exacerbated, or ameliorated that stagnation.

Trade between Asia and Europe was already expanding by 1650, so this evidence certainly does not rule out the possibility that the growth of the European infrastructure for trade (in the form of European ships and organizations) played a role in creating the gap between England and Asia—although it is more likely that overseas trade expansion helped the Europeans more than it hurt Asia given the relative size of the populations involved in and affected by overseas trade. This position is supported by the work of Daron Acemoglu, Simon Johnson, and James Robinson (2005), which shows that active involvement in overseas trade explains much of the divergence between European countries.

When considered together, the contradictions between the findings of regional historians and those of economic historians suggest that further work needs to be done breaking down growth patterns within the Indian Subcontinent. The subcontinent should not be treated as a unified or discrete entity in the early modern period. If anything, the combined research suggests that if a European presence in Asia had a positive effect, that effect must have been limited to specific regions and times, and also potentially to certain classes or groups within involved communities. While any positive effects of commercial growth may be attributed to both the English and Dutch Companies across much of Asia, the English Company bears more responsibility for the negative consequences of colonial policy with the exception of the islands in the Dutch East Indies.

## STATE CAPACITY

A distinct but related line of historical development in the early modern period is growth in state capacity. Tudor monarchs had limited despotic powers, whereas Benjamin Disraeli oversaw a vast administrative infrastructure capable of effective tax collection on several continents (O'Brien and Hunt 1999). At times, the increased capacity of the British state clearly benefited the East India Company. Beginning in the 1690s, the Company had turned to the British government for assistance in patrolling Eastern waters for pirates (Stern 2011: 186), and the late eighteenth-century conquest of Indian territory relied upon British government forces. Without the increased military powers of the British state such interventions would not have been possible. However the Company also contributed to the process through which the state and its military capacity was built up.

The increasing costs of warfare in the seventeenth and eighteenth centuries imposed new burdens on the government. Military costs were irregular and therefore difficult to manage through the steady incomes produced through tax collection. In order to cover the expense of new campaigns, governments of the early seventeenth century were forced to respond by imposing new taxes or raising existing rates. But however quickly taxes were raised, it was rarely possible to collect and deliver them in time to cover immediate military costs. It has been noted in several places that the creation of new and efficient financial institutions in the late seventeenth and early eighteenth centuries, created in large part through the expansion of overseas trade, gave Britain a crucial military advantage over other European countries (Bonney 1995: 377, Dickson 1967: 11, Neal 1977: 31 and 35, Cain and Hopkins 1986: 513, Mann 1993: 268, Carruthers 1996: 54). Crucially, these institutions facilitated the timely extension of large-scale, long-term, and low-interest credit to the government, used mainly for funding critical military operations.

The creation and implementation of new mechanisms that allowed for a significant expansion of the public debt—and a concomitant increase in state capacity—was part of a larger process known as the financial revolution (1688–1739). P.G.M. Dickson, who pioneered research in this area, summarized its main features as the development of long- and short-term borrowing, the creation of relations between the national treasury and the City (as the financial and banking center of London is known), the emergence of a market in securities, and investment in public loans (Dickson 1967: 12). It has since been persuasively demonstrated that the successful implementation of these financial innovations depended upon larger political changes that led creditors to the belief that the government would in fact honor its debts. These transformations include the adoption of representative government, the emergence of party politics, and the imposition of uniform national tax policy (North and Weingast 1989, Stasavage 2003, 2011, Dincecco 2011), as well as the emergence of a monied merchant elite with access to fungible capital (Stasavage 2011).

Prior to the creation of mechanisms for long-term loans to the government at reasonable or low rates of interest, the government was subject to the possibility of simply running out of funds, as occurred to Charles II in 1672 when he was unable to continue to honor the Orders of Payment that had funded the Second Anglo-Dutch War after the onset of the Third

Anglo-Dutch War (Dickson 1967: 43–44, Carruthers 1996: 61–69, Körner 1995: 525). By the early eighteenth century public outlays outstripped public income by over £2 million, and the shortfall was made up through public debt (Carruthers 1996: 54). The English East India Company played a significant role in this process, along with the Bank of England and the South Seas Company.

At the most basic level, the English East India Company was a major source of short- and long-term capital for the government. In the late seventeenth century, the English East India Company had long found it necessary to make repeated loans to the Crown in order to secure support for its monopoly privileges, but after 1688 the scale of the loans increased. From 1675 to 1679 Charles II received what would have been considered an extremely large sum of £200,000 through a series of loans from the Old East India Company (Sherman 1976: 336). In 1698, the New East India Companies loaned the government £2 million, and the United East India Company, which combined the New and Old Companies, had loaned the government an additional £1.2 million within a decade (Dickson 1967: 57). Thus the English East India Company directly contributed to the military successes of the British government by financing a significant portion of them.

However the needs of the state had outpaced what any one individual or even any one organization, however large and wealthy, could provide. The East India Company was able to supply these large funds to the government because of the concurrent development of the London stock market and the creation of new financial instruments. Because the East India Company was a joint-stock company whose shares were traded in a public market, they were able to transfer the cost of the public debt they funded on to third parties through the creation and sale of India bonds. As has recently been demonstrated by Pilar Marco and Camila Vam Malle-Sabouret (2007), these were sophisticated financial instruments that incorporated an early version of call and put options. India bonds were popular because they were extremely liquid, but still returned interest (Marco and Vam Malle-Sabouret 2007: 387–88). Thus, the English East India Company's sale of India bonds greatly increased the liquidity of public debt. Transferring government debts had previously been an onerous process (Carruthers 1996: 82). The East India Company's role was therefore not only to loan money, but also to facilitate the transfer of funds between private investors and government coffers.

Furthermore, because the East India directors were well represented in the Parliament, investors could expect that at least some portion of the government was committed to the repayment of debts to the Company. David Stasavage has argued that the representation of creditors in the offices of governments was crucial to a government's ability to signal a credible commitment to loan repayment (Stasavage 2003). Such representation clearly depends upon the adoption of a representative form of government, which was also a crucial component in the expansion of the state credit.[4]

Because the finances of the East India Company, as well as the South Seas Company and the Bank of England, were intertwined with those of the government, these large organizations and their investors were now tied to the interests of the new government (Carruthers 1996: 76). The financial and merchant classes had a direct stake in the continued success of the government, and indeed the government now had a direct stake in responding to the needs of the merchants and financiers.

In a less direct manner, the City became a site in which new money and old money, particularly aristocrats and wealthy merchants, were able to interact and form alliances that buttressed the state by integrating elite factions. Michael Mann charted out this process in the late nineteenth century. He argues that in the City, "capitalists in land, commerce, and finance fused as a single extensive political class, with national economic, familial, and educational (the 'public' schools) organizations, committed to a bureaucratic state and to free trade under British near hegemony" (Mann 1993: 129). But as P. J. Cain and A. G. Hopkins argue, this system of "gentlemanly capitalism" was in place well before the Industrial Revolution. The development of the banking profession attracted the aristocracy into lucrative positions that tied them to overseas ventures, such as the East India Company, and at the same time, taxes on overseas trade allowed the new government to expand revenues without raising land taxes and thereby alienating the same landed elites (Cain and Hopkins 1986: 518). Through these direct and indirect paths the rise of commercial institutions allowed for the fusion of interests necessary to support a strong, yet diffuse state marked by its commitment to free trade and economic liberalism.

Indeed, it has even been argued by George McGilvary that the success of the unification between Scotland and England (1707) depended upon a patronage system that funneled Scottish elites into positions of power within the East India Company (2008). In return for the opportunity to make their fortunes within the firm, the Scottish families put their political weight behind the English politicians and supported the continued success of the union. McGilvary further argues that the wealth brought back by Scottish families from the East brought prosperity to Scotland, winning further acquiescence to the new state of affairs. Thus the wealth brought from Asia in the ships of the Company seems to have welded potential breaks in the body politic along several possible fault lines.


## ECONOMIC THEORY

Accompanying the process of state centralization and financialization was the development and articulation of a new body of thought called political economy or economic theory. The sheer number of links between the

Company and the new political economists is somewhat remarkable. David Ricardo was a member of the Company's court of proprietors. Ricardo's close friend, James Mill, wrote his major life's work on the history of the British in India and went on to serve as assistant examiner of the India correspondence, a very respectable position within the East India Company. His even more influential son also worked for the Company. Thomas Malthus served as the chair of history and political economy at Haileybury, the East India Company's college for the education of young men. And, although eventually passed over, even Adam Smith at one time put considerable effort into seeking a position within the Company. These are only the more familiar names; the earlier, more obscure theorists of the seventeenth century with close associations to the East India Company include Thomas Mun and Josiah Child, both at different times directors of the Company, and Edward Misselden, who negotiated contracts on the Company's behalf.

Smith was the only one of these men to be passed over by the Company and also the most critical of Company policies, which should provide some insight into the general trend by which Company affairs influenced economic thinking of the day. Many of the economic writings of the seventeenth century were also vehicles whereby individuals attempted to build support for policies that favored their own affairs. Individuals heavily invested in or associated with the East India Company were no exception. The work of Thomas Mun provides a clear example.

Mun (1571–1641) was a successful London merchant, born to a family of merchants, as well as a sophisticated thinker who has become an important part of the history of economic theory. He was also a director of the East India Company when a silver shortage struck England in the early seventeenth century (Supple 1959: 222). Paper money was not yet in use in Northern Europe, and silver served as the currency of the day. This meant that a silver shortage was perceived as causing considerable hardship for the general population, who had difficulty getting their hands on enough currency to engage in routine market transactions. This situation caused particular trouble for the East India Company as its main export was silver. The shortage played into the hands of the bullionists, who insisted that any drain on bullion was bad for the country. With their prodding, general sentiment swung sharply against the East India Company (Muchmore 1970). By the 1620s the Company was at risk of losing its monopoly because of its export practices.

During the height of the silver shortage, Thomas Mun came to the defense of the Company by writing a tract titled *A Discourse of Trade from England unto the East Indies*. In this tract he argued convincingly that overseas trade did not need to directly increase the nation's store of precious metals because it indirectly contributed to economic health through profits made in the reexport trade and other intangibles, such as growing the shipping industry and employing dock workers. These arguments effectively persuaded many in the public and Parliament of the importance of the East Indies trade, thus helping to rescue the East India Company from its many critics (Barber 1975: 56). It also set Mun upon a path of work that would eventually ensure him a significant place in the history of economic thought for developing the theory of the balance of trade. It was in the interests of the Company to export bullion; Mun's economic works were part of the process by which the Company lobbied the government for support of this practice, by tying overseas trade expansion to long-term national prosperity.

Similarly, Edward Misselden, another early mercantilist, argued in *Free Trade, or the Means to Make Trade Flourish* (1622) that bullion export to Asia was a drain on the prosperity of England. Then, after gaining a position negotiating contracts for the East India Company, he argued in *The Circle of Commerce* (1623) that the trade to Asia was beneficial after all (Johnson 1937: 61). Together, and to a significant extent in response to the work of Gerard de Malynes, Misselden and Mun pushed their contemporaries away from a bullionist doctrine, which emphasized the role of the desire for silver or gold in commerce, to a belief in the balance of trade, emphasizing instead the role of international trade flows (Appleby 1978: 202). Although historians of economic thought have viewed balance of trade theories as outmoded by the eighteenth century, it may still be considered a step forward in the seventeenth. Mun in particular developed a perspective in which economic activities were conceived separately from the political or social, producing one of the first abstracted models of economic processes and leading toward the distinct conceptualization of "the economy" that has come to dominate modern thought (Appleby 1978: 47).

Sir Josiah Child, who has perhaps been unfairly credited with being an important thinker and a forerunner to free trade economists (Letwin, Child, and Culpeper 1959), owned an enormously large stake in the Company and, during his time, arguably exercised more personal control over the affairs of the Company than any single individual in its long organizational history. He argued for lowering interest rates, which would help reduce costs for the Company; he criticized bankers for discouraging commercial investment, but targeted bankers who opposed the Company's practice of exporting bullion; he argued against balance of trade theory when it could be used to criticize the Company; and he opposed a double tax on reexports because it would cut into Company profits (Finkelstein 2000: 140, 137, 141, 142).

As Andrea Finkelstein has pointed out, with the possible exception of Josiah Child, although these authors' works were largely rooted in various types of defenses of the East India Company trade, this did not define the full import of all that they had written—their work was not merely propaganda for the Company as it was the logic, consistency, and invention of novel or powerful concepts that led to their lasting impact (Finkelstein 2000: 55–88). The interests of the East India Company, however, were the springboard from which they were motivated to develop those larger concepts and theories.

Individuals who were not so directly tied to the Company itself, but were instead observers of the East India trade, made other important contributions to seventeenth century economic thought. Henry Martyn (1665–1721) was opposed to the monopoly privileges held by the East India Company but a strong supporter of the East India trade.[5] Although his contemporaries largely ignored his work, it grew more influential with time. In *Considerations upon the East India Trade*, he developed the idea that free trade benefits the economy even when the goods are manufactured elsewhere, that is, that there is an advantage to buying goods made abroad when they are cheaper than goods at home. This point is now considered an important precursor to the idea of comparative advantage (Maneschi 2002: 233). This argument was made in the face of opposition from the manufacturers of woolen goods, who opposed increasing the import of cotton textiles and argued that it depressed industry in Britain. Together with Sir Dudley North, Nicholas Barbon, John Houghton, and Sir Dalby Thomas, Joyce Appleby credits Martyn with developing the idea of consumer demand as an important driver of commercial growth (Appleby 1978: 173).

These authors were a part of a larger dialogue, but one that inevitably touched on the affairs of the Company, so much so that Joyce Appleby could summarize the seventeenth-century developments in economic thought by writing, "[I]n the debates over East Indian imports and recoinage, the conceptualization of the free market economy reached a new level of sophistication" (Appleby 1978: 248). However, the contributions inspired by the East India Company trade did not end with the mercantilist period. A new round of scholars in the late eighteenth and nineteenth centuries dealt with the ramifications of the Company acquiring sovereign powers in Asia.

Soon after the Company acquired political control of Bengal, in the aftermath of the 1757 Battle of Plassey, the region began to experience severe silver shortages, thought to disrupt both the local economy and the English export trade. From 1769 to 1773 a devastating famine struck the area. The Company was criticized both as a potential cause of the famine and for providing inadequate relief to the population. By taking political control of Bengal, the Company had finally found a way to end the debate over exporting bullion, by using Bengal tax revenues as a source of silver. However, it was now open to a new line of attack and the grounds of whether a company could serve as an adequate governor. Again the issues at stake revolved around the relationship between the state and commerce. Increasing calls for a division between the two came to dominate the discourse as doubt was cast as to whether a commercial actor could rule without rampant corruption. James Steuart, the political economist who wrote *An Inquiry into the Principles of Political Economy* (1767), and Edmund Burke roundly criticized the Company, arguing for a strict separation of the spheres of commerce and sovereign power (Burke and Marshall 1981).

William Barber devoted a book to how development economics was influenced by debate on the Company (1975), including a detailed chapter on the complete reconstruction of the history of the Indian Subcontinent by James Mill, who was interested in defending the right of his employers to rule as sovereigns in the East. According to Barber, Mill recast the history of what we now know as India. In the seventeenth century, the region was popularly understood in Europe as a thriving center of trade and manufacture. After Mill, it came to be viewed as a static, if not backward, traditional economy—a stereotype that has persisted to at least the twentieth century (Barber 1975: 126–40).

The Company was not solely responsible for the twists and turns taken by the formation of the discipline of economics in Britain. The existence of the Company gave many individuals a stake in a particular perspective, which led them to engage in a debate that shaped economics in its earliest stage of development. The Dutch did not produce a similar line of scholarship, though their Dutch East India Company was as large and consequential in the Netherlands as the English Company was in Britain (Van Niel 1988: 21). Andrea Finkelstein argues that the unique combination of commercial expansion, conflict between Parliament and Crown, and distance between merchants and the ruling political body found in England created the need for public discussions of economic policy (Finkelstein 2000: 4). These domestic conditions, coupled with the large organizational presence of the East India Company, and the particularities of the East Indies trade encouraged self-interested behavior that evolved into a larger discourse bound by its own internal logic. Eventually its legacy came to haunt the Company, as free market philosophers successfully challenged monopoly privileges in the nineteenth century.[6]


## NEW FORMS OF COORDINATED BEHAVIOR

By the late seventeenth century, the Company had begun to take on the characteristics of a modern corporation. It was a multidivisional global firm with permanent capital, regular stockholders' meetings, and a large administrative bureaucracy (Anderson, McCormick, and Tollison 1983,

Carlos and Nicholas 1988). Although not entirely unique, these characteristics distinguished the English Company from most other instances of
economic organization in the seventeenth and eighteenth centuries. Some
version of a limited liability partnership has been available since the ninth
century (Harris 2009, Udovitch 1962: 203).[7] The partnership system, in
which one person could manage distinct contractual obligations across
several locations, arose in the fourteenth century (Padgett and McLean
2006: 1563). In Northern Europe, merchant guilds managed much of the
overseas trade from the ninth to the sixteenth century (Kieser 1989: 550,
Ogilvie 2011). Guilds were exclusive fraternal associations of merchants
or other businessmen pledged to support each other, through which price
coordination and some overseas protection could be achieved. By the thirteenth and fourteenth centuries, the organizational and legal form of the
corporation became increasingly common in commerce, and as early as the
1400s regulated companies began to take on a prominent role in overseas
trade. By the middle of the sixteenth century, joint-stock companies, which
combined the exclusive privileges of guilds and regulated companies with
pooled investment capital, had emerged (Harris 2009: 613, 615, Walker
1931: 98–99). The English East India Company was a particularly large,
complex, and successful instantiation of this new class of organizations.

As I argue in the following chapters, the English Company had one additional element that differentiated it from other joint-stocks of the time.
The incorporation of legitimated private trade into Company operations
affected organizational structure and dynamics. The decentralization represented by the private trade fostered network patterns of communication
and trade. These networks contributed to the flow of information within
the firm, increasing its capacity to adapt to the complexity of its environment in the East Indies trading world. The increased capacity to adapt
promoted the long-term expansion and success of the firm, contributing to
its ability to play a large role in world history.

## CONCLUSION

Although the English East India Company can be usefully compared to
other national monopolies of the seventeenth and eighteenth centuries,
its historical impact was largely unique. The Industrial Revolution and the
early efflorescence of economic thought were British phenomena. As demonstrated by the lack of such developments in the Netherlands, the mere
existence of a large and powerful East India Company was very clearly not
enough to call these events into being. In both cases the Company was an
important piece of a larger set of circumstances that produced the particular

trajectory of English history. In these cases the effect of the Company was conditioned upon other circumstances. The Industrial Revolution and the birth of the field of economics were unique and world-historical events. Similar events had not occurred earlier in history. When the Industrial Revolution and the systematization of economic theory did occur, all subsequent instances of economic development as well as contributions to the field of economics would have to be evaluated in relation to the initial events. Other industrializing nations explicitly considered the example of Britain and incorporated technologies developed there, and subsequent writings in economics responded to the early mercantilists; for example, the Physiocrats extensively criticized Mun and Misselden's theory of the balance of trade. It follows fairly simply that unique events are produced by unique, or at least extremely rare, circumstances. Otherwise, such events would be more common in our history. Since we cannot experimentally re-create the emergence of capitalism and economics, it is impossible to definitively say that the East India Company was a necessary component. However, at the very least it can be argued that the English East India Company affected the character of these transformations, and in doing so had a lasting impact on the course of human history.

The role of the East India Company in the process of financialization and state centralization as well as underdevelopment is less unique, but larger than the role it played in the Industrial Revolution. The process whereby state capacity was expanded through the creation of new financial instruments was pioneered in the Netherlands. Many of the techniques were probably brought from the Netherlands to England by the former Dutch Stadtholder William of Orange, or his advisors. The English Company was central to the process of implementing these techniques in England, as it both was a major debt holder and provided a unique vehicle for transferring public debt through the creation of the India bond.

The Company's role in processes of underdevelopment was also large, but not unique. Several other instances of underdevelopment or failed transition occurred throughout the world, in many cases under the colonial rule of European imperial powers. However in the particular case of India, the East India Company must be considered a central factor in the trajectory of development. With state centralization, financialization, and the underdevelopment of Asia and the Americas, events that occurred within the Company framework may be regarded as symptomatic or of a piece with larger historical currents, without entirely disregarding the unique contribution of the Company to events in Britain and India.

At first glance, the relation of the Company's history to the emergence of new forms of coordinated behavior should be the most conceptually generalizable of the causal chains it was involved in. The concept of institutional innovation is not tied to a particular time or place in the same way as the Industrial Revolution, the emergence of the modern nation-state, or the birth of economics. New organizational forms have been invented throughout history. Even in its own time, the East India Company was one of the very first multidivision, multinational companies, but it was neither the first company nor the first joint-stock. I would argue however that its incorporation of private trade produced a uniquely decentralized organizational structure for the time. Viewed in this light, this book functions to illuminate one of many cases of the invention and adoption of new forms of coordination, similar to John Padgett and Paul McLean's Florentine elites (2006) and Quentin Van Doosselaere's Genoese merchants (2009), as well as part of the process whereby different types of coordination are documented in the past, in order to better understand their evolution and change, as perhaps better describes Julia Adams's analysis of patrimonial merchant capitalism (2005) and Avner Greif's project in *Institutions and the Path to the Modern Economy* (2006b).

One question posed by this line of work is the link between social and cultural environs and firm structure. By focusing only on innovations, an image is built up in which new institutional forms (i.e., means of coordination) emerge and grow in complexity over time—one leading to another. However it is not clear that once an innovation is introduced it is available for all future generations. There was a long hiatus between the creation of East India Company and the modern rise of the multinational in the twentieth century, indicating that this organizational form did not immediately become part of a portfolio of viable options for commercial enterprise. Instead the kind of organization that the East India Company became depended to a great extent upon its environment. Nevertheless, there is an increase in similar though modern forms of decentralized, networked, global firms in the twentieth and twenty-first centuries, which operate under ostensibly different conditions. I believe that this indicates that although the East India Company's organizational structure was moored to specific historical circumstances, it may be worth attempting to compare those circumstances to those of other points in time (Emigh 2005: 378–80). In this I am suggesting that the relationship between the organization and its environment may also be a case worthy of comparison, with the object of understanding how decentralized organizational capacity emerges at different points in time or across distinct cultural contexts.

*Chapter 3*

# THE EUROPEAN TRADE WITH THE EAST INDIES

The core commodities of the European trade with the East, carried by all East India Companies, were spices, textiles, coffee, and tea. The relative share of these goods changed over time and across Companies as the firms attempted to identify and exploit new areas of profitability. Spices were the chief concern for the first fifty years, with textiles growing in importance as the century progressed. Coffee and tea became increasingly important during the course of the eighteenth century. Bulk goods, like indigo, saltpeter, and chinaware, as well as thousands of other smaller commodities, filled out the lists. A short sample of less common goods might include sugar candies, diamonds, rubies, rose attar, shiraz, dragonsblood, lac, galls, rose maloes, sal ammoniac, assafoetida, bezoar, and brimstone. The timing of shifts in the commodity content of the East Indies trade across Companies highlights the innovative nature of the English Company, particularly when contrasted with the Dutch.

The trade in spices had long been carried on along the overland routes from Asia to Europe. The European companies merely diverted this existing trade to the seas. European markets for cotton, tea, and coffee, however, had to be created. Cotton had been a staple of Asian trade for centuries, but was rarely found in the West before the seventeenth century. The Dutch Company actually participated in the cotton trade within Asia, in order to finance their spice trade, but did not realize the potential for exports to Europe (Glamann 1981: 133). In contrast, the English Company had shifted aggressively to cotton by midcentury. In 1664, cotton accounted for 73 percent of the total value of the English trade and over a quarter of a million pieces (Chaudhuri 1978: 282). By comparison, the Dutch trade in cotton until the 1670s could be described as modest (Glamann 1981: 133). The English also realized the potential of finer grades of cotton goods well before the Dutch (Glamann 1981: 141–42). Cotton became immensely popular so quickly, that contemporaries referred to a "calico craze" in European society. Historians have associated this rapid increase in demand with the advent of consumer culture in the West (O'Brien, Griffiths, and

Hunt 1991, Lemire 2011: 226). The English Company took the lead in creating and supplying this rapidly expanding new market (Moreland 1923: 123, Chaudhuri 1978: 282–84, Glamann 1981: 138).

A similar story unfolded around the import of coffee, which was extremely rare in Europe prior to the mid-seventeenth century (a situation painful to contemplate). The Dutch and the English both encountered coffee from the Middle East soon after they ventured around the Cape. It was also possible to buy coffee as a reexport good from many ports in India, and in fact the Company purchased much of its early store of coffee in Surat (Chaudhuri 1978: 366). Neither the Dutch nor the English immediately realized the potential for coffee as a marketable good in Europe. However the English significantly expanded their trade in coffee before the Dutch, who were left complaining about an English advantage in procuring it (Glamann 1981: 186). The Dutch Company also notoriously lagged behind the English in establishing and sustaining direct commercial ties to Canton (now Guangzhou), the market for tea (Chaudhuri 1978: 386).

The capacity for innovation is demonstrated but not exhausted by the introduction of cotton, tea, and coffee. Within each of these categories was an almost infinite gradation of quality and type. This was particularly evident in the cotton trade, where profitability was determined not just by quality but also by the decorative pattern woven into or painted onto the cottons. Different weavers produced different patterns in different regions. Novel designs generally brought the highest prices in Europe, while different types of textiles allowed the Company to circumvent import restrictions in England (Chaudhuri 1978: 283, 278).

Many scholars who have studied the East India Companies have noted that the English excelled at incorporating new goods and creating or adjusting to new market demand, particularly in comparison to the Dutch, who had great difficulty shifting their focus from the spice trade. H. V. Bowen emphasized the English Company's "restless search for commercial advantage and profit [that] ensured that it sought constantly to exploit new opportunities and advantages" (Bowen 2002: 19). Larry Neal explicitly contrasted the flexibility of the English Company with the rigidity of the Dutch (Neal 1990: 220).

Explanations of the difference between these firms, however, have been located in specific circumstances. The early establishment of a stable Dutch settlement in Batavia (now Jakarta) is frequently credited with the Dutch attachment to the spice trade. Similarly, English innovation has been attributed to the accidental: pushed out of Indonesia by the Dutch, they had no choice but to focus their efforts in India, which happened to also be the world's largest textile producer. Local versions of the same argument have also been made: the Dutch were present in India prior to the English; however, they had established themselves in Coromandel, leaving the English no choice but to settle in Bengal, which was, coincidentally, the more vibrant economy (Glamann 1981: 138). The specifics of these arguments ignore the larger pattern, in which the English Company consistently introduced new goods to the European market, and the Dutch (as well as the Portuguese) consistently failed to do so.

Innovation is a central problem in organizational theory, and it has long been recognized that larger, established organizations have greater difficulty innovating. Over the long term this leads to declining productivity and eventually the failure to adapt to changing markets. The problem is faced by every organization. The English Company was founded nearly coincidentally with the Dutch Company—but was reinventing itself well into the third century of its existence. Therefore an important puzzle is how the English Company was able to retain its innovative capacity for so long.

In this chapter I consider this question by investigating how the English Company varied from other European organizations operating in the East. The English Company's two main competitors were the Dutch and the Portuguese. Both organizations were large enough to have significant impacts on the overall conduct of overseas trade, so I give them greater attention, both in order to construct a comparison with the East India Company as well as to describe the context in which the English Company was operating. The smaller companies are considered as well, but allotted less space as they had less impact. As the comparison demonstrates, the companies differed in terms of their relationship with the state, their level of militarization, and their acceptance of employees' participation in the private trade. I begin by describing the way in which the English Company conducted its trade in the East, paying particular attention to private trade practices.

## THE ENGLISH EAST INDIES TRADE

Passage to the East from Downs or Portsmouth, where the Company ships docked, usually took around six months. Ships often stopped at the island of St. Helena or South American ports along their way. Once in the area known as the East Indies, represented in figure 2, ships visited several different ports. Entire voyages, dating from departure from England to return to its harbors, frequently lasted two years or more. Only during the early decades of the seventeenth century did the Company actually own a fleet of ships. By midcentury it had chosen instead to lease them. The owners of the ship were called managing owners or ship's husbands. The position was both prestigious and lucrative. The managing owners were a particularly powerful faction within the larger body of shareholders.

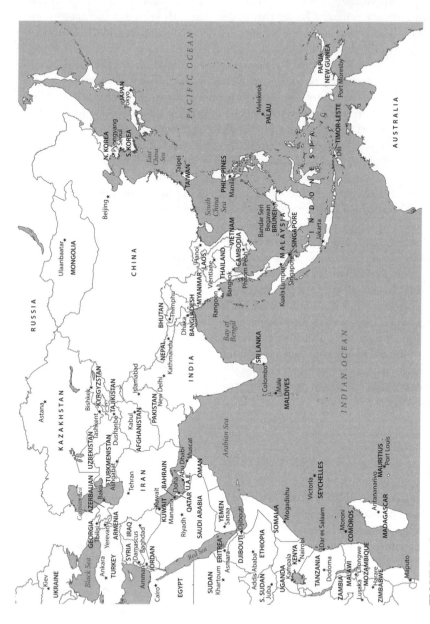

**FIGURE 2.** Current map of the area once known as the East Indies.

Life aboard the ships did not change significantly until the invention of the steamship in the early nineteenth century, although voyage length decreased over time. The size of the ships increased from the seventeenth to the nineteenth century. Lemon's curative effect on scurvy was discovered surprisingly late in the eighteenth century. Nevil Maskelyne invented the lunar method of determining longitude in 1761. Much, however, remained the same. On every voyage there were sail adjustments to be made, cables to be hauled, decks to be mopped, and firearms to be cleaned. Different parts of the ship were constantly in need of repair. The cargo and provisions had to be checked daily for leaks and water. The depths could be sounded if shore was near. There were often deaths to be mourned, or perhaps simply marked by a short ceremony. Occasionally a distant sail or shipboard intrigue relieved the tedium. There were also celebrations, including double rounds of grog on crossing the equator and in observance of royals' birthdays. A remarkable amount of ammunition was used in salutations, which were recorded in meticulous detail. Schools of sharks, flocks of birds, and flying fish were sighted. Days out from harbor, the seafloor could still be seen in clear waters. The captain often noted down the color of the sands in their log (red, blue, gray, yellow, and white), and whether it was clear, pebbled, or sparkled in the light.

At port it was necessary to get both goods and provisions, such as water, wood, and meat. In early voyages, the captains often ventured out in longboats to negotiate the necessary deals to take on new cargo. All of the European companies quickly realized that this practice was unsatisfactory. When trading from a ship, merchants had only a limited amount of time to fill their holds—so prices rose to meet the sudden large increase in demand (Chaudhuri 1978: 136). It was frequently complained that merchants were raising their prices as soon as they saw the sails of their ships.

To resolve this issue, the English Company installed semipermanent merchants at important ports. These merchants were called factors. The factors oversaw and often resided at Company buildings called factories. Although its use has changed over time, the term "factory" then meant a permanent warehouse for storing goods. In most Eastern ports, local rulers had long been aware of the needs of overseas traders; they accommodated those needs by awarding each foreign group a different area for long-term settlement. The size of the settlement depended upon the size of the trade in the port and the wishes of the local government. Some English factories were large and well established (for example, Madras, Bombay, and Calcutta) and some were simple lean-tos. Once established, many larger factories became the center of permanent settlements. Instant cities sprang up around the factory walls, often with populations reaching the hundreds of thousands, large administrative staffs, English courts of law, churches, garrisons, and hundreds of Indian employees. Other factories were limited

to temporary settlements of one or two English Company merchants attempting to establish trade in new areas. In still other cases, ships arrived
at ports, established temporary factories, which we might call storehouses,
and dismantled these constructions when departing. In a few ports in the
Far East (Japan and China), local rulers restricted access to the population,
so that even though the trade itself was of considerable importance to the
English Company, they were not allowed to create permanent settlements.

The most expensive investment in a port was fortifications; however
the Court of Committees was limited in its ability to exercise control over
the process of construction. The decision to establish large fortified settlements always began with the Court of Committees, but inevitably devolved
into circumstantial considerations and local decisions made by Company
employees. The first layer of these consisted of diplomatic negotiations
with local authorities, in order to acquire permission to build fortifications.
This process was rarely straightforward. The second layer was a negotiation with the overseas officers of the Company. For example, the Court of
Directors ordered the construction of a fortified settlement at Armagoan
(originally Durgarazpatnam) in 1626. When the fort was complete, the
employees stationed there abandoned it, complaining of the quality of the
construction and a poor choice of location (Stern 2011: 19). The employee
who was meant to be the chief factor at Armagoan, Francis Day, negotiated the rental of Madraspatnam instead. This became the site of Madras,
one of the most prosperous of the Company settlements. Similarly in the
late seventeenth century, the directors desired a fortified settlement somewhere in the vicinity of Bengal. It was the chief factor of Hugli, Job Char-
nock, however, who selected the three towns of Sutanati, Govindpur, and
Kalikata as sites for settlement, and he is credited with founding Calcutta.

Other countless smaller decisions—even those that involved land
leases—were made by lower-level Company employees. There were exceptions to this bottom-up process. Bombay was established by direct
order: it was a part of the dowry of the Donna Infanta Catherina when she
married Charles II. Not having much direct use for it, he gifted the port
to the English Company. Under routine circumstances, London principals
exercised direct control over factories and forts by shutting them down.
However, even these orders were not always followed (Sutton 2010: 83).


## PRIVATE TRADE OF THE ENGLISH IN THE EAST

The private trade came in many different forms, and these forms were
granted varying degrees of legitimacy by the Company at different points
in its organizational history. Some types of private trade, however, were

routinely treated as significant threats to the continued existence and profitability of the Company. The Company was, for example, very consistent in its attempts to curtail the activities of private individuals whom it believed were infringing upon the Company monopoly on goods transported between Asia and Britain. These private traders, which the Company would have considered smugglers, included persons unaffiliated with the Company, but citizens of the British Crown, who either traded in Asia or brought Asian goods to Europe by way of the Cape route. This category included non-British citizens who attempted to sell goods shipped directly from Asia in Britain—that is, goods that did not go through legitimate channels of the reexport market. For example, passengers unaffiliated with the Company but traveling to the East aboard their ships were searched for smuggled goods. One such search aboard the *Macclesfield* in 1732 yielded 126 ounces of gold hidden away in the pockets of Mr. Flower, a passenger aboard ship (Thomas 1999: 280).

The Company made strenuous attempts to enforce the rule against captains of the Company unloading goods at Kinsale, the Isle of Man, the Channel Islands, or any other British port before returning to the Company docks in Portsmouth or Downs or meeting with other ships to illegally transfer goods while still at sea. Patrols were sent out to monitor for illicit rendezvous with other ships while still at sea. If patrols caught non-Company ships with East Indian goods, the goods, and possibly the ship, were confiscated (Thomas 1999: 282–84).

The Company believed, or at least frequently argued, that the individuals engaging in this type of trade were not only breaking the law by violating the Company's charter, but also defrauding the Crown out of taxes due on overseas trade. The Company brought charges against many of these perpetrators in the courts of London (Stern 2011: 47–48), offered rewards for their detection, and appointed individuals to survey and monitor coastal ships as well as their own ships once in dock (Sainsbury 1922).

Even when the British government officially sanctioned other East Indies trading ventures, the Company was active in its opposition to these groups. The largest of these sanctioned groups—that were however considered interlopers and smugglers by the Company—were the Courteen Association and the New English Company. The Courteen Association was founded in 1635 and gained Crown support because of its stated purpose of creating settlements in the East Indies (the East India Company was understood as having neglected its duty to the Crown in this regard) (Foster 1912). By 1657 the English East India Company had forced an advantageous merger with the Courteen Association. A similar pattern of events unfolded after the creation of the New English Company, founded in 1698. Through some involved machinations, the Court of Committees of the old Company was able to force a union between the two companies,

effectively absorbing the New English Company into the old. The resulting combination was then christened the United English East India Company in 1709.[1]

In more ambiguous cases, English merchants sometimes renounced
their citizenship in order to participate in companies chartered by other
European nations. Such was the case with the Scottish merchant Colin
Campbell, who took up residency in Sweden in order to work for the
Swedish East India Company (Koninckx 1980: 50). The English Company
regarded this practice as illegitimate, but had much greater difficulty pros-
ecuting these cases. In one instance, Captain Thomas Hall joined the rival
Ostend Company and made a personal fortune through the private trade.
Hall was allowed to rejoin the English Company as a managing owner
after formally apologizing and paying the firm £2,100 (Sutton 1981: 22).

The Company did demonstrate some leniency toward its own employees even in the highly valued intercontinental trade. The Company
had always awarded small freight allotments to the captains, officers, and
crew, for their own private trade. The Captain had far and away the greatest allotment, up to five times the amount allowed to the first mate. In
1715 this allotment was three hundred pounds of goods to one hundred
tons of Company freight for the captain versus sixty pounds of goods for
the first mate. Each rank made successively less, with seamen allotted ten
pounds per ton (Mentz 2005: 130). In 1767, the disparity between allotments seems to have increased. John Wyche, the captain of the *Salisbury*,
took on board £4,660 in private goods, whereas the first mate shipped £305
(Thomas 1999: 151). This type of private trade was legitimate, but subject to strict oversight. Cargos were inspected in England to ensure that
employees were not exceeding their allotments, and all goods returned to
England were sold through the Company auctions in London.

Although the Company did not charge freight in most of these cases,
other fees inevitably drove the costs up for those engaged in legitimate private trade. Captain John Stevens brought twenty-eight tubs and ten chests
of hyson tea, twelve chests of benjamin (benzoin), fifteen chests of cassia
lignea (Chinese cinnamon), two chests and 159 tubs of camphire (henna),
one chest of white pepper, one cask of tamarind, five lots of oranges, twenty
casks of arrack (wine), and 6,336 rattans back with him to London on the
Godolphin in 1749. Stevens made £7,240 from his goods at the auction,
but paid out £380 to the Company in fees tied to the storage and auction-
ing of goods. When customs, duties, and a donation to a charity fund were
included, he was able to take home £4,760, which does not take into account the initial cost of the goods (Sutton 1981: 157).

The goods that Stevens brought to England were not untypical imports in the private trade, but quite different from the type of goods regularly exported to the East by employees. John Wyche's goods, shipped on

the outbound passage of the *Salisbury*, consisted of braziery, cards, and stationery, a chariot filled with hats, clocks, and toys, coach springs, cutlery, drugs (three chests), glass beads, glassware, gold and silver lace, grapnels and anchors, hosiery, lead, looking glasses, nails, paint, perfumery, prints, red and white lead, saddlery, wine, wrought plate, and wrought silks (Thomas 1999: 152).

Captains, officers, and crew who exceeded their allotments or shipped the wrong types of good were engaging in illegitimate trade, although this was generally treated as a minor infraction. Indeed a completely accurate count of all the goods aboard ship was probably difficult for captains to achieve while at port overseas or rushing to return to England before the weather turned. In many cases, the Company simply fined captains an additional £28 for each ton over the limit (Mentz 2005: 129).

## THE EXPANSION OF PRIVATE TRADE PRIVILEGES

Though the Company's position on trade between Asia and Europe changed little over its existence as a commercial organization, its position on the country trade, that is, trade confined to the East Indies region, changed more dramatically. It was in this respect that the English Company's relationship to private trade varied from those of other European chartered companies operating in Asia. In the early years of English Company history, though employee private trading was not formally allowed, there also was not much effective control over its practice (Chaudhuri 1965: 118, Watson 1980b: 74, Marshall 1993: chap. xiii, 278–80). In 1661, the Company officially withdrew from the country trade and opened parts of that trade to its employees (Watson 1980b: 75). As with many of the private trade regulations that were enacted between 1660 and 1680, this act legitimized an existing practice.

In 1662, Englishmen operating outside of the Company were formally allowed to trade on their own account within the East Indies, as long as their own trade did not interfere with the Company trade (Marshall 1993: 279). In 1667, trade in certain commodities was opened between Europe and Asia and all country trade, with the exceptions of pepper and calicoes, was made legitimate (Watson 1980b: 75). By 1679 the restrictions on pepper and calicoes were lifted, opening all country trade to private individuals and employees (Watson 1980b: 77). These acts essentially ratified the autonomy that overseas employees had already claimed for themselves by using their time in the Company in the attempt to amass personal fortunes through the private trade. They formalized the decentralized aspects of the otherwise hierarchical structure of the firm. The overarching argument of the book is that this decentralized organizational structure, and its formal extension into the eighteenth century via the private trade allowances, had a profound effect on the way in which information was received and communicated within the English Company.

The most immediately visible impact was to stimulate the private trade by allowing for the resolution of two specific problems. One of the largest of these problems had been the issue of transferring wealth between Asia and England. Prior to 1660, private traders faced significant difficulties in remitting their fortune—if they had made one—back to England. Such fortunes had to be hidden from the Company since there was no legal means by which individuals would have been able to acquire them. When the country trade was legalized, employees acquired a reliable means of remitting money back to England: they could use Company bills of exchange.[2] Bills of exchange also made it possible for private traders to draw upon resources and loans in England to finance new ventures while still in Asia. Mentz estimates that £955,280 was remitted from London to Asia for starting capital in the private trade from 1675 to 1683, or around £100,000 annually (Mentz 2005: 95).[3] Although considerable, this would not capture the full outlay for private trade in the East as many British merchants also borrowed from Indian moneylenders to finance their purchases in Asia (Marshall 1993: 39).

Since the risk of dismissal due to participation in the country trade was removed, the scale of private trading operations could be expanded. Whereas factors would have had to furtively hire ships or smuggle goods aboard Company ships to engage in country trade before the 1660s, with the more lenient regulations they could amass small fleets of country ships without fear that other employees might inform on them. At Cochin (Kochi) alone, Holden Furber found records of fifteen English private country ships in 1719; this number grew to twenty-nine in 1740 (Furber 1976: 272). Bal Krishna estimates that by 1680 private country trade was a quarter of the formal Company trade and equaled it by 1710 (Krishna 1924: 125). A fraction of this trade belonged to English merchants unaffiliated with the Company. A small number of free merchants, who were private British citizens, established residences in some of the larger Company settlements as they grew into major trading hubs in the eighteenth century.[4] Some of these individuals made large fortunes by participating in the country trade of Asia, most famously Thomas Pitt.

The allowances of the 1660s and 1670s also affected the trade of the employees serving on board the East Indiamen. Since larger fortunes were being made in the East, the freight of the captains, officers, and crew became an additional avenue through which capital could be transferred back and forth between country traders in the East and the commercial networks in Britain (Mentz 2005: 51).[5] However the captains and officers did not confine their activities to facilitating the transfer of capital between

London and the East. They actively participated in the country trade, diverting the paths of their ships to buy and sell goods. Such diversions were within the boundaries of legitimate behavior as long as they did not significantly delay the progress of the voyage. The trade of the captains and crew was necessarily smaller than the Company trade itself, since it occupied a smaller proportion of the same cargo space. Following Krishna's estimate, it therefore must have also been smaller than the country trade of Englishmen aboard private vessels by 1710. It was however a regular fixture on English ships, and therefore almost certainly overshadowed the less systematic incursions of private interlopers challenging the Company's East-West monopoly. Because the captains and officers used the East India Company ships to conduct their private trade, their pursuits changed both the structure and dynamics of the larger Company trade network. Chapters 4 and 5 are devoted to analyses of these impacts.

Although the private traders, across all periods, were acting in their own interests, they were rarely acting entirely independently of the Company. This is particularly true of the employees of the Company who engaged in both licit and illicit private trade. The Company negotiated diplomatic accords with foreign powers in order to establish legitimate access to different ports and markets and in many cases to reduce tariff rates, thus legitimizing the presence of English private traders, whether they were Company servants or not, as well as reducing their customs burden. Once in port, private traders employed by the Company depended heavily upon one crucial infrastructural investment made by the Company: the factory. Many of the private traders also relied upon the ships leased by the Company, not only for transport to and from the East, but also for transporting goods in the intracontinental trade of Asia. Private traders also at times— and clearly illegitimately—made use of Company capital to cover short-term outlays. The Company provided a vehicle for transmitting private fortunes back to Europe, protection against aggressive competitors and probably greatly increased the profits to be made on good smuggled back to England through its attempts to enforce its monopoly privileges there. Thus the private trade, as it was conducted, depended on the monopoly and cannot be understood simply as a version of free trade.

## CONTEMPORARY AND COMPANY VIEWS ON THE PRIVATE TRADE

Contemporary readers may be surprised at the prevalence of licit and illicit private trade among Company employees. Its pervasiveness was grounded in both different common notions of what was considered acceptable behavior and limits to the Company's ability to enforce its own rules and regulations, particularly when they were at odds with common practice. Tudor and Stuart England were patrimonial monarchies. Their political systems were founded upon and operated by virtue of a very different standard of conduct than the impersonal, meritocratic ideal embraced after the rise of large state bureaucracies. Stuart England in particular has been held up as a model of "proto-corruption" (Scott 1972). Patrimonialism is a system where rights and privileges are granted vis-à-vis personal ties with the ruling political authority (Adams 2005). Such a system does not discourage, but is instead based around the principles of favoritism, nepotism, and clientelism. Once granted, office, rights, and privileges are treated as personal property. In feudal systems, political offices and their attendant rights and privileges are heritable and confined to an aristocratic class. France, Spain, and the papal states formally instituted a system of venality, where offices were treated as commodities for sale in an open market (Gorski 2003: 144–54). Venality was never openly legislated in Stuart England, but the principles of venality were nevertheless incorporated into the operations of the state.

These practices had their critics even in the seventeenth century.[6] However many individuals straightforwardly equated the public good with the good of the Crown, providing an entirely consistent justification for practices such as clientelism or simple favoritism (Génaux 2002: 108). State and individual actors simply were not subject to the same set of normative pressures that came to pervade the cultures of advanced industrial nations. Particularly the ideal of disinterested loyalty made little sense in the premodern, patrimonial context. In his review of the period, James Scott briefly outlined many of the central differences:

> Thus seventeenth-century English politics fostered a proliferation of practices we would now consider corrupt. Seeking offices for one's clients regardless of their qualifications was an integral part of the patron-client loyalties of the period. The purchase of sales and office, the exchange of favorable government decisions for cash or kind, the enrichment of family and friends from the Crown's coffers, and the abuse of less powerful or less well-connected citizens was typical of English government in this phase of its development. (Scott 1972: 44)

The East India Company was instituted through and based in the same patrimonial principles of patronage as the Stuart monarchy. The merchants that composed its Court of Committees curried favor with the sitting monarch through direct loans and political support in order to ensure the continuation of its charter privileges. Individuals were appointed to important offices within the Company, such as shipowner or commander, through the patronage of powerful figures from the Court of Committees. Once the charter had been granted, the Company was able treat it as private property, and indeed could have leased the privileges to others if it had adopted a regulated structure. Thus it should not be surprising that once granted office within the Company, employees felt it was their prerogative to make use of the rights, privileges, and resources granted to them through their employment in order to further their own interests. In doing so, they were simply following the standard set of practices followed by merchants in their relations with the state. It was of course generally understood that acting directly against the interests of your employer was improper conduct—in the same way that acting against the interests of the Crown was condemned. The question then for the employees and Company alike was whether engaging in the different types of private trade actually harmed Company interests. Then, as now, it was not trivial to flesh out a clearly defined answer to this question and bring all interested parties into complete agreement.

The backdrop of moral ambiguity behind the private trade helps explain employees' engagement but cannot entirely explain why the Company came to accept limited forms of the private trade as an open and legislated practice. The Company was in the business of profiting from its monopoly privileges and as late as 1670 a proposal was made by William Allington to prohibit all private trade and debated on the floor of the general court (Sainsbury 1929: 356). Monopoly and control of competition were the dominant "conceptions of control," default strategies used by the directors to resolve problems (Fligstein 1990: 12).

Ideological shifts may have played a limited role in the decision to extend private trade privileges even at this early date. An undercurrent of opposition to the idea of monopoly rights existed in seventeenth century and probably gained some traction among the general court of shareholders in the late seventeenth century. Many contemporaries of the Company argued that monopoly privileges were in violation of the common law and Magna Carta (Roover 1951: 507, Stern 2011: 47–48). When a new class of rising young merchants was installed in the board of the Company in the aftermath of the Civil War, a number were former interlopers and free trade proponents (Brenner 2003: 516–18). They may have supported the expansion of trading rights on principled grounds.

Much more important, however, seems to have been structural limitations to the Company's power. Distance of course played a significant role. All overseas companies had tremendous difficulty exerting sufficient control over overseas agents in this period. It regularly took six months for any Company headquarters to even receive a notification of any transgressions. The transmission of a response would take another six months to get back to the East. More complex investigations could stretch on for years.

The logistical problems posed by long distances did not stop other companies from the attempt to regulate the trade of their employees, although it clearly made it more difficult. In the case of the English Company, the separation between the state and the Company meant that the organization was less militaristic than the Dutch or Portuguese operations and therefore had fewer resources (Furber 1976: 39). The combined lack of capital and military authority diminished the effectiveness of control efforts within the English Company (Bassett 1960: 34)—making indirect incentives, such as the private trade, more attractive. Ian Bruce Watson and P. J. Marshall both cite the Company's desire to escape the costs associated with the country trade as an important part of the decision to withdraw from some of the monopoly privileges (Marshall 1993: chap. 12, 281, Watson 1980b: 77).

When the issue is addressed directly in the court minutes during the pivotal years in which the private trade concessions were made, the committee and directors appear to be addressing the reality of private trade by enacting legislation meant to contain and channel it. In a 1662 petition to the Duke of York regarding private trade practices, the Company wrote that to "prevent this abuse [of the private trade] the Company have provided reasonable and legal covenants to be entered into by all their commanders, officers, and seamen" (Sainsbury 1922: 276). Two years later, existing misbehavior is again the only clearly stated reason as to why private trade allowances are being expanded:

> [The Company] have found by experience that many unauthorized persons, under colour of said owners and mariners, engage in a considerable trade . . . for the encouragement of trade, and that all persons may act openly and freely in what the Company shall permit, it is this day ordered that all persons may send in the Companies ships for the Indies any jewels or other fine goods and things of great value but small bulk on paying the Company for permission and freight two per cent. (Sainsbury 1925: 18)

By waiving fines, freight, and tax on some goods, the Company was attempting to divert the private trade away from those goods that were considered most profitable. The Company selectively lowered the costs for some items and raised the costs of others by enacting specific acts prohibiting goods that were considered too profitable for the private trade (Sainsbury 1922: 352, 1925: 233, Chaudhuri 1978: 386–87). Regulating rather than prohibiting allowed the Company to make a small profit on goods, via freight charges, taxes, and fines, that if illegal would inevitably find their way into England along other routes unseen by Company officials or customs houses.

The Company also used private trade allowances interchangeably with wages. Private trade allowances were offered as remuneration for exemplary service. The well-known journalist Nicholas Buckeridge had his private trading fines waived for the exceptional performance of his duties. The officers of the *Happy Entrance* received similar treatment (Sainsbury 1922:

363). In other instances, salaries were negotiated with respect to private trade privileges. Captain John Hunter was granted an exceptionally high salary in return for a commitment to "abstain from all trade, and devote himself wholly and solely to the Company's business" (Sainsbury 1922: 43). The crew of the *Return* was granted an additional month's pay when their stay in Fort St. George was abruptly terminated, cutting short their opportunities to engage in the private trade (Sainsbury 1932: 17). And the Company regularly waived fines associated with private trade goods for the widows of men who died in service (Sainsbury 1922: 185, 243, 1932: 84).

Although it is tempting to ask whether the directors strategically introduced private trade allowances in order to encourage the continued exploration of new ports and goods and diffusion of that information through the organization via peer networks, the question runs the risk of being anachronistic. The records of the court minutes indicate that the private trade allowances were a pragmatic response on the part of the principals of the Company to the limitations they experienced in terms of (1) their ability to control the private trade of their employees and (2) their ability to offer proper remuneration for the service of their employees. Despite the fact that directors were responding to more immediate concerns, the period in which employees' rights were legitimized and expanded appears to have had long-term consequences, as it was coincident with the beginning of the expansionary moment in English Company history, from 1660 to 1700 (Chaudhuri 1978: 82).

## THE END OF THE ERA OF EMPLOYEE PRIVATE TRADE

For nearly a century after the extension of private trade allowances, little changed in the management of Company affairs overseas other than expansion and growth. Beginning in the 1740s, the French East India Company began an aggressive campaign of territorial expansion on the Indian Peninsula. Eventually the complex politics surrounding the French Company's expansion and the response of the English Company and Mughal state culminated in the 1757 Battle of Plassey. The victory of the English forces led directly to the Company's accession to the position of de facto territorial sovereign of Bengal.

The assumption of political power in Bengal had tremendous significance for the conduct of overseas trade, the Company's internal organizational structure, and its relationship with the British state. The most immediate change was to the Company's need for silver bullion. Since the Company's inception, its most important export was silver bullion. Historically, there was not a strong demand in Asia for European goods, and the heavy woolens that were England's main export in Europe were a particularly hard sell. This meant that the Company had to trade in bullion in order to acquire Asian goods. Many influential policy makers at that time espoused a dogmatic brand of mercantilism based around the idea that exporting bullion drained the nation's wealth. Their opposition embroiled the Company in a series of debates over the public benefits of overseas trade expansion, which helped to shape modern economic theory (Barber 1975, Khan 1975: 48–51, 185–92, 299–305, Appleby 1978: 37–41, 125, 216).

The constant need for bullion overseas, and the political difficulties caused by exporting it from England, pushed the Company to search for alternative sources throughout its long history. In fact, the Company's continued embrace of the private trade was linked to the need for fungible overseas capital. Private traders brought capital with them to the East and, if successful, accumulated more during their stay. William Monsoon was sent by this father, Lord Monsoon of Lincolnshire, to the East in 1725 with £1,000 in silver bullion (Mentz 2005: 80). More experienced traders brought larger reserves. Robert Nightingale recorded the difficulties he had in locating a reliable method to transport somewhere between £12,000 and £20,000 to the East (Mentz 2005: 85). When faced with serious shortfalls, the Company turned to private traders for short-term loans (Cheong 1979: 9). On a more regular basis, employees drew bills of exchange from the Company in order to transfer earnings home to London. These remittances were a valuable source of overseas capital for the Company (Adams 1996, Mentz 2005: 146–47).

The Battle of Plassey led to the Company's appointment to the position of tax collector (*diwan*). This office provided it with an alternative and potentially vast source of bullion: the land taxes of Bengal. The managerial board in London was overjoyed at the prospect of reducing the Company's dependency on external sources of bullion as well as finally silencing the critics of their export policy. Investors were impressed as well, and stock prices shot upward—in the short term (Yapp 1986: 44). Tax collection began to rival commerce as the principal occupation of the firm, and the Company became more interested in territorial than commercial expansion. The new resources it had acquired through land revenues and political partnership with the British Crown reduced its dependence on the private interests of captains and shipowners, and the Company moved to end its long-standing compromise with employees.

There was a general process of organizational restructuring in which control was progressively centralized (Furber and Rocher 1997, Marshall 1993, Chaudhuri 1965, 1993). By 1787, Company servants were almost entirely excluded from the country trade (Webster 2007: 9). This period in Company history was notable for the way in which moral standards of conduct were redefined. Where the intermixture of private and public interests, represented most singularly by the private trade of Company employees, was an entirely accepted mode of conduct prior to the 1760s, by the 1780s it was considered a source of corruption (Marshall 1965, Nightingale 1985, Wilson 2012).

The private trade of individuals unaffiliated with the Company, or "free traders," grew in this period (Webster 2007: 9). Shipbuilding in Asia expanded, which fed into the private trade as overseas British free merchants used local ships for their country trade. Calcutta, which according to P. J. Marshall was the largest producer, experienced a boom in the 1780s. Seventy-seven vessels were constructed in the Calcutta shipyards from 1781 to 1802, between three or four ships annually (Marshall 1993: 296). A new Anglo-Indian institution, the agency house, arose to take the place of the employees who had once dominated the country trade. Agency houses invested in overseas trade on behalf of others, while also offering banking and insurance services, and even at times became involved in the manufacture of goods (Tripathi 1956: 11). Their customer base was largely composed of the same Company employees who were now barred from direct participation in trade.

Company ships and their officers continued to play an important role in the private trade. Freight allowances on board ships were increased. From 1785 to 1793, goods sold for commanders at Company auctions came to £6,000,000 (Sutton 1981: 81). However, captains' freight allowances were increasingly tied to the process of remitting capital between England and Asia. The agency houses depended upon and cultivated contacts with captains in order to keep this important avenue open (Webster 2007: 10). Captains' autonomous engagement in the country trade, however, was targeted and curtailed by the board of directors.

In the 1760s and 1770s, the board launched investigations into identifying effective means through which to control overseas operations. In 1776 the board of directors passed an act that strictly forbade any deviations from ships' ordered routes (Cartwright 1788?). Captains found guilty of altering their routes were ordered to appear before both the private trade committee and the shipping committee to explain their actions. The 1776 act significantly reduced the captains' control over their greatest resource—the ship. Additional reforms followed, such as the enforcement of a long dormant act banning a formerly lucrative market in the buying and selling of captaincies (Cotton 1949: 25, Sutton 1981: 72–73). Reforming the process by which captains were appointed clarified the chain of command, increasing the threat of dismissal should they violate Company rules. It also signaled a step away from the informal patterns of patronage and venality that had characterized Company operations. Together these acts undermined the captains' ability to engage in and direct their own private trade—which is exactly what they were intended to do.

The general contours of these shifts suggest three main periods of Company private trade: 1600 to 1660, illicit and uncontrolled private trade; 1660 to 1760, legitimate and growing private trade concerns; and 1760 to

1833, illicit and increasingly contained private trade combined with the growth of free trade outside of Company auspices.

## ESTADO DA ÍNDIA

The Portuguese Estado da Índia was the first of the large European organizations to enter the Asian overseas trade. Unlike the English, the Portuguese were interested in the spice trade, but largely motivated by political concerns. Most of the goods that traveled overland from Asia to Europe profited the enemies of the Portuguese state. They were taxed by the Ottoman and Mamluk Empires as they passed through their lands on the way to Europe. By reaching around the coast of Africa, the Portuguese hoped to exclude the Muslim nations from the European-East Indies trade, thereby reducing state revenues and, therefore, their capacity for war. The Portuguese also envisioned that a tactical advantage would be created by outflanking the Middle East. This strategy failed to have an immediate impact, but eventually the shift from the overland to the Cape route would take a heavy toll on the finances of the Ottomans (Barkey 1994: 50). Ironically, even though the Portuguese fought the entrance of other Europeans into the East Indies trade for more than a century, the decline in the overland route had more to do with the eventual success of the English and Dutch Companies than any direct action taken by the Estado or its related commercial ventures (Braudel 1992c: 447, Steensgaard 1974: 155–69).

In order to pursue their military goals, the Portuguese entered the Indian Ocean with the intention of conquering strategic sites from which they could control trade. For example, Malacca, taken in 1511, was targeted because it sat on the southwestern tip of the Malaysian Peninsula, overlooking a narrow passage between the Spice Islands, the South China Seas, and the Indian Ocean. Hormuz, taken in 1515, possessed only salt and sulfur, but sat on the edge of the narrow strait that guards the entrance of the Persian Gulf. Other important strongholds taken by the Portuguese were Goa, Sofala, and Mozambique. Farther east the Portuguese were forced into a less militaristic and more commercial pattern of operations (Subrahmanyam 1990a: 92). For example, in 1557 the Portuguese bribed a Chinese port official to allow them to take possession of an island at the entrance of the Pearl River Delta. This island was to become Macau. The Portuguese built fortifications and established a bustling trade from the island, but on the condition of acquiescing to the demands of the powerful and wealthy Chinese Empire.

Where they were able, the Portuguese imposed a self-styled rule within their own settlements and over the oceans. King Manuel of Portugal proclaimed himself "Lord of conquest, navigation, and commerce of Ethiopia,

India, Arabia, and Persia." Crown forces began to enforce the *cartaze* system off the western coast of the Indian Subcontinent: ships were forced to buy a pass from Portuguese authorities in order to engage in trade. The pass, unsurprisingly, cost a significant fee. The Portuguese also demanded that ships dock at a Portuguese port in order to purchase the pass, during which time they were obliged to pay duties on their cargo. Failure to carry the pass or the trade of restricted merchandise could end in extremely serious reprisals. A Muslim family was sold into slavery after being discovered piloting a boat without the Portuguese document (Subrahmanyam 1990a: 104). Ships and goods were regularly confiscated.

As a result, Asian merchants went to considerable lengths to avoid Portuguese ships and ports. The *cartaze* system did not make the fortunes of the Portuguese. Instead it rerouted trade away from the once rich and cosmopolitan destinations of Hormuz, Goa, Sofala, and Mozambique. The basis for these cities' wealth had been their thriving overseas trade. Bereft of this, they slowly decayed, putting significant financial strain on the Estado as they did (Silva 1974: 154).

The commercial fortunes of the Estado did not fare better than their settlements. The entire organization was owned and operated by the Portuguese Crown. The Crown participated in the intercontinental trade between Europe and Asia, but not successfully. Commercial difficulties led officials to experiment with other approaches to the trade. When the Portuguese began to realize their severe financial straits in the late sixteenth century (before other Europeans had even entered the trade), they created a system of concessions. The concessions were granted to former officers of the Estado as a reward for loyal service and gave them the right to trade exclusively on specific routes in Asia—that is, between two designated ports (Subrahmanyam 1990a: 112).[7] The problem with this system was that the Estado had not really established effective monopoly control over any of these trade routes, and their ability to maintain limited control eroded over time (Subrahmanyam 1990a: 201). Thus the privileged access granted by the concessions was largely a fiction and was soon treated as such.

The Crown attempted to revive the fortunes of the overseas trade a second time with the creation of a short-lived chartered company in 1628. Within five years the company had failed due largely to its inability to attract private investors, who feared Crown involvement. Political infighting and corruption, both of which seem to have been perennial problems for the Estado, had plagued the venture from the start (Disney 1977: 248–51). Despite these halfhearted attempts to innovate, the Estado demonstrated a pronounced inability to adapt to new market conditions, incorporate new products, or successfully alter the status quo (Silva 1974: 195, Disney 1977: 251). Traditionally tight Crown control has been blamed for these problems. My argument suggests that Crown control was linked to the failure of the Estado, but that Crown control was problematic because it centralized control over operations, restricted access to markets and profits, and suppressed local initiative.

Although the Portuguese establishment was notoriously corrupt (Disney 1977: 248–51), the private trade did not flourish within the organization. The concession system was a failure, and other avenues for employed officers of the Estado to participate in trade were limited. Portuguese officers and men were allowed to stow goods for their own personal trade—the private trade—in small chests called *caixas de liberdade*. Unlike the English voyages, which made frequent stops along their way through the Pacific (in North and South America as well as West Africa, the Cape Verde Islands, St. Helena, and throughout the East), the ships that sailed the *carreira da India* were under strict orders to proceed directly from Lisbon to Goa. Intermediate stops were forbidden except under extraordinary and life-threatening conditions. These orders were necessary to keep the men from deserting, but also curtailed private trade opportunities. The one concession wrung from the Crown was a stop at Bahia for provisioning, which channeled the private trade into a predictable pattern of the exchange of silks, teas, spice, and ceramics from Asia for the gold extracted from Minas Gerais (Boxer 1969: 206–18).

Portuguese settlers had a habit of breaking away from the Estado. This pattern produced several settlements of independent Portuguese traders composed of former officers and merchants of the Estado and their descendants. Pulicat and Negapatnam (Nagapattinam) were among the largest. In the early sixteenth century, these independent traders were often composed of deserters and not initially looked upon with favor by the Portuguese establishment (Subrahmanyam 1990a: 106). As the merchant settlements expanded and became more prosperous, legitimately retired officials of high standing began to make these ports their permanent home as well. The official standing of the settlements rose in the estimation of Portuguese authorities. The settlements, however, seemed to remain skeptical of the Estado. Sanjay Subrahmanyam describes them as a "stateless and adaptable commercial group" (Subrahmanyam 1990a: 225). In Negapatnam, the Portuguese settlers refused to allow the Estado to erect fortifications, even ostensibly to protect the town from recent Dutch threats. Thus, Portuguese free traders formed an important merchant community in Asia, but one that had little connection to the official Portuguese establishment.

## THE VEREENIGDE OOST-INDISCHE COMPAGNIE

The Dutch Company was much closer in form to the English Company than the Portuguese Estado. The Dutch East India Company itself was not chartered until 1602; however the Dutch had been organizing regular

voyages around the Cape since 1597. In 1602 several Dutch regional partners consolidated their operations into one very large and well-provisioned
company—at that time the largest in the East.

The Dutch government was composed largely of a merchant elite,
which had close ties to the Dutch East India Company (Khan 1975: 6,
Irwin 1991: 1307–8, Adams 1996: 15). Unlike the English Company, the
Dutch Company was able to sign treaties with other sovereigns, acquire
land, and construct forts from its inception (Irwin 1991: 1300). The Company had commercial goals, but used military means to achieve them. Niels
Steensgaard argued that the Dutch Company "integrated the functions of a
sovereign power with the functions of a business partnership" (1996: 135).
In 1605 they captured two nutmeg-producing ports, Tidore and Amboina,
from the Portuguese. In 1641 they took Malacca. In 1658 they conquered
several Portuguese ports in Ceylon, thereby cornering the cinnamon market. By 1667 they had largely forced the Portuguese out of the spice trade.
The strategy was clear: the Company was attempting to achieve a true
monopoly in the spice trade through conquest.

In one of the many tragic moments of European colonization, the
Dutch decimated the entire population of the Banda Islands in order to
take control of the nutmeg groves. In place of the native economy, they set
up slave plantations and patrolled the islands for unauthorized cultivation.
In all of their colonial possessions, which were concentrated in the Indonesian Archipelago, the Dutch installed systems of forced labor, pushing the
population into agriculture and away from trade. Other merchants were
considered potential smugglers and treated as threats. Using these draco-
nian measures, the Dutch were able to achieve a near monopoly in cloves,
mace, nutmeg, and cinnamon.

Despite this overt militarism, the Dutch Company was formally a private organization, albeit one that issued regular reports to the government
and whose upper management were required to swear oaths of fealty to
the Dutch state (Parthesius 2010: 35). The Dutch Company had a complicated organizational structure, which mirrored the complicated structure of the Dutch state itself. At the top of the hierarchy sat the Seventeen Gentlemen, or the Heeren Zeventien. These men were drawn on
a proportional basis from six regional boards of directors representing
Amsterdam, Middelburg, Delft, Rotterdam, Hoorn, and Enkhuizen. The
mayor of each town was responsible for appointing representatives to
these regional boards. Directors were invariably drawn from elites, which
included merchants in the Netherlands. At first merchants dominated the
board, but in the eighteenth century politicians came to outnumber them
(Boxer 1965: 47).

As if compensating for the pluralistic structure of the Company in
the Netherlands, the Dutch consolidated control in the East into one
city: Batavia. Under the direction of Jan Pieterszoon Coen, and against

the orders of the Heeren Zeventien, the Dutch Company captured Batavia from the Sultan of Bantam in 1619. Batavia became the seat of the
governor-general (who was at that time Coen). The governor was assisted
by a *raad van politie* (polity council), second-in-command, head accoun-
tant, *fiscaal* (judge), and military commander. Other Dutch settlements
had a similar organizational structure, but fell under the jurisdiction of
Batavia. The government at Batavia oversaw all of the Dutch Company's
affairs in the East. It was the center of strategic and operational power
(Furber 1976: 50, Steensgaard 1996: 136). By the early seventeenth century, all ships traveling between Europe and Asia arrived at or departed
from Batavia, which also made it the central transshipment point for the
large country-trading network developed by the Company (Parthesius
2010: 116).

The means by which the Dutch handled the private trade was similar
to those of the Portuguese. A small chest was allotted to the seamen and
officers for intercontinental trade. The country trade was not open to the
officers because it played an integral role in the Dutch Company's commercial strategy, financing the intercontinental voyages. For a brief period
in the 1620, the Dutch Company considered leaving the country trade
open to free merchants (known as *vrijburgers* or *vrijlieden*), often former
employees who remained in the East to engage in the private trade, but
in 1627 decisively moved to ban their participation in the country trade
(Parthesius 2010: 41).

When the Dutch Company installed strict regulations over the private
trade, they had an advantage over the English in enforcing them. Company
officials, housed in Batavia, were much closer to potential offenders and,
due to the large military presence within the Company, they had more
resources at their disposal to monitor activity and enforce rules. When the
director of Surat, Pieter Laurens Phoonsen, was suspected of illicit private
trade, his salary was docked and he was ordered to report to Batavia. The
prospect of returning to Batavia under scrutiny must have been unpleasant;
Phoonsen took his chances by fleeing to Bombay and died in poverty two
years later (Winius and Vink 1994: 94).

Despite problems, this system worked for more than a half century.
However, the closure of the country trade meant that instead of drawing
new ports and goods into the trade network, Dutch sailors (i.e., private
traders) directed their energies into smuggling goods back into Europe.
Embezzlement of Company funds occurred regularly (Boxer 1965: 202).
The English private trade offered additional avenues for remitting illicit
funds, exacerbating the problems the Dutch Company had in controlling
its employees (Adams 1996: 23–24, Winius and Vink 1994: 94). The positive synergy between private and Company trade found in the English system was absent.

## SMALLER COMPANIES

The French Company, *la Compagnie française des Indes orientales*, played an important role in the colonial history of India and Britain, but its commercial life was brief. There were, in fact, several French Companies, each organized along slightly different lines, but all were short-lived in comparison with the English and Dutch Companies (Wellington 2006). The first set out as early as 1600. It was a private venture consisting of one voyage of two ships, the *Croissant* and the *Corbin*. Monopoly rights to the Eastern trade were granted in 1615, to the *Compagnie des Moloques*, but allowed to lapse in 1627. The *Compagnie d'Orient* was granted a monopoly in 1633. Its activities consisted of a disastrous attempt to colonize Madagascar. A royal company, founded by Jean-Baptiste Colbert for the French Crown, was chartered in 1664. Although finally able to pull away from the doomed efforts to establish a settlement in Madagascar and focus on trade, the company produced consistently mediocre returns and faced insolvency by the early 1700s (Wellington 2006: 23–47). The infamous John Law reorganized the company in 1719, newly christening it the *Compagnie des Indes*. As was his signature, there was a short speculative fever and an abrupt crash in 1720 (Manning 1996: 27). In 1721 the *Conseil des Indes*, a government committee, was formed to run company affairs. Its formation gave the state direct control over the commercial affairs of the company.

Catherine Manning has shown that although the state directed company affairs, there was a positive dynamic between private and company trade in this period. While official company trade was strictly controlled by the state, French company vessels were leased to employees so that they might pursue their own trade—and the state often acted as a primary investor in these ventures (Manning 1996: 78). The crew was also accorded the standard cargo allotment, in this case free freight of 4.9 percent, on official voyage for private trade purposes (Manning 1996: 85).

In the French Company, private and corporate interests were not intertwined as they were in the English Company. Private investors had little influence over company policy as it was run by the state, and it is unclear to what extent the information gained through private voyages was able to penetrate and influence official trade policy. Nevertheless the French Company survived, and even briefly prospered in the 1730s, before being diverted into colonial and militaristic pursuits by the government after the War of Austrian Succession (Manning 1996: 29–31).

A straight comparison with the English Company is difficult to make since there are many factors in play. The success of the French Company during this brief period in the eighteenth century provides some support for observing a general advantage from increased private trade allowances across East India companies in this period. However the strict separation between private and Company use of ships in the French Company was markedly different from the practices that evolved over time in the English Company, and that were so central to the transfer of local information between ships in the East. It is also true that a brief period of prosperity, as finally experienced by the French Company in the 1730s, is quite different from the persistent innovation and expansion of the English Company. It is difficult to tell whether the success of the Compagnie des Indes would have continued past the 1740s if the French Company had not turned to colonial pursuits. Indeed it can be argued that by engaging in territorial aggression the French changed the rules of the game for the large European companies operating in the East, putting into jeopardy organizations that were not able to compete militarily as well as commercially.

The Ostend Company, based in Austria, existed from 1715 to 1731. It was monetarily successful, but folded due to external political pressure from England. The English East India Company had long resented the competition and believed the company was simply a foil for illegitimate continental English private trade (Hertz 1907). Since its eventual failure had little to do with the commercial organization of the company, its history does little to shed light on the problems addressed here.

The Swedish Company was created soon after the dissolution of the Ostend Company in 1731. Indeed many individuals seem to have transferred their assets from the Ostend Company directly to the Swedish Company, although little evidence exists to show that the Swedish firm was a continuation of the Ostend operation (Koninckx 1980: 52). As with the Ostend Company, British involvement in the venture was high despite the fact that participation violated British law (Koninckx 1980: 80). One of the more important investors was the Scottish-born Colin Campbell (Koninckx 1980: 50). The charter specified that the names of the shareholders and company accounts were to be kept secret (Koninckx 1980: 45–46), likely to protect the English investors.

The Swedish Company was much smaller than the English or Dutch Companies and had no colonial aspirations (Koninckx 1980: 55). It is unlikely it could have afforded them. In its first fifteen years, it sponsored twenty-five voyages (Koninckx 1980: 53). It grew, becoming a joint-stock in 1753 and sending out thirty-nine ships between 1766 and 1786. Decline set in after 1786, and the last ship was sent out in 1804 (Koninckx 1980: 65).

The crew was allowed a private trade allotment (Koninckx 1980: 325), though private trade by directors and principal shareholders was forbidden (Koninckx 1980: 62). This restriction is significant because directors and shareholders served as ships' captains. Private trade was curtailed in other ways. The ships bound for China did not engage in an appreciable country trade beyond taking on provisions (Koninckx 1980: 119–34), and fifty-five of its sixty-one voyages went to China. In all, the Swedish Company enjoyed moderate success by exploiting European inroads into the market at Canton.

The Danish Company went in and out of existence for nearly two hundred years. In many ways it was the Dutch equivalent of the Ostend and Swedish Companies. It was nominally Danish, but relied heavily on Dutch interlopers for capital and staffing (Furber 1976: 212–13). Bernt Pessart, formerly of the Dutch Company, became head of operations in 1636 (Subrahmanyam 1990a: 186). It was first active from 1616 until 1650, although for a significant portion of this time its trade was restricted to the country trade of Asia because it lacked the capital necessary to finance intercontinental voyages (Subrahmanyam 1990a: 186). It was in this second period that the Danish Company established a fort at Tranquebar (Tharangambadi). The company eventually failed entirely, only to reappear in 1670. In this period, the company achieved moderate success, but had nearly failed again by 1721, at which time it leased out its monopoly privileges. It re-emerged in 1732 and followed a similar path to the Swedish Company, trading heavily and successfully with Canton. In 1772, the Danish government lifted monopoly privileges to India, opening it to individuals and other organizations. According to Furber, private Danish ships after this time often carried English private cargo and were staffed by any number of foreign sailors (Furber 1976: 212–15). The English private trade became increasingly important to the Danish Company's operations as the eighteenth century drew to a close and the nineteenth began (Feldbæk 1976: 233–34). The company continued to trade profitably until 1808.

Ole Feldbæk, who has written a comprehensive history of the Danish Company in its later period (1772–1808), described its trade as conducted "on extremely rigid lines" (1969: 14). Country trade appears to have been negligible, at least in this later period, which has received the most attention. Contrary to the free trade advocates, the example of the Danish Company provides some support for the idea that the large company form had advantages over officially licensed private traders. It was, after all, able to hold its own after the Danish East Indies trade became an open market. It is also true that its modest but profitable trade may have been linked to the restricted focus and high degree of specialization of the company (Feldbæk 1969: 233) and that it relied heavily on access to local capital brought into the region by English private traders (Hodacs 2013).

In 1695, the Company of Scotland, trading in Africa and the Indies, known as the Scots Darien Company, was incorporated (Bingham 1906: 214). The Darien Company was granted a national monopoly to Asia, as well as Africa and Asia, but foundered in an attempt to establish a colony in Central America.

## CONCLUSION

When compared with its two largest competitors, the English Company was both less militaristic and significantly less centralized. Its employees systematically enjoyed more autonomy and greater private trade privileges, and it was not subject to direct state control. These are all potentially important factors in the long-term success of the English Company. The comparison across European East India Companies provides a means by which to evaluate the importance of each, although any conclusions are limited by the small number of companies, their relationship to each other (i.e., the nonindependence of observations), and the relatively large number of potentially important factors (relative to the number of cases).

State control is often seen as a factor in the decline of the Portuguese and French Companies; however the Dutch enjoyed significant autonomy from the state and yet experienced difficulty adapting to new market conditions. With the exception of the French Company, the smaller firms were all less militaristic than the Portuguese and Dutch. These companies tended to go in and out of business, each time exploiting niches in well-established markets, such as the Canton trade. They did not demonstrate the adaptability of the English Company, although it is difficult to say what they might have accomplished with access to a larger pool of capital. There were synergies between the company and private trade in these other smaller organizations, including the French; however, private and company interests seem uniquely intertwined through the country trade of the captains of the English Company ships.[8]

Specific historical circumstances have been used to explain the difficulties faced by the early overseas companies; however in the case of the Dutch and the Portuguese their failures were part of a larger pattern by which large and successful organizations have difficulty adapting to changing environments. The incorporation of forms of private trade seems to have helped many of the smaller companies, while lack of direct government oversight and pacific, rather than militaristic, strategies were not in and of themselves sufficient to propel companies to long-term success. Thus the comparison between East India Companies suggests that the private trade and its concomitant decentralization of the organizational structure of the English Company played a role in increasing its adaptability and continued growth. The next two chapters are devoted to exploring the mechanisms by which the private trade promoted innovation and decentralized coordination within the English Company.

*Chapter 4*

# SOCIAL NETWORKS AND THE EAST INDIAMAN

---

The English East India Company began the seventeenth century much like a smaller, less confident version of the Dutch Company. Over the course of the next two centuries the situation was reversed. Where the Dutch appeared to be trapped by the routine behaviors and the sunk costs of their significant investment in establishing control over the islands of the Indonesian Archipelago, the English Company adapted to shifting market conditions by incorporating new ports and goods into its trade. In the East Indies trade one of the largest problems the companies faced was expanding beyond their initial pursuit of pepper and spice. As K. N. Chaudhuri puts it, "By the third quarter of the seventeenth century it must have become clear to all those who were concerned with the East India trade that there were other and more valuable Asian commodities which could be brought to a profitable market in Europe. But few of them would have been prepared to concede that the national stake in the European pepper trade should be relinquished in favour of rival foreign countries" (Chaudhuri 1978: 313). Despite the fact that the Dutch Company was larger, more powerful, and better provisioned, it was the English Company that moved first to incorporate cotton piece goods as a central component of their new trade strategy. This innovative, and incredibly successful, introduction of a new good to the European markets was not an isolated occurrence, but indicative of a larger pattern. In this chapter I explore how the private trade allowances of the 1660s and 1670s helped to sustain mechanisms of information diffusion that allowed the English Company to build innovation and exploration into durable aspects of the firm.

Organizational theorists have suggested that multinational firms operating in complex global environments profit from decentralized organizational structures that allow local knowledge to filter into the firm's knowledge base (Bartlett and Ghoshal 1989: 68, 131–54). Implemented in a new context, that is, within the boundaries of the organization, this local knowledge is innovative (Burt 2004, Padgett and McLean 2006). The problem is that large organizations inevitably have difficulty receiving information from the world around them. Following Max Weber, this difficulty arises because organizations depend upon existing rules and routines to ensnare individuals and press them into service (Weber 1991: 196–240). Inflexible routines and rules prevent the incorporation of new information brought in by new employees. Following Niklas Luhmann, this difficulty arises because organizations are at their base tools for reducing the complexity of the lived environment (Luhmann 1995). Structurally the centralization of control that accompanies the creation of most bureaucratic administrations limits the amount of information that can be processed by decision makers, that is, the fewer the decision makers, the less information it is possible to process. Centralization also increases the distance of decision makers from local conditions on the periphery.

To the extent to which an answer to this problem exists, a structural approach suggests decentralization, or the increased autonomy of local actors. But, for the organization to continue to act as an organization, which is a form of coordinated activity after all, there must be some integrative mechanism linking the actions of these semiautonomous actors. Therefore, to successfully encourage adaptation and innovation, decentralization must facilitate the transfer of information between local agents and into the larger pool of knowledge that exists within the organization. The analysis in this chapter looks at the transfer of information between East Indiaman ships engaged in the East Indies trade and whether that information was incorporated more generally into company operations.

## INFORMATION

The problem of gathering information is always acute in foreign trade and was even more problematic for the early modern trader. Goods and markets were dispersed. Prices and supply fluctuated wildly. Political conditions varied. Depending on the degree to which it affected state coffers, political leaders might encourage trade, but in times of hardship or scarcity, the local population could swing violently against foreigners. Tax rates and exemptions changed frequently. Enemy ships might haunt the harbors. And unchartered shoals could founder ships. A word of warning or information on how to hire a pilot could save a vessel from disaster or commercial failure.

As might be expected, information on market conditions occupied much of the correspondence of Company employees: "The private correspondence of the East India Company's officials, some of whom were country traders on a large scale, are full of very detailed messages on the number and timing of the local shipping and the effect of their arrival and departure on markets and prices" (Chaudhuri 1978: 192). According to Miles Og-born, who has specialized in the written communications of the firm, the written correspondence was supplemented with informal networks: "[T]he official correspondence between the directors and the factories also had as its constant shadow an extensive network of private communications, both within India and between India and London" (Ogborn 2007: 95).

Timely information was of particular importance. Correspondents repeatedly request that every possible haste should be made in getting them the most current information possible. Robert Cowan, future governor of Bombay, directed a friend to always send news via Madras ships, as they arrived sooner (Chaudhuri 1986: 102). In 1778, director Laurence Sulivan wrote to his son "never to fail me by any possible conveyance giving me the earliest notice in cypher of every material circumstance" (Buchan 2003: 109). Written correspondence between two distant confidantes had to suffice if there was no alternative, but face-to-face interactions, which tend to drop out of the historical record, were more timely, more direct, and also a more trusted means of conveying information (Sood 2007). As is still true today, conversation and face-to-face interaction were essential to setting in motion the wheels of commerce.

The importance of conversation and direct interaction made public meeting places crucial components of the maritime trade. The coffeehouses of London were hubs of information and interaction, central to the evolution of the insurance business and overseas trade. Edward Lloyd's coffeehouse, the most famous of these gathering spots, produced Lloyd's of London, Lloyd's Register, and Lloyd's List, a journal of shipping news. The owners and commanders of the East Indies trade gathered at the Jerusalem Coffee House.

In the politically eventful decade of the 1760s, Sutton describes typical topics at the Jerusalem as including Indian politics, disagreements within the overseas council, and private trade rumors (Sutton 2010: 102). In 1768 word apparently raced through the coffeehouse of a shortage of glassware in Madras. Outbound ships loaded their freight to take advantage of the opportunity, in the end producing so much oversupply that prices fell to unprofitable levels (Sutton 1981: 83). The event was a cascade, a situation in which some initial event triggers contagion-like behavior among socially connected individuals, either through the spread of influence or information. It is a typical outcome in active, highly clustered social networks.

Though not all ports held coffeehouses, they all provided ample opportunity for interaction. Given the preoccupation of those abroad with making their fortune in trade, it is not surprising that conversations would turn to trade. While attending a dinner with the factors of Anjengo, William Larkin, then first mate of the *Durrington*, "learned what price he would get in ports up the coast for his fine Bengal silks, what Anjengo pepper and fine cloth and betelnut would fetch at Surat and the rate of exchange of the great variety of coins used in the trade" (Sutton 2010: 59).

Captains would also have communicated information about the conditions and dangers of different harbors. Well into the eighteenth century, the Company did not provide adequate sea charts. Instead, captains would have to piece together their own information. Much of this was done through conversation: "Reliable printed sailing directions were very sparse, too, at this time, though commanders and officers with experience of sailing to the eastern seas would have acquired a vast body of lore through discussion" (Sutton 2010: 22).


## SHIPS, CAPTAINS, AND DECISION MAKING

As captains drifted into tropical waters, they had several considerations to weigh. They were piloting a roughly thousand-ton wooden ship into distant waters. Most frequently, their crew of one hundred or more men had already been dramatically reduced from death due to scurvy, malaria, or a host of other illnesses and parasites.[1] Those that remained alive might not be operating at full capacity. The captain and crew braved these generally horrific conditions because they were attempting to secure a fortune to support an early and prosperous retirement.

On their first voyage the captains and officers were usually already in debt. It was common practice to pay the ship's owner in order to obtain a potentially lucrative position, such as captain or officer (Sutton 1981: 72–73).[2] Uniforms and incidentals were costly. In addition, initial capital was needed for individuals to participate in the private trade—in order to buy goods. Captains were paid only ten pounds a month for most of the Company's history (Sutton 1981: 73). They might make additional money by carrying passengers, whose fares went into the captain's pockets, but only the profits made through private trade could compensate them for their initial outlay.

After securing their position and readying their ship, captains received their shipping orders from Company headquarters at the East India House (Sutton 1981: 104). In 1720 the *Cassandra* was sent to Bombay. The Captain James MacRae's shipping orders included directions to take twenty-three tons of ballast, forty tons or more of specified goods, which, if the ship was dispatched from Surat, Bombay, Karwar, or the Malabar Coast, must be one-third pepper. In addition, the ship was not to stop at Madeira or the Canary Islands and was allowed four months for lading in India (Chaudhuri 1993: 64). As with most things in the Eastern trade, patronage played a role as captains and managing owners fought to obtain the better assignments for their ships. The managing owners would also have advice and directions for the captains of their ships (Sutton 2010: 20).[3] Roughly six to eight months and often several lives later they would be facing their first commercial decisions in the East.

Once at sea captains had a significant amount of control over the course of their ships. There is no question that they were determined to make their fortunes while in the East. On the other hand, their continued employment depended upon arriving at the port, or ports, assigned to them at the East India House in London. They had to consider the advice they received from their patron: the shipowner. They might receive additional orders from Company factors and directors in the East, and on some occasions they may have been transporting important officials in the Company, who could complicate the authority structure onboard ship. The formal destinations were determined by the directors in London, set in formal orders, and inscribed on the first page of the ship's logbooks.

In theory, captains could trade their own goods at the ports given to them by Company officers in London. And many did. Captains traded liquor and mechanical trinkets, such as magnifying lenses, for their own profit alongside the Company's larger trade in tea, indigo, and cotton at well-established ports, such Bombay, Madras, and Canton. It was also a common practice to divert ships to private trade destinations. Captains could—and did—legitimately fit in other ports of call on their way to obligatory destinations.

Captains might drop anchor at St. Augustine's or at any one of the several ports along the southern coast of Madagascar. There they could restock their provisions and buy slaves for sale in the Middle East or India. Even more frequently English captains headed to Portuguese or Dutch ports to sell liquor bought in Madeira or the Azores. Edward Barlow, officer and captain of the English Company, recorded in his journals the many trips he took to Goa under orders from his commanding officer, who was pursuing a lively trade in the distilled liquor arrack (Barlow and Lubbock [1703] 1934: 372). Captain Cummings of the *Royal Duke* missed the seasonal passage to China and determined to spend the time plying the trade along the Malabar Coast (Sutton 2010: 64). Whether pursuing Company or private trade, the captain would need to find a safe haven and good prospects for trade in order to conduct a successful voyage.

The analysis in this chapter considers whether captains' decisions about where to pilot their ships were informed by the experiences of other Company ships. Specifically I ask whether local information traveled laterally from ship to ship within the East Indies—without having to travel back to headquarters in London. Given the value of information in overseas trade, timely information would have been a significant advantage in pursuing both Company and private trade. As captains were operating under conditions of considerable uncertainty, the transfer of information between ships might also be considered a process of rational imitation, where captains imitated the last voyage of successful captains they encountered at port because they lacked information about the full set of commercial opportunities available to them across all Eastern ports (Hedström 1998). Second, the analysis considers whether the organizational structure of the firm, which varied over time, had an impact on this lateral transfer of information, that is, the use of these social networks to communicate information across ships. These two steps investigate the aspects of captains' social environment that conditioned their final decision to travel to a given port.

Finally, I consider what impact these social networks had on the overall structure of Company trade. This final stage of the analysis links the individual decision-making process of the captains to macro-level outcomes. The entire process then can be considered as a concatenation of dynamic network structures influencing a conditional-choice process at the level of captains (Rolfe 2009), which cumulate into new patterns of network structure. As a decentralized means of communication, social networks can serve as conduits for the transmission of vital local information that a large company, if receptive, may use to innovate and adapt to new market patterns. In this case, there is evidence that social network exchange did facilitate organizational learning at the Company level.

## DATA

The data used to address these problems were gathered from the shipping records of the East Indiaman ships. I used these records to identify communications between ships as well as the organization's incorporation of information previously transmitted through informal links, that is, lateral communications between captains. The data on the voyages of the East Indiamen ships have both methodological and substantive advantages. First, the Company systematically recorded the passage of the ships through their logs. Many large historical patterns can be revealed only by systematic data. The only other comparable sources are the shipping registers kept at various European ports. The problems with these shipping registers have been discussed in detail elsewhere (Das Gupta 1979: 280–92, Subrahmanyam 1988: 179–88, Arasaratnam 1989: 104–6, Prakash 1991, Mentz 2005: 197, Parthesius 2010: 125). Registers are available only for certain ports at certain times, and even within those periods there are inconsistencies and grounds to suspect large biases in what was recorded. Although registers provide valuable insight into the life of certain ports, the problems in the data would be magnified in any attempt to collate the various registers into one large data set in order to consider the larger system of trade.

In contrast, the records of the voyages of the English Company ships are drawn from the shiplogs themselves, which are reliable records of the paths of the ships.[4] There are also data on Dutch Company shipping (Bruijn, Gaastra, and Schöffer 1979–87); however these data have been collected from the shipping registers rather than the logs and are not directly comparable to the English Company shipping data. The English shipping data do not allow for an analysis of the larger pattern of all maritime trade in the East Indies region because they include only English Company ships. They do allow for an examination of systematic patterns in the English Company trade, and I confine my interpretations of the results to the mechanisms by which knowledge was transferred and incorporated within the English Company itself. This helps to clarify the specific means through which decentralization within the English Company contributed to its commercial success. The shipping data are intraorganizational data and are treated as such.

The ships are a compelling site for analysis because they are one of the sites of the extreme decentralization of control that occurred within the organizational framework of the East India Company. Hypothetically, the private trade and Company trade could have operated as distinct areas, although occurring at the same time. For example, when the private trade was considered illegitimate, private traders had strong incentives to minimize its impact on Company operations in order to hide what they were doing. The same reason would lead them to keep their private activities secret, in order to avoid suspicion or reprimand. Even when legitimate, if the private trade and Company trade were simply managed as separate concerns, they might have little direct impact on each other. Because the captains engaged in the private trade and had a significant amount of control over the course of their ships prior to the reforms of the late eighteenth century, they represent a site in which private and Company interests were intertwined.

The data on the ship's voyages came from the print volume, *Catalogue of East India Company Ships' Journals and Logs, 1600–1834* (Farrington 1999b). This volume integrates information from the journals, logs, ledgers, imprest books, pay books, receipt books, absence books, Company papers, and voluminous correspondence of the Company. The initial stage of the project involved the electronic transcription of the information pertaining to all voyages of the English Company, supplemented by the collection of geographic data for the 264 East Indies ports visited. The result includes a list of 1,480 ships (4,725 voyages) that were engaged in the English East India Company trade from 1601 to 1835 and geographic coordinates for all 264 ports. This includes ships whose voyages originated in Asia, the ships of the New East India Company, and country trade voyages on East India Company ships. All ships list the trading season in which they were active, and 99 percent include the intended destination. The captain of the ship is systematically listed and present in 95 percent of the voyages with ports recorded. Of the entries for voyages, 85 percent contain a complete set of ports visited. Of the missing 724 voyages, 188 were terminated due to rotting, wreck, acts of aggression, and other misadventures. Inland trade is not included, however both private and Company trade was generally restricted to the coast until after 1800 (Marshall 1993: 292).

This list of port-to-port trips is the centerpiece of the analysis since it forms the basis of the evolution of the trade network—each trip between ports constitutes the creation of an edge in the network, and travel to a new port adds a node. As such, I took the step of verifying that the data recorded in the Farrington volume accurately represent the ports visited by the East Indiamen ships by consulting the original logs. The British Library holds the original shiplogs in the India Office Records collection. A stratified sample of 107 logs confirmed that the ports listed as destinations in Farrington (1999b) were the same ports recorded in the original logs: dates and ports were correct in all cases.[5]

One may also question whether the purser and captain (the two officers usually responsible for maintaining the log and journal) recorded the actual passage of the ship. As described by the historian Miles Ogborn,

> [The journals] were to guarantee to the adventurers in London of the perfor-
> mance of what they had ordered to be done, or at least that decisions made
> on the voyage did not contradict those orders. Where possible, they were to
> provide the foundation of succeeding voyages by providing knowledge of winds
> and shoals, useful ports and places of refreshment, good routes to take, sup-
> posedly friendly or treacherous peoples, good commodities and markets, and
> the extent of Portuguese and Dutch power as well as the orientations of Asian
> politics. These journals were collated, archived, and used by the Company in
> increasingly systematic ways in order to provide "navigational" knowledge for
> subsequent voyages. (2007: 49)

The "guarantee" mentioned above raises the possibility that the captains and pursers might omit ports from the logs that were not consistent with official orders and regulations—in order to hide transgressions from Company officials. There is no evidence of such omissions. Instead, Portuguese and Dutch ports, legitimately off-limits to English Company traders, are recorded in abundance. Prior to the late eighteenth century, the Company was simply not very concerned with regulating the course of entire voyages, as long as the ship did go to the port to which it was formally ordered at some point. Company officials were much more concerned with keeping the voyages on time, but changing the text of logs could not hide delayed arrivals in London.

There was also a practical reason for faithfully recording the voyages as they occurred. The log served as a navigational tool during the course of the voyage, tracking weather conditions as well as position. Without an accurate record, the ship would be lost, and therefore at risk—good reason to keep an accurate record. Captains also directly relied upon data collected on previous voyages and stored in the logs. For example, William Larkin used William Dampier's account of his travels when navigating through uncharted waters between Sumatra and Japan, and much of Alexander Dalrymple's valuable work was based on close readings of East India Company logs (Sutton 2010: 83).

As an additional check on the validity of the data contained in the Farrington volumes I compared the voyages listed in the *Catalogue of East India Company Ships' Journals and Logs* (Farrington 1999b) with the record of ships trading in China compiled by Hosea Morse (1926). Morse's records came from the diaries of the supercargoes until the formation of the Council of Supercargoes, at which time the council's records were used. Of the 211 ships listed by Morse, only four do not appear in Farrington's data. These ships, the *Dragon*, *Sunne*, *Catherine*, and *Anne*, are unusual in that they were sold at Macao. Remaining discrepancies between the two lists include the 1702 voyage of the *Macclesfield*, the 1702 voyage of the *Union*, and the 1741 voyage of the *Royal Guardian*. In these cases, according to Farrington, these ships did not visit China. Morse notes that the *Royal Guardian* was sent back from Bombay, and there are two consecutive dates associated with Bombay, November 29, 1740, and January 9, 1741, so it seems likely that a stop in Canton may have been dropped from between these two other port listings. The records of the *Macclesfield* and the *Union* do not offer a simple explanation, and both ships had a relatively busy schedule of ports listed for their 1701 voyages. Morse, on the other hand, does not report thirty-five voyages that are included in the Farrington volume. A small minority of these may be accounted for by four occasions in which Morse includes a line stating "several others from Indian Settlements" or some variation thereof. All of this indicates that the voyage data are indeed significantly more reliable than the ships' registers.

Despite what may appear to be problems associated with historical data, the ships' records actually have some notable advantages when compared to contemporary data on social networks. The voyages carried goods and individuals, and through the individuals aboard, they carried information. The interaction between individuals was, at this time, the main channel for the transmission of information and goods (there were no modern methods of communication). Though emergency information could be communicated over a land route if seasonal weather patterns obstructed travel (Furber and Rocher 1997: chap. 5, 105–6), as late as 1803 essential news regarding a declaration of war with France came to Canton via the brig *Ganges* (Sutton 2010: 215). These circumstances make this data set exceptionally useful for tracking the flow of information in international trade. Whereas today multiple information networks overlap and feed into each other, in the early modern period people, in this case carried by ships, were the central means by which information, written or verbal, was transmitted. The passage of information, goods, and capital was consolidated along a smaller number of available channels than is the case in the modern world, and the English voyages were a central conduit (Mentz 2005: 220). This is a great advantage of the data.

## ANALYSIS

Given the uncertainty and volatility involved in overseas trade in the premodern period, the problem of how captains made decisions to travel to one port or another is interesting in its own right. One might for example be interested in whether captains relied upon personal experience more than they trusted information gathered from others. Nevertheless the central theoretical question in this chapter is whether increased employee autonomy increased or decreased horizontal communication between ships. Employee autonomy varied over different eras in the history of the organization. It was high during the early exploratory period and the subsequent period, from roughly 1670 to 1757, in which private trade allowances were legitimated in Company bylaw, and the final colonial period in which employee autonomy was depressed. Thus the relationship between the transfer of local information via network exchange between captains and each of these organizational eras is of central interest in the analysis.

To test the relationship between information types and the decision to travel to a port, the data were structured with a choice set. The dependent variable reflects the existence of a tie between port A and port B. If a ship travels from port A to port B, the dependent variable is coded as 1. When the ship travels from port A to port B, it necessarily does not travel to the set of other possible ports (for example, ports C, D, E, and F). The dependent variable in these cases is coded as 0. Thus the unit of analysis is the set of possible trips based on the number of trips between ports actually made by each ship. It is worth noting that each voyage was composed of several trips between ports. The set of possible ports is determined by including all ports that had been visited by an East India Company ship five years prior to the first visit and five years after the last visit. This means, for example, that Singapore, which was founded in its modern incarnation in 1819 by Sir Thomas Raffles, does not enter the choice set for any port until the nineteenth century, as is appropriate. All ports that were never visited from a target port are also dropped from the choice set. For example, if there is no history of travel by any East India Company ship from port A to port D, this port-to-port pair is not included in the data as part of the choice set for the actual trip that occurred between port A and port B, although of course port D may appear in the choice set for another port—which did have a history of direct travel to port D. Additional models were estimated where ports entered the choice set five and ten years prior to the first visit and exited the choice set five and ten years after the last recorded visit. The results of these models were very similar to what is presented here.

At an elementary level, captains had three potential avenues through which to gather information: they could trust the orders given by the Company and use them as a means by which to identify profitable centers of trade (for the Company and for themselves); they could rely on information given to them by other individuals participating in the trade; once they had amassed some experience, they could draw upon their own past familiarity with ports in order to make informed decisions about new prospects for trade. The statistical model incorporates these options as independent variables representing exposure to different types of information sources as well as several controls into a logistic mixed effects model.[6] The logistic model is appropriate as the dependent variable is a binary outcome, that is, if the ship travels to a given port or not. The model reported here incorporates crossed random effects for captains and port-to-port pairs, a control for the distance between ports, and a time-varying control for the traffic between any port-to-port pair.[7]

INDEPENDENT VARIABLES

*Networks*

When engaged in risky ventures, many individuals turn to information drawn from social networks to make financial and commercial decisions (Powell, Koput, and Smith-Doerr 1996, Powell 1990, Gulati 1995, 1998, Raub and Weesie 1990, Fried and Hisrich 1994, Sorenson 2003, Burt and Knez 1995, Baker 1984, Faulkner and Anderson 1987, and many others). Trust plays an important role in the decision to form and use social networks. The strength or durability of a relationship leads actors to trust the information they receive through social contacts. If captains used informal networks in their decision to travel to foreign markets, it is likely that they relied on the information passed through the network of the voyages of their compatriots, who shared a common culture and language and generally traded in the same type of goods. This preference is indicated by contemporary research on homophily and trust (Lazarsfeld and Merton 1954, McPherson, Smith-Lovin, and Cook 2001) as well as historical work on trust bound by (or constructed through) ethnic and religious similarities (Bosher 1995, Breen 1985: 84, Curtin 1994, Grofman and Landa 1983, Hunt 1996: 22–23). Organizational theorists also suggest that it is more likely that trust and cooperation develop in social networks within firms when organizational affiliation is a meaningful category for individuals in foreign environments (Simon 1997: 278–95), as was the case with the English Company.

Although they were operating in a cosmopolitan environment, the majority of employees of the East India Company were bound by strong community ties.[8] The rank of captain was a significant role in the Company that brought with it considerable prospects for amassing wealth through the private trade. In the highly stratified society of Britain at this time, this meant that the position was reserved for individuals of higher social status with existing ties to powerful interests within the Company. For most of the Company's history, captaincies were bought and sold by the managing owners. Exceptions occurred when the captain died en route (Sutton 1981, 61, 70–72). In these cases, the captain would be replaced by the first mate, who would also have had to be a person of at least some significant social standing—if not as highly connected as the captain. Captains were therefore bound by both similar class standing and a network of indirect ties linking them to shipowners.

The crew of outward-bound ships also appears to have belonged to a distinct community. According to Jean Sutton the crew was chosen from the families that had settled along the Thames. The men were identifiable by their striped clothing, canvas jackets, and brightly colored ribbons (Sutton 1981: 85). The fact that captains and crew were bound by strong within-group social ties makes it extremely plausible that they would have at times communicated trusted information to each other. It has even been argued that the success of British merchants depended to a large extent upon their "unbounded trust to one another" as a contemporary Dutch merchant put it (Price 1989: 273). As Jacob Price notes, this trust was crucial to the credit supply. In reviewing the tight links between the economies of London and the private traders of Madras, Søren Mentz has summarized the situation by saying, "Company servants left England to seek social mobility, but they did not abandon their social network and cultural background when they took off on board the Company vessel destined for Asia" (Mentz 2005: 49).

If social ties make it likely that captains would have communicated information to one another, historical evidence, discussed earlier, has provided direct evidence that face-to-face interactions were used to transfer valuable market information. All of this indicates that peer interactions were a source of information for employees abroad. Existing historical knowledge does not, however, give a systematic picture of the impact of social networks on the organization and its trade. In order to gauge the importance of social networks, a statistical model is necessary. By including control variables, the model allows for an examination of the relative importance of social networks compared to other information sources and additional factors that might have affected captains' decisions. It does so by controlling for these factors. And, importantly, it allows for an evaluation of how organizational structure, specifically the decentralization of control over ships, affected the use of social networks.

Using a model requires operationalizing the social networks that linked the ships of the English Company. This means identifying the mechanisms through which information may have been laterally transmitted between different units, that is, ships. East India Company ships were dispersed across Asia, but they came into regular contact with each other at ports. If informal relationships between employees were used to transfer information, regular opportunities to communicate arose when English captains and crews shared the same harbor.[9] If the port held an English factory, that factory served as the living quarters for all Company employees in that area. In many ports, local governments curtailed English access to the larger social and residential life of the area. The English, as well as most other foreign merchants, were consigned to merchant ghettos, called *natios*.[10] In these cases, the factories became the center of English social life overseas. At factories, Company employees ate together (Ogborn 2007: 88), further facilitating the collection and transfer of information. When senior officers did not stay in factories, but instead rented out private homes (such as in Madras), they were expected to engage in the busy social life of ports (which would have picked up considerably as ships came into dock) by attending events such as receptions and parties (Sutton 1981: 61). By the nineteenth century in Calcutta, they attended balls, public receptions, the theater, and concerts—all stops on what became a regular society social circuit (Webster 2007: 1). In Canton, captains, supercargoes, and passengers of note dined together every day at two o'clock in the afternoon (Sutton 1981: 61). In the evenings, they were often entertained on the lavish estates of Chinese merchants (Sutton 2010: 97).

It follows that each captain should have been able to access information about the ports visited by each of the other captains anchored or recently anchored at the same port. The set of captains who crossed paths at ports is effectively a reference group that allows network effects to be identified. Although competition between ships and captains must have existed, information hoarding and deception would have been unlikely given that the entire crew would have to agree to withhold all information or lie about their past whereabouts. In addition, ships that had just traveled from a port were less likely to be interested in returning to that port, so they would have more to gain from exchanging valid information about potential destinations, than in hoarding information of little remaining value to themselves.

The frequently overlooked issues of timing and scheduling, considered in greater detail by Christopher Winship (2009), are a crucial component of the larger mechanism of information diffusion within the shipping network. Overlap at ports is the basic mechanism that allows for the transmission of information from captain to captain. Taking the timing of port overlap into account injects a significant amount of dynamism and complexity into the network structure, which cannot be captured by static structural analysis that in effect combines many actors' viewpoints into one larger map. That is why, in this chapter, network structure is operationalized as the local structure perceived from the vantage of each ship as it sat ready to embark on a new port-to-port trip. This local structure is then incorporated as a variable into a decision-making model of captains' choices to travel to different ports.

The exact overlap between voyages at the different ports is unknown in many cases because the data systematically report only arrival dates. However 1,012 of the 14,065 trips that were completed between ports within the lifetime of the organization did list arrival and departure dates. A sample was used to estimate the standard duration for voyage overlaps. The sample was drawn from all voyages, but only voyages with complete departure and arrival dates that occurred within the sample were used to calculate the final estimate. For these seventy-two trips the average stay in port was 3.62 months.

If the factories provided a home away from home for the English overseas, residents of the factories should have been able to store information that could then be transferred from ship to ship without direct overlap. However, the information would have to have been timely to be useful. In order to address this possibility, I considered the probability that a captain would be influenced by information left at a port one month, two months, three months, and so on prior to arrival at the port. There was a sharp increase in the number of times captains traveled to ports recently visited by other captains who had departed four months prior to their arrival, which leveled out at five months onward. This natural break indicated that information continued to be most useful for periods of four months, but had little influence on captains after that period—most likely because it was no longer timely. The model includes this additional four months when calculating the potential for information transfer between ships, although model results are robust to variations of this estimate.[11] A small number of voyages originated in Asia. In these cases it is assumed that they gathered information in the port four months prior to departure to make preparations.

Using the supplied arrival times and the imputed departure times, and taking into consideration the possibility that factors—or others in the factory—may have held and transferred information between ships, it is possible to assess which captains had an opportunity to get information from the travels of other ships. If a captain both was exposed to information about a port by his colleagues and chose to travel to that port, the variable *network* was coded as 1. For example, Captain Robert Hurst brought the *Averilla* into Bencoolen on November 30, 1714. One month later, while the *Averilla* was still at port, the *Banjarmassin* arrived in Bencoolen under the command of Captain Thomas Lewis. The *Banjarmassin*'s first stop in the East Indies had been at Batavia. Three months later the *Averilla* departed Bencoolen bound for Batavia as a last stop before returning to the Atlantic. Since the ships sat in port together, captains and crews had the opportunity to share information about their voyages. Because Captain Robert Hurst seems to have acted on that information, the *network* variable is coded as 1. If he had gone to a port not visited by the *Banjarmassin* on its current voyage, it would have been coded as 0. The model controls for other factors that could have influenced Captain Hurst, such as the distance between ports, seasonal weather patterns, port popularity, and personal experience.

It is worth noting that the variable is capturing the use of information made available through relations between employees in the East, not the presence of relationships. Instead, relationships are assumed as employees came into regular contact with each other at port and were known to engage in extensive social activities with each other. Also, information could be gained from outside of the English network of trade via other Europeans or Asians. Similar systematic data on the voyages of European and Asian ships are not available and therefore cannot be included in the analysis. However there are reasons to believe that the rate of potentially profitable information transferred between resident Asian merchants or other Europeans and English East India Company employees would be lower than within-firm rates of transmission.

Other Europeans were present in many of the ports visited by the English Company; however they were not housed in the same quarters, as was the case with Englishmen. Therefore there is no regular mechanism for face-to-face interaction. Other Europeans were also potential trade partners, from whom a profit could be made, but they were not necessarily likely confidantes as rivalries dominated relations between companies. Similarly although English factors would have come into regular contact with Asian merchants while in port, it is less clear to what extent captains would have had the same opportunities. There also seem to have been significant boundaries to the construction of cross-cultural relations. The relationships between factors and resident merchants were consistently strained. For example, in Madras, the English factors suspected each merchant they dealt with of some form of treachery (Mukund 1999: 64, 68, 70–72, 109, 111–12, 115). Similar complaints were made of the Hong merchants in Canton. Evidence of generalized forms of discrimination, that is, racism, were also present. Madras for example was racially segregated. The generally poor treatment of elite Asian merchants, extremely poor conditions for *lascars* (Asian sailors who often manned return voyages to Europe) (Lahiri 2002: 180), and the use of racially charged epithets all indicate racism had entered the larger discourse of the English in Asia as early as the 1700s, if not before (Nightingale 2008: 61).

It is more likely that captains would have trusted information gathered by other British officers or traders on private trade voyages conducted off Company ships. Unfortunately there also are no systematic data on smaller private English vessels owned by factors or free merchants. Very prosperous English private traders could amass small fleets of country trading ships. Mentz considers a contemporary's estimate of the size of Richard Mohun's fleet, fourteen ships, to be an improbably large figure (Mentz 2005: 166).[12] It came from the letter of an individual accusing Mohun of misconduct and was probably intended to ruin his reputation in London. The existence of private trading ships does mean that the results of the analysis are a potentially conservative measure of information transmitted between Englishmen, although the information would have come from individuals acting outside of the Company framework.[13] Because I cannot include data on private voyages of European or Asian merchants, I restrict my claims to the transfer of information within the firm—rather than across firm boundaries.

### Organizational Eras

The model is divided into three periods, representing different stages in the organizational history: *exploratory, private trade,* and *colonial.* As reviewed in chapter 3, from 1600 to 1674 the English Company was in an initial exploratory phase—the firm's main goal was simply to establish itself in the complex commercial worlds of Asia and the Middle East. Private trade was not entirely legitimate, but also not well controlled. From 1660 to 1680 several pieces of internal legislation were passed expanding the private trading privileges of the Company employees, with a major piece of legislation enacted in 1674. The model incorporates 1674 as a marker for the beginning of this second phase in the Company's history. In the second phase, the Company reached maturity while also incorporating a large amount of autonomy for its employees through private trade allowances. I often refer to this period as the private trade period. In 1757, the Battle of

Plassey was fought, beginning the colonial phase of the Company's history. As described in chapter 3, the autonomy of the captains was significantly reduced during this later phase. The regulatory shift lagged behind the organizational shift, as shown by the Act of 1776 outlawing route deviations. However it was in 1757 that the organizational goals and incentives were redirected.[14]

## CONTROL VARIABLES

### Experience

Besides peer networks, captains also had access to the store of information they accumulated during their own travels in the East. The disadvantage of personal experience is that it is limited when compared to the information available through social networks and more likely to be out of date. On the other hand, personal experience may reflect trusting relationships across firm boundaries or a deep cultural knowledge of sites that cannot be easily transmitted to others. In this sense, personal experience could reflect a different set of social networks, those networks stretching outside of the firm's boundaries. In other words, personal experience could also be conceived of as the accumulation of past relationships created outside the boundaries of the firm.[15]

It is possible to see personal experience in an individualistic light. It is reasonable to expect that in competitive circumstances, individuals will prefer to rely upon their own experiences, rather than trust others for reliable information. Up-to-date information about prices and goods was invaluable for making the fortunes of foreign traders: there was frequently a large difference in profits between the first ship to port and the second. This difference makes it possible that captains might have hoarded commercial information. The expectation that captains would rely solely upon personal experience is most in line with classical assumptions about decentralized actors in market situations. Following Adam Smith, it is the self-interested actions of individuals that create the greatest value for the whole. Narrowly conceived, this would lead to the expectation that captains relied exclusively upon personal experience to pursue their own interests; social networks did not drive the trade. If this was the case, the distributed autonomy of the captains and crew would not have contributed to the overall efficiency of the organization through coordinated activities.

In either case, personal experience is a potentially crucial source of information for captains that must be disentangled from information transmitted through peer networks. In a trade network such as this, information is not only transmitted through the network, *it traverses the network* as

actors move from location to location.[16] Personal experience captures the
movement of information as it is carried and accumulated by the individuals who traverse the network. It is recorded in the data as a binary variable:
1 if the destination port is part of a captain's past repertoire, 0 otherwise.

### Voyage Count

Distinct from the experience captains had in specific ports is the profes-
sional experience acquired by each captain within the organization. Captains' tenure in the organization was measured by the count of voyages he
had taken prior to the current voyage.

### Formal Orders

Captains were ordered to proceed to particular ports by Company managers at the outset of their journey. If they were to abide by the terms of their
contract, captains were obligated at some point in their voyage to journey
to the destinations indicated by the board of managers in London.[17] However, as described earlier, there was leeway as to exactly when the ships
touched ashore at these ports.

   The formal destination for each voyage was noted in the first pages of
the ships' journals, and systematically recorded in the comprehensive catalogue of ships' voyages (Farrington 1999b). However, these directions were
occasionally vague. When an area was listed rather than a port, the site of
the major English factory in that region was used. For example, if Bengal
was listed, Calcutta was used as the formal destination of the voyage. The
reasoning behind these decisions was that imprecise directions are possible
only when general knowledge is high; therefore, vague directions are given
only if the most obvious answer is the correct one. If the listed destination
was too imprecise, that is, the East Indies, it was not replaced. Centers of
English Company power, such as the presidencies (for example, Madras,
Bombay, and Calcutta), were also treated as formal destinations. Captains
pursuing their own trade were unlikely to make unofficial stops at these
official ports. A sample of shiplogs confirmed that uncommon destinations
were noted in the first pages of the logs.[18] Common destinations, that is,
Bombay and Madras, could go unnoted although they were part of the
official route intended for the ship by the board of directors. A dummy
indicates formal destinations. Since additional information about a formal
destination would be beside the point—and captains would be more likely
to have information about those formal destinations as they were heavily
trafficked—this is an important control.

   Factors or directors in the East may also have ordered the captain to
certain ports, although it is more likely that they would have consulted

with the captain—and other captains present at port—as to the best course of action. Factors were also heavily engaged in the private trade, so orders to captains may or may not have been related to official Company trade. Such orders would often have been verbal, and there is no systematic record of such orders, so they cannot be directly included in the analysis. In any case, factors' orders were part of the localized decision-making apparatus of the Company and provide further evidence of the decentralized organizational structure. In the analysis, they are conceptualized as a colleague's influence on the captain's decision and are discussed in the section on social networks.

### Additional Control Variables

As noted above, random effects based on captains are included in the model to control for clustering that in the data related to the expression of individual preferences at the level of the individual making decisions about where to travel. The logged distance between ports is included as a standard control for the costs involved in traveling longer distances. The log of distance is used as variation in smaller distances generally has a stronger effect than variation in longer distances. For example, the relative distance between my two local grocery stores has a large impact on my decision to travel to one or the other despite the fact that the distance between groceries is much smaller than the difference in the relative distance between Los Angeles and San Francisco, which has very little impact on my decision to fly to one or the other from the East Coast.

A fixed effect for season was originally included in the model but was insignificant at all levels and was subsequently excluded. An extremely important control for the rates of traffic between two ports was included. This control essentially acts as a substitute for time-invariant direct port-to-port fixed effects. The rate of traffic captures thirty-five years of travel and is calculated as the thirty-five years of traffic prior to the ship's departure date from the first port—thus it varies according to the rate of traffic between each port-to-port pair at the time that each trip is taken. Incorporating this time variance is important as the popularity of the ports both grew and declined over the nearly three centuries of Company history. Surat, for example, was a major port in the seventeenth century that drew very little traffic in the eighteenth, whereas many of the major English ports, such as Bombay, Madras, and Calcutta, grew exponentially in the eighteenth century. As an additional check, the model has also been estimated with controls for traffic rates defined over periods of twenty, sixty, and eighty years with similar results. Shorter periods run the risk of controlling for exactly the short-term changes in port popularity that arise from the effects of formal orders, personal experience, and social networks.

Additional potentially confounding variables are included to control for war, changes in the commodity composition of trade, and periods in which the Company monopoly was under threat. During times of war, timely information is at a premium. Running into hostile ships could be dangerous, as well a hindrance to trade. When Henry Middleton brought his ship into a promising port in the Bay of Cambay he was surprised to find Portuguese ships in harbor. The ships did not openly attack, but picked off stray English attempting to cross from the ship or shore, successfully blocking access to much-needed provisions (Sutton 1981: 63). More than a century later, the *Edgecote* was able to successfully evade French ships trolling off the Coast of Malacca after picking up information warning of them at the port of Queda (Kedah), where the *Hardwick* and *Wager* had recently stopped (Sutton 1981: 110).

When conditions shifted suddenly, dated information from London, captured by formal orders, was likely to be less useful, whereas timely, local information carried through social networks was likely to carry more weight. Therefore, wars are likely to reduce the importance of formal orders and increase reliance on social networks. However, wars with Asian powers were generally fought on land and may affect the trade less than wars with the major European powers. Thus variables for war with European powers were included in the model and coded 1 only if a war was in progress.[19]

The initiation of trade in a new commodity could also have potentially affected patterns of information use. Attempts at quickly finding the best sources for valuable new commodities may increase reliance the benefits of timely information from social networks while reducing the value of formal orders. There were several periods in which a rapid expansion in the trade of a particular commodity took place. The importance of cotton increased dramatically from 1660 to 1685. Tea consumption in Europe rose from 1717 to 1722. Coffee's share of the trade rose from 1700 to 1710. These shifts in commodity and port composition are controlled with dummy variables, coded 1 in the period of expansion. Although the East Indies trade included hundreds, if not thousands, of specific exotic items of trade, these commodities cover the essential, large-scale shifts in import patterns.

Finally, there is a control for the period when the Company's charter privileges were not renewed by Parliament and a rival company was formed. The Company's charter failed to pass in the Commons in 1694. In 1698 a rival company was formed. Through various strategic machinations on the part of the old company, the two were merged in 1709. Political contention over the management of the Company continued through 1711 (Carruthers 1996: 149). Because this confused situation could have reduced the power of the principals, and hence reliance on formal orders, this period (1694–1712) is included in the model (*two companies*).[20] Table 1 reports descriptive statistics for the variables.

Table 1. Descriptive Statistics

|                      | Count[a]  | Mean  | SD      |
|----------------------|-----------|-------|---------|
| Networks             | 49,631    |       |         |
| Formal orders        | 16,277    |       |         |
| Experience           | 30,474    |       |         |
| Voyage count         |           | 2.269 | 1.53    |
| War                  | 192,250   |       |         |
| Cotton               | 2,458     |       |         |
| Tea                  | 5,232     |       |         |
| Coffee               | 10,264    |       |         |
| Two companies        | 15,523    |       |         |
| Distance             |           | 2,659 | 2,096.9 |
| Port-to-port traffic |           | 7.229 | 32.154  |
| Exploratory era      | 13,515    |       |         |
| Private trade era    | 100,874   |       |         |
| Colonial era         | 221,685   |       |         |

a. Counts are reported for binary and categorical variables.

## RESULTS

Table 2 presents the basic results in the column labeled model 2. *Networks, formal orders*, and *experience* are all highly significant. *Formal orders* has the largest effect, indicating that captains were indeed obligated to follow formal orders at some point during their voyage. The log of distance is negative, as would be expected, and the rate of traffic between port pairs is positive, also as expected. The significance of other controls seems to indicate heightened activity in moments of expansion into the new commodity markets of *cotton* and *tea*. In model 2, interaction effects with *voyage count* have been added. The results suggest that the importance of both formal orders and social networks declines over the career of a captain, while the importance of experience increases. As an example, the effect of formal orders at different levels of organizational experience, captured as *voyage count*, can be calculated using the interaction between *voyage count* and *formal orders*. The effect is calculated by adding the coefficient for formal orders with the product of the interaction term (for *formal orders* and *voyage count*) and the different values taken on by *voyage count* in the data. In the case of a captain on their first voyages this would equal 2.516 + (–0.22 × 1), which equals 2.296. In the case of a seasoned captain on their sixth voyage this equals 2.516 + (–0.22 × 6), producing an estimated effect of 1.196. These gation" 98 CHAPTER 4

Table 2. Coefficient Estimates Describing Relationship Between Independent and Control Variables and Travel to a Port

| Travel to port | Model 1 | Model 2 | Model 3 | Model 4 |
|---|---|---|---|---|
| Intercept | −2.136*** | −1.879*** | −2.078*** | −2.005*** |
| | (0.044) | (0.049) | (0.05) | (0.05) |
| Networks | 0.211*** | 0.439*** | 0.421*** | 0.187*** |
| | (0.024) | (0.042) | (0.041) | (0.05) |
| Formal orders | 2.069*** | 2.516*** | 2.489*** | 2.411*** |
| | (0.024) | (0.042) | (0.042) | (0.051) |
| Experience | 0.615*** | 0.403*** | 0.476*** | 0.540*** |
| | (0.027) | (0.059) | (0.058) | (0.063) |
| Voyage count | −0.021*** | −0.133*** | −0.082*** | −0.092*** |
| | (0.0) | (0.011) | (0.01) | (0.01) |
| War | 0.004 | −0.028 | −0.0448* | −0.028 |
| | (0.023) | (0.022) | (0.022) | (0.022) |
| Cotton | 0.976*** | 0.842*** | 0.616*** | 0.656*** |
| | (0.101) | (0.098) | (0.092) | (0.093) |
| Tea | 0.38*** | 0.287*** | 0.164* | 0.195* |
| | (0.083) | (0.081) | (0.076) | (0.077) |
| Coffee | 0.043 | 0.043 | 0.032 | 0.024 |
| | (0.098) | (0.094) | (0.087) | (0.087) |
| Two companies | 0.563*** | 0.433*** | 0.288*** | 0.296*** |
| | (0.082) | (0.079) | (0.074) | (0.075) |
| Log of distance | −0.262*** | −0.263*** | −0.277*** | −0.279*** |
| | (0.006) | (0.006) | (0.006) | (0.006) |
| Port-to-port traffic | 0.021*** | 0.021*** | 0.022*** | 0.022*** |
| | (0.0) | (0.0) | (0.0) | (0.0) |
| Networks × voyage count | | −0.115*** | −0.114*** | −0.084*** |
| | | (0.016) | (0.016) | (0.016) |
| Formal × voyage count | | −0.22*** | −0.212*** | −0.199*** |
| | | (0.016) | (0.016) | (0.017) |
| Experience × voyage count | | 0.173*** | 0.145*** | 0.138*** |
| | | (0.017) | (0.017) | (0.017) |
| Exploratory era | | | 1.256*** | 1.071*** |
| | | | (0.04) | (0.052) |
| Private trade era | | | 0.411*** | 0.296*** |
| | | | (0.016) | (0.031) |
| Networks × exploratory | | | | 0.444*** |
| | | | | (0.017) |
| Networks × private trade | | | | 0.420*** |
| | | | | (0.051) |
| Formal × exploratory | | | | 0.312*** |
| | | | | (0.093) |
| Formal × private trade | | | | 0.108* |
| | | | | (0.053) |
| Experience × exploratory | | | | −0.206 |
| | | | | (0.158) |
| Experience × private trade | | | | −0.105 |
| | | | | (0.059) |
| Groups | 13,503, 1,561 | 13,503, 1,561 | 13,503, 1,561 | 13,503, 1,561 |
| N | 335,905 | 335,905 | 335,905 | 335,905 |

Note: Mixed effects logistic regression, clustering at the level of captain (1,561) and port-to-port pairs (13,503) included as crossed random effects.
*p < .10. **p < .05. ***p < .01.

are the coefficients, which in a logistic model are the exponentiated odds ratio. These coefficients indicate that the estimated odds of traveling to a port given formal orders to do so is 9.934 for an inexperienced captain on his first voyage. The estimated odds fall to 3.306 in his sixth voyage. The same exercise for *networks* yields an odds ratio of 1.383 for captains exposed to network information in the first year, and 0.778, which indicates a reduced probability of tie when captains are exposed to information via peer networks in their sixth year. As experience within the organization grows, less attention is paid to others, whether principals or peers. This finding provides additional reassurance that the network indicator is capturing the transfer of information between peers—since we would expect this to decline with experience.

Model 3 adds categorical variables coded for the era of organizational history. In this case, the colonial period acts as the reference category so it does not appear in table 2. Model 4 presents the main findings regarding how the impact of formal orders, personal experience, and peer networks on captains' decisions changed over the organizational eras. Since the colonial era acts as the reference category, the interactions should be interpreted with respect to this category. In this model, the variables capturing types of information transfer across trips (*network, experience,* and *formal orders*) were interacted with the period variables to capture how their impact changed within the different organizational regimes.

The central finding here is that the interaction between *networks* and *exploratory era*, and *networks* and *private trade era* are significant and positive. Thus the odds of forming a tie when exposed to network information increased relative to the probability of forming a tie when exposed to network information during the colonial era. In contrast, *experience* shows less responsiveness to organizational change. The interactions are not statistically significant. Hence, it appears that personal experience with ports played a significant but stable role in the trade. The model indicates that formal orders on the other hand increased the likelihood of a tie in the initial exploratory phase, but differed little in impact across the colonial and private trade period.

## IMPACT ON TRADE

In this section I evaluate the larger impact of social networks on Company trade and present evidence that the circulation of local information in the East increased the number of ports engaged in trade with Company ships in any given year.

In the overseas trade of the Company, routes between ports represent commercial opportunities for trade. For example, the frequent passage of

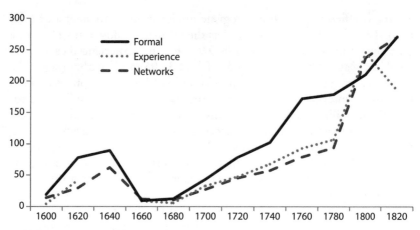

**FIGURE 3.** Average traffic rates of ports.

ships from Calcutta to Canton indicated the high price of Bengali opium in the Chinese marketplace. For the English Company, exploiting existing opportunities meant sending more ships on previously established routes, in order to pursue well-known profits. Figure 3 demonstrates that formal orders from the principals consistently steered the trade to ports with above-average rates of traffic, measured as the number of visits to that port in the prior twenty years. Social networks on the other hand directed trade to less-well-served ports, with the exception of the last forty years of the Company's life when social networks had a significantly reduced effect on captains' decisions about where to trade.

Information transmitted through social networks created a larger set of known options for captains to choose from when directing the paths of their ships. The information they received was reflected in the choices they made, and their individual choices cumulatively impacted the trade network as a whole. In order to see this effect first consider a simple chart of the number of ports visited by English Company ships, represented in figure 4. The initial burst of exploration evident at the beginning of the Company's existence is sustained for the first few decades of the seventeenth century, but inevitably dips during the political turmoil of the 1640s and 1650s. In this period, very few ships were actually sent out to sea. After securing a political alliance with Oliver Cromwell, the Company rebounded and we see the only period of consistent expansion. This prolonged episode occurred in the private trade period (1674–1757). In 1760, at the peak of the Company's power in the East and the point at which the owners were able to reassert control over the captains, we see a marked decline in the number of ports visited.

**FIGURE 4**. Number of ports in the trade network.

A simple count of the number of ports included in the trade network on a yearly basis does not entirely capture the number of ports currently engaged in trade with the English Company. The Company had limited resources, particularly in the early years, so although it could have a good trading relationship with a given port, it may not have been able to send a ship to that port every year. Ports actively engaged in the Company trade are therefore not necessarily the only ports visited within a given time frame. They are instead those ports to which the Company repeatedly returned. Repeat visits indicate the sustained engagement necessary for a trading partnership. Figure 5 reports the number of ports actively engaged in trade, that is, those ports to which the Company repeatedly returned over time. These ports also drop in and out of the trade network when the Company ceases to consistently return to a target port.

Figure 5 clarifies what occurred to the trade network in the 1640s and 1650s. Although the Company was not able to visit all ports each season —or even every two or three seasons—they did not give up trade with those ports. In fact, after the initial exploratory burst of the first years in the East, the Company was able to sustain a relatively stable number of trading partners. Another exploratory burst occurs in 1700, and again, the Company manages to sustain relationships with a relatively stable number of ports from 1700 to 1760. In 1780, the number of ports peaks and we see the only sustained period of decline in the trade network from that point onward. Reliance on formal order concentrates the trade on a small number of ports. In contrast, in the earlier periods, information that flowed

**FIGURE 5**. Number of active ports in the trade network.

through social networks increased the likelihood that captains traveled to more destinations, particularly destinations off formal routes, thereby increasing the total number of ports engaged in trade—given the resources available to the Company.

This relationship becomes particularly clear if we plot the number of active ports against the number of ships the English Company was able to send out to sea.[21] The lighter line in figure 6 represents the total number of ships employed by the Company. The investment in ships was initially small, so the level of participation in Eastern trade was low. The Company began to pick up steam in the late seventeenth century. Steady growth occurred throughout the next century and investment spiked rapidly in the final years of the 1700s. The number of active ports, by contrast, began to peak in 1750, when the investment in ships was still relatively low, and less than half the number reached at the turn of the century. Figure 6 reveals that not only did the Company sustain trade with more ports when social networks were active within the firm, it did more with less. The change in the number of ports does not necessarily mean that Company profits fell; it does however indicate a clear shift from a pattern of exploration to one of exploitation, in which the firm concentrated its efforts on known competencies, in this case ports and markets (March 1991).[22]

The direct role of social networks on incorporating many of these ports into the larger trade network is documented in the next graph. Figure 7 breaks down ports by how information was first distributed about them

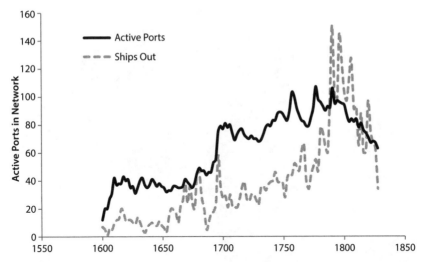

**FIGURE 6**. Active ports against number of ships deployed in trade.

when they entered the Company trade network. Ports are marked as formal order ports if formal orders first directed ship captains to that port. Similarly for personal experience and social networks.[23] The result is striking: of new ports, 45 percent were visited based on information transmitted via social networks.[24] New ports often meant new goods, and a similar process was at work with commodities. Goods that consistently proved profitable when carried in small amounts to England by private traders often migrated onto the roster of restricted goods as the Company moved to incorporate them into their larger bulk trades, as for example when white pepper was excluded from legitimate private trade because it "has become much esteemed and used" (Sainsbury 1925: 233).

The use of social networks had direct consequences for the pattern by which the firm pursued trade. These patterns had structural consequences for the larger network of global trade within Asia and between Asia and Europe. Social networks expanded the portfolio of active ports and reduced the concentration of trade on any one port. The captains effectively used their autonomy to explore local opportunities, straying off established paths. When the Court of Directors asserted control, from 1757 to 1833, past experience with certain ports continued to influence captains' decisions about where to trade, but the effect of *networks* decreased and the concentration of resources on a few ports dramatically increased. The use of networks increased the size, scope, and sustainability of global trade, but the prevalence of network exchange was conditioned on the organizational structure of the firm and employee autonomy.

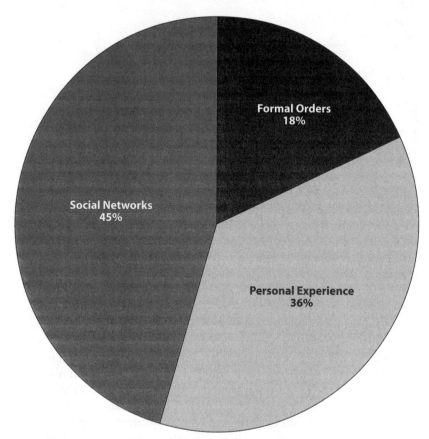

**FIGURE 7.** Proportion of ports by method of information diffusion.

## CONCLUSION

The directors of the English Company long suspected the existence of dense, shadowy networks of conspiratorial actors attempting to direct the course of the Eastern trade (Ogborn 2007: 98). How those networks actually affected the formal trade of the English Company escaped them. It turns out that social networks in the East circulated information about potential ports of call. When captains drew from their social networks to make decisions about where to trade, they tended to go to less-traveled ports. Because these ports would have otherwise disappeared from English routes, captains' use of social networks increased the overall size of the English Company's trade network.

We know from documentary evidence that country traders, not necessarily operating on English ships, kept an English presence alive in Siam (Thailand) (Bassett 1989: 633) and initiated trade at Hanoi (Bassett 1989: 634). Also, information passed from informal ventures to formal operating decisions. For example, D. K. Bassett documented that Kedah was given preference over Aceh as an outlet for opium and piece goods based on the informal advice of private traders (Bassett 1989: 640). The research in this chapter shows that informal networks were a regular feature of the process of information procurement and disbursement.

Networks mattered for the development of trade because they expanded the range of possibilities open to any one individual. Social networks might be expected to increase clustering and regionalism within trade, and in a larger sense they do—networks do not bring new ports or regions into a trade network. By definition, they pass along information about ports already present within the network. However, by circulating information about any one port throughout the network, they increase the likelihood that smaller ports were incorporated into the larger trade on a permanent basis. For example if a merchant in Quang Nam gave an English captain a good price on a shipment of porcelains in the hopes of breaking into the European market, he was affected by the use of networks within the English firm. If social networks in the English firm were depressed, the porcelain merchant had to rely upon the one captain for continued business. If networks were in use, news of the successful transaction could filter out to other English captains, who were then likely to visit the port. And each additional voice was another chance that London might hear of good trade prospects as well.

Captains who drew on their social network for information were inevitably presented with a larger portfolio of information on possible ports of trade, thereby increasing the options available to them. This process led to an increased English presence in a larger number of ports—a factor that contributed to the success of the English trade. Going to new ports exposed the Company to more types of goods. The entire process of information diffusion and circulation involved several smaller mechanisms, including dynamic network processes, decision making conditioned on social environment, social trust, as well as schedule coordination between ships, which was largely a by-product of traffic at more popular ports. When the private trade period ended, with the onset of the colonial period in 1757, crucial pieces of this larger process stopped functioning and the effect of social networks decreased.

After the Battle of Plassey, and particularly in the nineteenth century, inland trading became increasingly important to the Company and its servants (Marshall 1993: 292). One alternative hypothesis explaining the shift in social networks use is that informal networks moved to the interior. The question of increasing inland trade is not at stake in this analysis, but, as figure 6 should make clear, in terms of the number of ships, the maritime trade of the Company expanded in the colonial era, although in a concentrated fashion. Since there was no decline in maritime trade, there would be no reason to expect a decline in networks—unless of course the new organizational structure suppressed them. This suppression was one of the unintended consequences of the centralization of the organizational control that accompanied the Company's conversion into a political and territorial entity.

*Chapter 5*

# DECENTRALIZATION, CORRUPTION, AND MARKET STRUCTURE

In the preceding chapter, the analysis showed that when the English Company had a decentralized organizational structure, which is to say that significant autonomy lay in the hands of employees, social networks encouraged the transmission of local information and led to the incorporation of more ports and goods into the English trade network. A heterogeneous mix of captains and private traders participated in these social networks. Many captains successfully wove their personal business interests in with the Company trade without directly disturbing the conduct of official business. Others put their personal profit ahead of the obligation to abide by Company rules. This chapter focuses on these malfeasant private traders.

Unknown to the Company, opportunistic employees who passed beyond the boundaries of legitimate behavior provided another un-looked-for benefit by increasing the connectivity of the English Company trade network in Asia. They linked the firm, ports, and regional economies into a complex multilateral network of exchange that increased the potential for information flow within the firm, thereby helping to integrate unit operations. Through their explorations of private business opportunities, these employees also brought new ports into the trade network.

The effect of the malfeasant private traders can be measured through further analysis of the trade network they helped to create. Decentralization affected local communication patterns and increased the number of ports included in trade. Through malfeasant actors, decentralization also impacted the global, or macro, structural pattern through which ports were linked together. The trade network of the Company spans the 234 years of the Company's existence as a commercial enterprise, from 1601 to 1835, and represents the set of port-to-port linkages (26,000+ trips) for the 4,572 voyages undertaken by the Company and recorded by Farrington.[1] By looking at images of this network as it evolves over time, it is possible to observe the emergence of a dense, fully integrated global trade network—and to piece out the effect of malfeasant private traders on the structure of that network.

Without the opportunistic free riding of the malfeasant captains taking advantage of high levels of decentralization, the Company's trade network would have fallen apart into discrete, disconnected regional clusters. When the English Company rounded the Cape, markets across Asia and Europe were linked, but did not form a cohesive whole. The structure of overseas trade was "horizontally" integrated through overlapping segments. The global economy was fragmented into linked but substantially separate markets.

In Asia, the gradual erosion of past trade relationships and disconti-nuities introduced by the Europeans have led researchers to speak of the various "systems" (Lombard 1981: 181), "networks" (Marshall 1993: 294), "commercial regions" (Chaudhuri 1978: 193), or "worlds" (Braudel 1992c: 533), to refer to "a network of inter-connected systems" (Arasaratnam 1995: 15) or "interlocking circuits" (Barendse 1998: 5), or to describe them as "dispersed," "loosely-jointed" (Das Gupta and Pearson 1987: 42), or seg-mented (Prakash 1997: xvi). It was not one "system" in the sense that we think of the existing global economy. This is not to say that trade in Asia had not been better connected in ages prior to 1600. Significant evidence suggests that the economies of Asia had been better integrated, but cohe-sion was declining when European began to use the sea route to Asia. This decline may be one reason the Europeans were competitive, as it provided a structural opportunity for arbitrage.

With the help of the opportunistic employees, the English Company wove these loosely integrated commercial regions into one densely con-nected network that increased the potential flow of information between English ports in Asia as well as those ports and England itself. Increases in information flow would have helped the Company plan for and adjust to the fluctuating markets of the premodern period while tightly coupling the economies of England and Asia, and thereby changing the structure of trade within Asia as well. Translated into the language of network analysis, the micro-level activities of the malfeasant traders caused the development and elaboration of complex multilateral exchange circuits that gave rise to densely integrated network components.


## HOW I LEARNED TO STOP WORRYING
## AND LOVE FREE RIDING

Rational actor theory dictates that in the absence of supervision, actors will divert resources to pursue their own private interests. In the context of both seventeenth- and twenty-first-century firms, principals (owners or managers) usually try to control their agents (or employees) in order to keep them from doing exactly that. Since Mancur Olson, social scientists have for the most part used the term "free riding" to refer to a collective action problem: how to get individuals to contribute equally to a group effort. The term was originally coined to refer to a specific type of principal-agent problem: how to keep employees from taking advantage of their employers. Employers patrol their employees to keep them from violating their contract and free riding off of resources provided by the principals, that is, slacking off on their work, not contributing to the larger effort, and using company time for their own purposes.[2]

The form this free riding problem took in the European-East Indies trade was excessive employee investment in private trading. The private trade of employees caused problems for all the overseas European companies, which is in keeping with the rational-actor model. It was difficult for employers to observe and regulate the actions of employees who were operating up to six thousand miles away. This situation made it possible for employees to take advantage of their employers by pursuing their own interests. What was not always evident to the directors of the East India Company was that, in this case, the free riding had a net positive effect on Company operations. Individually the employees seemed to be free riding, but collectively their actions produced a positive outcome for the Company, which was attempting to quell the behavior responsible for its success at the individual level.[3] The opportunistic and self-interested activity of Company employees was actually helping the Company collect information from and distribute information between the factories and presidencies of the East.

As outlined in chapter 3, the private trade took on many different aspects. This chapter is focused on the private trade of the captains and crew and even more specifically on a practice called "losing the season." Losing the season distorted the system by which the Company obtained goods in Asia. It was a particular trick of private traders employed by the English Company in which they purposefully prolonged their voyages past the deadlines set by Company officials. They did so in order to continue to pursue private trading opportunities while in the East. The English Company's permissive private trade policies had created a perverse incentive for the captains and crew. They were allowed to pursue private trade, and so they devoted themselves to various business opportunities. As they became more deeply embedded in the commercial life of the East, they were tempted to prolong their voyages in order to bring these opportunities to fruition. Because travel around the Cape was restricted to particular seasons, when weather conditions permitted safe transit, all the captains had to do was miss their target departure date by a few weeks and they were safely stuck in the Eastern Seas for another four to five months. Losing the season is a simple case of organizational and environmental opportunity structure channeling individuals' behavior. However the perverse outcome, at odds with the professed aims at the organizational level, highlights the importance of considering not only organizational rules and institutional structures, but also individual responses to those rules and norms.

While stuck east of the Cape, captains used their greatest commercial advantage, command of a comparatively large, fast, and well-armored vessel to transport goods—meaning they did not sit in port, but traveled across Asia, buying and selling goods. Ultimately, it was this behavior that increased levels of cohesion within the Company trade—helping to integrate overseas operations. This malfeasant behavior—or the lack of official control over captain's actions in the East—led to long-term gains for the Company by increasing the flow of information about prices and goods, market conditions, and even the activities of their employees.

Despite this un-looked-for benefit, the common practice of losing the season was in tension with formal Company policy. Timely delivery of goods was—and is—a central problem in overseas trade. For example, the East India Company's first voyage was a tremendous disappointment despite the fact that they had managed to bring huge quantities of pepper back to London. The Company was unable to turn a profit on the voyage because the market had been flooded with pepper previous to their goods' arrival—and prices dropped accordingly (Furber 1976: 39). In order to avoid flooding the market in London, the directors introduced a quarterly auction system (Chaudhuri 1978: 37). Rather than dumping supplies immediately onto the market, the directors put the goods into storage and auctioned portions of their supply off at four regular intervals throughout the year. These auctions evened out the flow of supply and stabilized prices.

The quarterly system helped, but could not fully compensate for annual irregularities. A steady annual turnout still mattered a great deal to the smooth operation of the quarterly auctions. Thus the directors in London were concerned with keeping the captains on a regular schedule. In addition, the Company incurred serious short-term losses from late ships. The English Company leased their ships and paid demurrage fees for delayed voyages. Costs associated with demurrage have been calculated to account for up to 36 percent of the total profits within sailing seasons (Chaudhuri 1993: 54).

Therefore it should be no surprise that the Company records and correspondence include demands for "quick despatch" and "speedy passage" as well as complaints about ships having purposefully missed the seasonal passage around the Cape of Good Hope (East India Company 1689, Chaudhuri 1978: 73–74, Jones 1988: 291). In another attempt at regulation, the English Company offered gratuities to timely captains (Anderson, McCormick, and Tollison 1983: 233n7, Datta 1958: 134). The directors perceived the purposeful delay of voyages as malfeasance and sought to curb the practice, succeeding only when the environmental and contractual obstacles to the exercise of their authority were overcome.

Many captains ignored both orders and positive incentives in part because they could escape punishment. By convention, captains were hired by shipowners. Since the English Company leased vessels, the owners retained the right to sell the captaincy as a transferable and inheritable good, and the rights to the captaincy usually fell into the hands of the captains themselves (Furber 1976: 195), thus limiting the Company's capacity to enforce regulations. The directors were able implement reforms to this process only after 1790.

In addition, there were barriers to authority faced by all European companies engaged in overseas trade. Captains and crew operated very far from Company headquarters in life-and-death circumstances. Once seasoned, they were highly skilled workers with invaluable trade experience. Finally, with roughly 35 percent of employees dying overseas in Company service (Hejeebu 2005: 509), they had every reason to focus on the present—in this case by maximizing personal profit and eliminating the need to return to the East for further commercial gain.

In this case, however, the captains who disobeyed orders by prolonging their voyages built on and elaborated the stable infrastructure of the English Company, bridging the regional clusters that the English Company had earlier reproduced through participation in the country trade. The dynamics underlying the structural cohesion of the English Company's emergent global trade network arose through the ability of the captains to pursue their own trade. This decentralization of control led them to new ports as well, thereby securing steady supply streams and potentially lowering prices, while increasing the capacity for communication within the Company.

The mechanism at its most basic level was that the autonomy of the captains produced increased variability or randomness in voyage patterns. When malfeasant captains created a situation in which they were left to their own devices and at least momentarily freed from scheduling constraints imposed by the Company, they were more likely to travel between ports that were not routinely connected in the course of normal Company operations than by rule-abiding captains. These random links increased the overall connectivity of the network. In this sense, the process can be seen as a small-world mechanism, where a small number of random links dramatically reduce overall path length (Watts 1999).

## INDUCING THE TRADE NETWORK

In the last chapter the analysis focused on reconstructing social networks that shuttled timely, local information between English captains on board official voyages. The analysis in this chapter uses the same data, but takes a different approach to the analysis of networks. Instead of analyzing peer communication, the paths of the ships are used to create a network representation of the structure of the English–East Indies trade between ports. The data capture both patterned interactions between individuals in different ports and the movement of commodities, capital, people, and information. The paths of the ships constitute the transportation and communication infrastructure of firm operations; the records of the voyages provide a material trace of the system of exchange. The resulting network of ships and ports represents three active elements: the ports, or local merchants; the official English trade; and the unofficial trade pursued by Company employees.

In the networks used in this chapter, the points (or nodes, vertices, etc.) represent ports and links between points schematically represent the paths of the ships. Figure 8 presents a simple example. It includes the famous exploratory voyages of the *Susan*, the *Dragon*, the *Ascension*, and the *Hector*, commanded by Sir James Lancaster, against a backdrop of ports active later in the history of the English Company. In this case, nodes are coded so that their placement represents their geographic location—the outline of the Indian Subcontinent should be recognizable in the center of the image. These early ships traveled east searching for pepper. Accordingly, they set sail on February 13, 1601, for the Indonesian Archipelago, making stops at the Canary Islands, the Cape of Good Hope, Madagascar, and the Nicobar Islands along the way. At Aceh they engaged a Portuguese carrack and separated, some proceeding to Priaman (Pariaman), and some proceeding farther to Bantam. The last ship returned to England on September 11, 1603. As may be quickly observed, the Atlantic ports are excluded from the image; they are also excluded from the analysis as the focus is on the monopoly trade in Asia.

The nodes represent ports and arcs schematically represent ships' routes: adjacent nodes are linked by trips. Arrows indicate the direction of travel, which indicates that the network is directed. The process of converting the data into graphical form yields fifty-eight networks of equally weighted ties directed according to the path of the ship, each capturing four years of voyage activity. The fifty-eight networks provide snapshots of the structure of trade over the period of English Company activity. The level of detail included in the data allows a nearly day-to-day re-creation of the location of ships (through reference to arrival and destination ports), which spans 85,838 days from the granting of the royal charter, December 31, 1600, to the return of the last ship, the *General Palmer*, on March 3, 1835. In this chapter, the analysis uses four-year intervals to represent the network over time.[4]

The British Library has also published a complete record of the career histories for all twelve thousand East India Company employees who

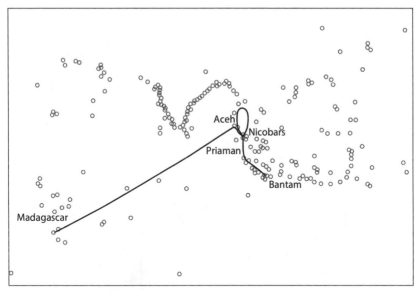

**FIGURE 8.** The Susan, the Dragon, the Hector, and the Ascension, 1601–3.

served on ship and reached the rank of sixth mate or above (Farrington 1999a). These data were used to check the validity of the private trade proxy data.

## NETWORK STRUCTURE OVER TIME

The transformation of the structure of the English East India Company trade network is shown in figure 9, panels A though F. These panels report the complete network for six trading seasons, 1620–24, 1660–64, 1720–24, 1760–64, 1796–1800, and 1820–24. The sequence covers the entire period of the English Company's commercial engagement in the East. As in the network representation of the first voyage, ports are represented as circles located with respect to latitude and longitude and voyages are represented as lines.[5] These figures do not capture the expansion of Company trade into the interior of India, which would have occurred in the nineteenth century.

As schematic as they appear, these network images reveal much about the history of the Company. For example, the dense network of lines linking ports in the Indian Subcontinent, Indonesian Archipelago, and Middle East in panel A reflects an early engagement in the country trade—the

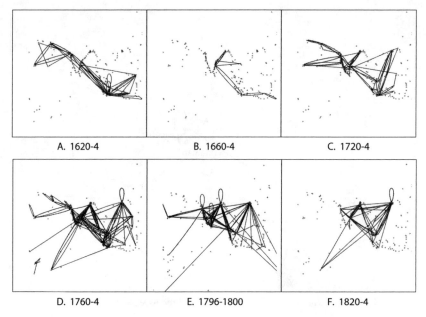

**FIGURE 9**. Development of Eastern trade over geographic regions in snapshots of six 4-year periods: 1620–24, 1660–64, 1720–24, 1760–64, 1796–1800, and 1820–24.

overseas trade within Asia. It is also evident from the images that regular trade with China had not been established in the first sixty years. When the English Company withdrew from the country trade in 1660, their footprint in the East was significantly reduced—as is clearly evident in panel B. Substantial growth and expansion was evident by 1720 (panel C): integration increased and the geographic reach of the network expanded to the Persian Gulf, through the Indonesia Archipelago, and into the Far Eastern markets of China. Historians have argued that the engagement of the private traders in the country trade drove this intense period of expansion (Furber 1965: 46, 1976, Asaratnam 1995: 16). By 1760 (panel D), at the end of the Company's private trade period, the English Company trade network had fully integrated the previously loosely connected trading regions of the East, linking the Red Sea, the Persian Gulf, West India, Bengal, Ceylon, Indonesia, Malaysia, the Philippines, and China through numerous redundant paths across ports. Centralization, consolidation, and control of trade are evident by 1796 (panel E). This trend increased, as shown by the representation of Company trade in 1820 (panel F). By this time, the number of paths and regions was drastically reduced as the Company's trade became focused on major ports within the territorial domain of the British.

## MICRO-LEVEL PROCESSES

As discussed earlier, private trade allowances in the English Company created a perverse incentive: Captains engaged in the private trade often broke
Company rules in order to extend their voyages in the East to pursue commercial opportunities. Captains "deliberately 'los[t] the season' for their
return voyages to Europe by moving in a dilatory fashion from Bombay
to other Asiatic ports, investing and reinvesting their 'privilege'" (Furber
1948: 280; also see Furber 1976: 195, Watson 1980b: 71, Anderson, Mc-
Cormick, and Tollison, 1983: 233).[6] Similar to the way in which English
private traders illegally used the Company's tax privileges on the conti-
nent of India, and thereby deeply embedded the Company into the local
politics of the area, the malfeasance of ship captains when they were losing
the season embedded the English Company's intercontinental trade into
regional country trade patterns. Together the formal Company trade and
the boundary-spanning behavior of the captains seeking to bend the rules
in order to increase their private profits created a dense, fully integrated
global trade network for the firm.

In order to see the effect of this behavior, it is necessary to identify voyages in which captains lost the season. Captains engaged in the illegitimate
diversion of Company resources for private profit did not purposefully
document their malfeasance for Company records, but they did leave traces
of their disobedience. In particular, the co-occurrence of extended voyage
duration and cycling within voyages indicates that liberties were taken with
Company resources. Ships were expected to stay in the East for roughly
six months. Here extended duration is calculated as voyage durations that
exceed the average for each sailing season, measured from time of arrival at
the first port in the East Indies to time of arrival at the last port in the East
Indies.[7] Most of the ships eventually identified as losing the season stayed in
the East for more than a year. This estimate is therefore conservative.

Private traders engaged in the country trade, buying goods in one port
and selling them in others. In contrast, Company-directed voyages left
England for ports where English factors waited with goods for return shipment. When ships went from one port to another in the East, they did so
either to participate in the private country trade or to procure new goods
for freight back to England. Because time was of the essence, captains engaged in legitimate Company trade should have avoided doubling back to
ports to which they had already traveled, thereby inducing cycles within
their voyage. The main purpose of cycling was trade, and the traders in
the East—after the Company formally pulled out of the country trade—
were private traders. Consequently, voyages with cycles are categorized as
private trade voyages.[8] The combination of excessive voyage duration and

cycling between ports is therefore a close proxy for those captains who unnecessarily prolonged their voyages in order to pursue additional private
trading opportunities—those who lost the season. Inevitably this measure
captures some voyages that legitimately lost the season due to inclement
weather or other unforeseen circumstances. It is attempting to capture
illicit behavior designed to look indistinguishable from innocent action.
However it is also the best possible approximation for a pattern of behavior
recognized as typical by Company officials and employees alike that had an
appreciable impact on trade. Further analysis also supports the measure's
accuracy.

In the eighteenth century, the area defined by Europeans as the East
Indies was a vast socially and politically diverse expanse of thousands of
separate and distinct communities. Foreign trade protocols varied across
ports; each had its own set of officials, who required custom duties, gifts,
and bribes with varying degrees of specificity and ceremony. Norms varied
significantly across trading regions; experience on the Indian Subcontinent
was not easily transposed to the Spice Islands or China. Captains and crew
engaged in Company trade were able to rely on institutional knowledge to
negotiate these complexities. Private traders shouldered greater risk and
lacked the institutional safeguards in place for legitimate voyages. Consequently, private traders often had to rely on their personal experience
in order to pursue commercial opportunities. Since prior experience in
the East was critical for negotiating private trades, it follows that captains
engaged in the private trade ought to have had more experience specific
to the destinations of their current voyage than captains pursuing legitimate trade. The indicator of malfeasant behavior—voyages characterized
by cycling and extended duration—can be further assessed by generating
an experience measure for captains, specific to each voyage undertaken.
Private traders ought to have had wider prior experience. Table 3 shows
the association between experience and private trading, reporting a count
of the number of distinct regions previously encountered by a captain, for
each target voyage, for all voyages that set out from England between 1680
and 1760—the period when private trade within the Company was legitimate and the organizational structure most decentralized.

The results of table 3 show that the captains of malfeasant voyages were
more likely to have had greater levels of regional experience tailored to
their current voyage. And inexperience in the East was strongly associated
with extended duration. Captains without experience were much more
likely to miss sailing seasons than were those whose previous tenure in
the East was substantial. Thus, this assessment is conservative—the strong
association between losing the season and experience provides additional
assurance that the indicator is indeed measuring malfeasant private trade.[9]
Consequently, voyages characterized by cycling and excessive duration are

Table 3. Cross-tabulation of Malfeasant Voyages and Legitimate Voyages over the Regional Experience of Captains, Specific to Target Voyage, 1680–1764

| Experience | Legitimate trade | Malfeasant trade | Total |
|---|---|---|---|
| 0 | 224 (1.01) | 79 (0.97) | 303 |
| 1 | 301 (1.12) | 66 (0.67) | 367 |
| 2 | 178 (0.96) | 76 (1.11) | 254 |
| 3 | 65 (0.85) | 40 (1.42) | 105 |
| 4+ | 14 (0.19) | 27 (2.45) | 41 |
| Total | 782 | 288 | 1,070 |

Note: Pearson $\chi^2(4) = 54.4325$, $Pr < 0.0001$. Parentheses enclose odds ratio.

considered to have been captained by malfeasant actors who purposefully delayed their voyage to extend their private earnings.

The impact of the malfeasant private trading voyages can be assessed by removing these voyages from the fifty-eight networks capturing the development of the structure of English Company trade. This returns a new set of trade networks, referred to as the *legitimate trade graphs*. These are the trade networks without malfeasant private traders. The most straightforward way to measure the effect of the malfeasant private traders would be to compare the networks in which the malfeasant behavior occurred with the networks from which it was removed (the *legitimate trade graphs*). The removal of voyages, however, automatically reduces the density of the original networks. Thus the differences between the *legitimate trade graphs* and the complete graphs may simply be the result of removing voyages— that is, any voyages, not simply the voyages of malfeasant private traders. To ensure that the results are not an artifact of voyage deletion, a randomly selected set of legitimate voyages of equal number to the malfeasant voyages, matched by destination, was removed from the complete trade graphs. These are identified as "matched voyages." Removing these matched voyages from the complete data produced another new set of networks, the *malfeasant trade graphs*. A comparison between the *malfeasant trade graphs* and the *legitimate trade graphs* allows for a direct assessment of the impact of the private trade on the macro-structure that controls for the loss of voyages on crucial network characteristics.[10]

It may be useful to conceptualize the malfeasant behavior as a treatment affecting network construction. The macro-level structure of networks subjected to treatment is compared with the structure of networks serving as a control set. In this case, the *legitimate trade graphs*—those lacking voyages with private traders—should be thought of as the control group. They

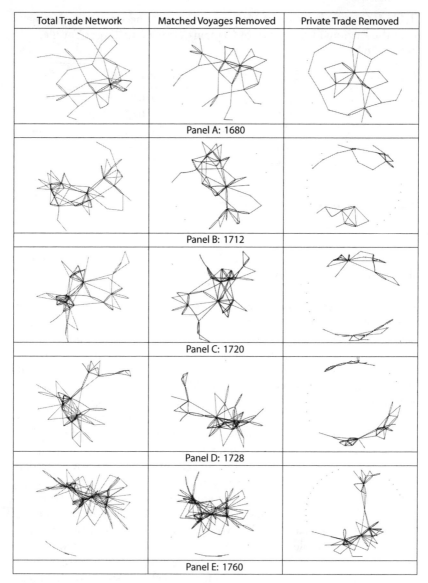

| Total Trade Network | Matched Voyages Removed | Private Trade Removed |
|---|---|---|
| | Panel A: 1680 | |
| | Panel B: 1712 | |
| | Panel C: 1720 | |
| | Panel D: 1728 | |
| | Panel E: 1760 | |

**FIGURE 10.** Network visualizations of the English Company's Eastern trade.

lack the treatment: malfeasant private trading. The *malfeasant trade graphs* can be considered the treatment group.

Figure 10 (panels A–E) shows the trade network at the beginning, middle, and end of the private trade period—1680, 1712, 1720, 1728, and 1760. Each panel allows comparison of the structure of the *legitimate trade graph* and *malfeasant trade graph*, revealing the impact of the private traders on the network. In this case, the ports are positioned using a standard and commonly used spring algorithm available in the popular network software package Pajek. The spring algorithm helps to reveal underlying structural differences (such as increases in density and connectivity) that are obscured by placing ports according to geography.[11] For reference, the complete trade network for each period is also shown.

With the exception of one exploratory voyage to Madagascar in 1760 (indicated in the bottom left of the complete trade network for 1760, panel E), the complete network is a single interconnected component over the entire period. A component is a network term for a subset of nodes within a network that are all linked by at least one path to each other (they do not have to be directly linked, but can be linked through chains of other nodes). This interconnectedness is significant because it indicates increased connectivity—all ports were linked to one large network that could efficiently shuttle information about prices, goods, and port conditions within the network and to London. The effect of the malfeasant behavior on this component is then of great interest. Focusing first on 1680, at the start of the private trade period, it is evident that the matched voyage removed and private trade removed graphs are essentially similar. In marked contrast, the impact of private trading is strongly evident in the middle of the period. The graphs for 1712, 1720, and 1728 (panels B, C, and D) show that without private traders, the entire system of Company trade in the East decomposes into two disjoint components, roughly divided by the Indian Peninsula. By 1760, as the Company reasserted control over the trading activities of captains, the effect of private trade is muted, but still visible. A single port connects two otherwise separate regions.

The absence of graph connectivity at the peak of private trading is readily apparent in figure 10. The key impact of private trading was to knit together otherwise disconnected regions. A modified measure of heterogeneity quantifies the extent of network integration, $H = \left(\sum_i^n (a_i/z)^2\right) + c,$ where $a$ represents the number of ports linked by $c + 1$ unique paths, $z$ represents the complete count of ports in the network, and $c$ represents the connectivity level of the graph or subgraph of interest. This means that a subgraph with one isolated node (i.e., no ties) has a connectivity level of 0, whereas a graph where all nodes have at least two unique paths between each other has a connectivity level of 2. This measure takes into consideration both the number of discrete components and the proportion of ports in each. For example, if the network were split into two components, but one component had only one port, overall connectivity would not be too drastically reduced—most of the ports would still be linked to one another. However if the network were split into two equally sized components, many ports would be cut off from each other—drastically reducing overall connectivity. A connectivity level of 1 indicates that all

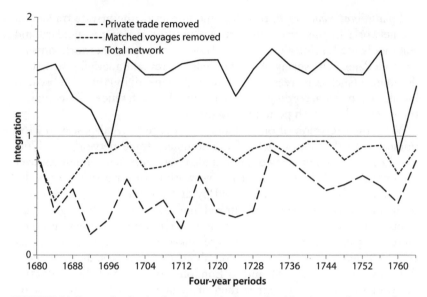

**FIGURE 11**. Integration levels of total networks, networks with private trade removed, and networks with matched voyages removed over four-year periods from 1680 to 1764.

of the nodes (ports) are integrated into a single connected component; a connectivity level of 2 means that all nodes are integrated into a single connected bicomponent. A bicomponent is similar to a component except that all nodes must be linked (directly or indirectly) by two separate paths. Increases in integration push the measure closer to the next connectivity level, for example from fragmentation to a single component (0 to 1) or from a component to a bicomponent (1 to 2). Figure 11 reports integration scores for the complete network, for the graphs with private traders removed and for the graphs with matched voyages removed.

Higher scores index greater integration. As is evident from figure 10, the total trade network from 1680 to 1760 is almost always a fully connected component. Only in 1696 and 1764 does the graph break into two components—note that the integration score for the total networks dip below one for these years. For all other periods, the total network is a fully connected component with a densely integrated core yielding integration scores well above 1.[12] The key finding is that the graph with the matched voyages removed is always more densely integrated than the graph with the malfeasant traders removed. The snapshots shown in figure 10 visually indicate the role of the malfeasant private traders in integrating the East Indian trade network. Figure 11 quantifies that impact, demonstrating that it is not an artifact of the network visualization. Malfeasant private traders

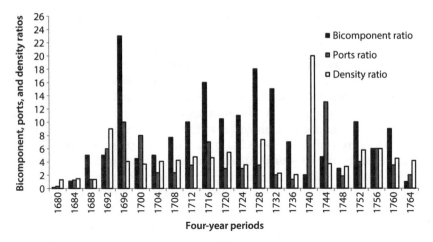

**FIGURE 12**. Relative impact of malfeasant trade on network density, the number of ports in the trading network, and largest bicomponent size in the East, 1680 to 1764.

contributed more to the integration of the overall trade network than did legitimate traders. Without these traders, the network fragments into large regional clusters dislocated from the main component.

While the inverted heterogeneity measure captures overall integration, the effects of the malfeasant employees are also evident in standard measures of network structure: density, size of the largest component, and size of the largest bicomponent. Figure 12 reports these results. For each, observed measures for the *legitimate trade graphs* and *malfeasant trade graphs* are first subtracted from observations taken on the total network. Each measure is then calculated as a percentage of the total network—that is, their impact. Relative impact, reported in figure 12, is the ratio of private traders impact over other traders. Where values exceed 1, private traders have greater relative impact on network structure than the matched voyages. As is readily apparent, this is the case for each variable at each moment of observation.

Density is simply the number of trips between ports relative to the total possible trips between ports. Consequently, a measure of weighted density mainly captures the increase in the number of ships at sea. To avoid this, the density of the directed binary port-port network is used. Ships may set out from one port and return—in cases of bad weather or other similarly unpredictable events. These loops are not included in the measure of density. As is evident above, malfeasant trade typically accounts for more than five times the density accounted for by the legitimate voyages. This means that in addition to linking regions, the activity of malfeasant actors significantly enhanced within region contact, thereby building multiple robust channels for the transmission of information on prices, conditions, terms of trade, and available commodities.

In addition to building within-region network infrastructure and cross-region trade networks, illegitimate traders directly incorporated markets into the existing network. The malfeasant actors consistently increased the size of the network: the sheer count of ports. This suggests that the process of establishing and sustaining ties to numerous markets was an ongoing by-product of the overcommitment of employees to their own private trade. Malfeasant employees are two times more likely than other captains to discover new ports subsequently integrated into the English East Indian trade network.

Finally, figure 12 considers the impact of private trade on the number of ports embedded within the largest bicomponent. Research on large complex networks (Moody 2004, Moody and White 2003, White and Harary 2001) has shown that bicomponents are well suited to assessing embeddedness and structural cohesion. In addition, networks characterized by redundancy—revealed through identification of graph bicomponents—are significantly less vulnerable to disruption. This structural element is critical for market contexts since uninterrupted delivery of goods and information is essential for market efficiency.

Redundancy also reduces information asymmetries. Bicomponents have more than one path between each node, so no one node is responsible for transmitting all information to any other node. For example, if all information about Eastern commerce was transmitted to London via one port, which is possible in a component but not in a bicomponent, there is a significant risk that those controlling that one port would manipulate that information to suit their own purposes—selectively transmitting or even fabricating information. This situation actually occurred in the Dutch East India Company. A select group of Dutch officers directed operations in Batavia, which was a central hub through which all Dutch communications were shuttled (Adams 1996: 19, Steensgaard 1996: 136). Their corruption of information about market conditions in the East is well documented and played an important role in the decline of the Dutch Company (Adams 1996: 21). The network structure created by malfeasant private traders created a situation in which this kind of illegitimate behavior was impossible without coordination across multiple ports. No one group or port had enough control over the total flow of information.[13]

## CONCLUSION

In 1738, Henry Kent set off on his first voyage with the East India Company—as second mate on the *Somerset*, destined for Bencoolen. Eight years later, in 1746, now captain of the *Dragon*, en route to China, Kent sailed through the Indonesian Archipelago, and landed twice at Tamborneo, a port on Borneo not previously encountered by any other English Company ship. After this trip, Kent sailed twice to India, with stops in Madras, Calcutta, Culpee (Kalpi), and Bencoolen. On these voyages Kent cycled between ports, but never missed a sailing season, returning to England roughly twenty-six months after departure. By 1752, Kent had sailed through—on different voyages—all the regions of East Indies.

On his last voyage, as captain of the *Dragon*, Kent left Downs on November 16, 1752, destined for Bengal. He made good time, arriving at the Cape in early February. By March 24, the *Dragon* sailed into St. Augustine's Bay. Rather than proceeding directly to Madras, Kent went up the coast of Madagascar to Morandava. From April to July, Kent stayed at Morandava, where, among other things, he helped establish a factory; exchanged guns, ammunition, and alcohol for meat, water, and slaves; engaged in a ritual exchange with the king and queen of Madagascar, who had traveled to meet him with their retinue; brought on board seventy-four slaves; dealt with mutinous crew members—three of whom were caught deserting in the ship's longboat—crushed a small slave revolt; and met up with another East India Company vessel (the *Swallow*, leaving Downs within days of the *Dragon*, captained by John Bell, also taking his last trip, for which very little voyage data are available in Company records). Leaving Morandava, Kent made a brief stop at the Morungary River, before setting sail for Madras. Once in Madras, Kent traveled to Calcutta and Culpee and returned to Madras, completing a cycle, before sailing for Bencoolen and cycling back to Madagascar (East India Company 1752). Along the way, he missed his sailing season, allowing him to stay in the East an extra year, and thereby incurring additional costs to the Company. What Kent did with the slaves is not recorded. The Company was not officially engaged in the slave trade.

Not all private traders engaged in the slave trade, but Kent was typical in other ways. Over the course of his career, Kent led legitimate and illegitimate voyages. Like other private traders, Kent discovered, and twice returned to, a new port, and thereby opened up potential new markets for the Company. The circuits he took wove together the Bengal trading region with the Indonesian Archipelago, and the vibrant trading world of the east coast of Africa. Only rarely can one see from these records into the world of the private trader as clearly as for Kent, but the trace of their activity is visible—long stays in the East and cycles between ports. To see this, one has to construct trade networks amenable to structural analysis. The paths of the ships constitute the transportation and communication infrastructure of firm operations. The records of the voyages provide a material trace of the system of exchange involving the English Company merchants. Those paths produce an image of the Company trade over time, thereby allowing the reconstruction of legitimate and illegitimate private trade.

The result reveals a convoluted story. Good intentions went bad and bad intentions went good. At the core of these processes is the increase in autonomy experienced by captains when the English Company legitimated private trade. By withdrawing from the country trade, the Company opened up an avenue of opportunity for their employees, who were all too willing to use it by tying up valuable Company resources. Even when the captains disobeyed direct orders, they contributed significantly to the overall success of the Company trade. Private traders wove local interactions into a global institution (the Company itself), creating the dense structures we associate with globalizing processes. They produced a larger, more integrated internal network of trade for the English Company.

The larger mechanism described in this chapter incorporates four smaller components into one larger chain bridging micro behaviors and macro outcomes. When individuals are placed in a competitive market situation, they can be expected to act to maximize their profits. Organizational control is incomplete and loss of control is exacerbated under conditions of physical distance and poor communication. Individuals acting in pursuit of personal, not corporate, goals (in this case personal profit) will introduce random perturbations into the regular conduct of organizational affairs—in this case producing a small-world effect where random links increase overall network connectivity.

The cohesive structure of trade produced by malfeasant captains produced a better vehicle for improved communication with London as well as communication between factories within the East, and the Company and English private traders alike would have benefited from hearing of the new ports that entered the network through the malfeasant voyages. Because social networks played an important role in the Eastern trade, the connected network created by the malfeasant traders would have served as an important, if unseen, resource for the legitimate, rule-abiding captains as well. Since captains drew information from their social networks when making decisions about where to trade, the robust, ultra-connected networks created by malfeasant captains would have done a better job of shuttling information to peripheral actors. The end result was an additional benefit from the private trade, a dense social network that provided information to legitimate and illegitimate traders alike.

*Chapter 6*

# THE EASTERN PORTS

As a general rule, organizations are shaped by the environment around them. The East India Company was particularly susceptible to external influences. It was not based on a preexisting template. The company form was novel in the seventeenth century. The East India Company also did not appear as a fully formed, fixed entity. It began as a series of joint investments that coalesced over time into a stable organization with a pool of permanent capital. The administrative apparatus, the Company's relation to the British state, and its operating procedures shifted and evolved over time in response to changing environmental pressures and opportunities.

Many of the external pressures that shaped the institutional trajectory of the Company were located in Britain and Europe. The formative push and pull between the British state and English Company is a central theme in Lucy Sutherland's work on the transition to colonial power (1952), James Vaughn's research revisiting and revising our understanding of the relationship between the metropole and Company imperialism (2009), Philip Stern's examination of the Company's adoption of sovereign forms of power (2011), and Rupali Mishra's detailed work on the evolution of the Company in its first decades (2010). In the background of these works is a broader stroke picture of economic history that has linked specific institutional developments in Europe, such as the development of property rights, to its economic takeoff, of which the fortunes of the East India Company were a part (North and Thomas 1973).

Without supplementary work on institutional contexts in Asia, this work can leave crucial assumptions unquestioned—particularly that the institutional and organizational innovations of the Company derive entirely from Europe. Such interpretations are not the fault of the research listed above, but instead derive from the larger symbol system of Western society, in which openness, tolerance, and market liberalism are reflexively coded as Western, and tyranny, hierarchy, despotism, and communism are considered Eastern. Because of this cultural schema, many may intuitively associate the private trade and employee autonomy of the firm—and the commercial development they contributed to—with larger cultural patterns in England. Two important recent works in comparative historical sociology have directly questioned the link between European influences and the development of tolerant, democratic, and economically progressive institutions in European colonies. Julian Go and James Mahoney have both emphasized the importance of the institutional environment of the colonies in creating the institutions and modalities of colonial rule—rather than assuming a one-directional flow from Europe to the colonies (Go 2011, Mahoney 2010).

The body of work that deals with Company affairs in Asia—rather than Europe—has not yet questioned the link between the European institutional setting and the organizational innovations of the Company. Instead the focus has largely remained on other questions, also important, regarding the effect of the Company on Eastern ports as well as European companies' incorporation and reliance on preexisting trade patterns. In the following two chapters I challenge the idea that the organizational innovations of the Company derive from Europe by considering the environment of the Eastern ports and their relationship to the decentralization of the English Company.

Although the analysis has largely focused on the board of managers and private traders of the Company, they should not be held as primarily responsible for the decentralized structure of the firm. The success or failure of English trade depended to a large degree on commercial sophistication in the East and the opportunity structure in place for foreign traders. If there were multiple opportunities for multiple traders, produced by decentralized access to foreign trade, English trade tended to be a success. The private trade could not have flourished without access to economically decentralized markets in the East. Since the decentralized organizational structure within the English Company was intertwined with the private trade, the increased flow of information and innovations documented in chapters 4 and 5 is tied to the institutional environment of Eastern ports. Although the two chapters describe significant institutional variation across ports, there is one simple analytical mechanism operating: opportunities structure behavior (Petersen 2009).

The temptation to read the high levels of employee autonomy and open stance on private trade back to the cultural predispositions against monopoly practices in England should be resisted. Whatever role it may have played, such an emphasis ignores the much stronger influence exerted by Eastern ports. The openness and toleration of many Eastern ports made the commercial expansion of the Company and its employees private trade possible. In the end, the innovative decentralized structure of the English Company—and its attendant commercial benefits—depended upon the commercial organization of Asian commerce.

The importance of the East in shaping the organization also has implications for the way networks are studied. Network mechanisms and structures, such as those identified in chapters 4 and 5, are often analyzed by network researchers in isolation—which is to say that they are treated as separate and separable from their environment. Although the effects of different network structures may be abstracted to the point where they can be generalized across different contexts, the dynamics behind the creation of those network structures are inevitably linked to the particular time and society in which they occur. People create networks by building relationships with one another. How they build those relations and with whom they build them will always be fundamentally affected by the society in which they live, its cultural predispositions, prejudices, habits of mind, and routine behaviors. Even network ties within organizations will be affected by the societies in which they operate, as was the case with the English East India Company. This chapter therefore begins to explore the institutional environment of the East and its impact on the English trade.

## THE EAST INDIES

The sophistication of Asian ports prior to the modern era is well established. Several areas in Asia appeared to have been on the brink of something like the Industrial Revolution. Many believe that the basic conditions necessary for sustained economic development had been present in China since the tenth century. In the Sung Period, the introduction of a new kind of rice in the Yangtze Valley brought about an agricultural revolution that triggered a long period of prosperity, expansion, urbanization, and innovation (Findlay and O'Rourke 2007: 60–67). There was a large class of powerful and prosperous merchants, the government had invested deeply into building an infrastructure to support trade, and there was major growth in the steel and iron industries. It seems to have been just as likely a time and place for the rapid takeoff we associate with England in the nineteenth century. The economists Robert Findlay and Kevin O'Rourke have argued that what might have been an early transition in China was unnecessarily cut off by the Mongolian invasion.

India was also reaching a peak of economic development. In 1602, when the English rounded the Cape of Good Hope, the Mughal Empire was at its zenith. Emperor Akbar had conquered northern India, including Malwa, Bengal, and Gujarat, as well as the beautiful and still contested Kashmir. His empire extended from the area now known as Afghanistan, through Pakistan, across northern India to Bangladesh, and as far south as Maharashtra. Under Aurangzeb (r. 1658–1707), the empire reached to the southern tip of the subcontinent. If not an incipient global superpower (as China might have been), India was home to an extraordinarily powerful manufacturing industry, a complex and thriving commercial economy, and a relatively stable government that encouraged commercialization through its taxation policies (Findlay and O'Rourke 2007: 268). After all, the rich markets of the East are what drew Europeans into the long overseas ventures in the first place.

Another set of historians has revealed the importance of Asian merchant groups in the economic integration of the East and West. Drawing from Philip Curtin (1994) and Fernand Braudel (1972, 1977, 1992a, 1992b, 1992c), they emphasize the importance of commercial partnerships between the English and Asian merchant communities (Furber 1948, 1976, Lach and Kley 1965, Ferrier 1973, Kling, Pearson, and Furber 1979, Chaudhuri 1985, Chandra 1987, Subramanian 1987, Frank 1998). In the story of the English Company's sustained success, the economic development of Asia and the willingness of local merchants to work with the English Company as well as English private traders were crucial elements. In the seventeenth century, overseas traders were simply entrepreneurs looking for new markets. They were starting up trade enterprises, and their chance of success depended heavily upon the social and cultural characteristics of the ports to which they had traveled: cultural barriers, linguistic barriers, legal restrictions, and institutional regulations. The number and type of commercial opportunities typically available to an Englishman in an Eastern port determined the success of the Company, just as much as the private trading employees, because they were necessary to the development of the private trade.

## THE PORTS

The relatively autonomous local agents of the English Company (i.e., the private trading captains and factors) needed relatively autonomous actors in ports with which to trade. Ports had to be able to handle the large-scale requests of the Company as well as the smaller-scale commerce of the private traders—both decentralization and commercial sophistication were necessary to satisfy the demands of employees and firm. And the English overwhelmingly chose to trade with ports that were both commercially sophisticated and decentralized.

The East Indies was a tremendously large and diverse area. Ports varied from the dusty, moveable bazaars of Mokha (Mocha) to the misty rivers and hostile ships of the Cagayan Sulu (Mapun). There were isolated villages and large metropolises. The English settled successfully in some, and unsuccessfully in others. In this chapter I introduce a typology of ports based on the institutional features governing overseas trade by describing representative ports. This categorization was inductively derived from the most salient features of social organization touching upon foreign trade. The categorizations are meant to represent ideal types, and each port inevitably possesses unique features. The ports are grouped into categories most representative during the early years of an English trade presence. The descriptions are not meant to describe the large-scale transformations wrought by the English themselves because the interpretation is focused on piecing out the effect of the environment of the ports on the English Company. The port descriptions motivate and ground the analysis of port interactions based on the full ships' data presented in chapter 7.

The ports presented here are Madras, Bantam, St. Augustine's Bay, Guangzhou, Batticaloa, and the Straits of New Guinea. Also discussed are English experiences in two European colonial ports, the Portuguese stronghold of Goa and the Dutch colonial capital of Batavia. Madras is representative of a broad set of ports with well-developed and defined commercial classes acting with relative autonomy from the state that I call *market societies*. Bantam also possessed a well-developed commercial class, but differed from Madras in its status as a city-state and a center of free trade in the East. Bantam and similar ports are referred to as *open cities*, although they have also been called emporia. Trade in St. Augustine's Bay had a close relationship with state organization, military power, and social status. I refer to this type of port as a *regulated reciprocity*. Canton was extremely sophisticated, and the government held a tight grip on foreign trade. I refer to this as a *regulated market*. Papua New Guinea sits at the opposite end of the spectrum from Canton, with little regulation and little commercial sophistication. This and similar ports are referred to as sites of *unregulated reciprocity*. In Batticaloa, the royal family directly controlled all overseas trade, thus it represents a *royal monopoly*. Finally, Goa and Batavia are representations of social patterns in non-English *European colonies*.

Each of these ports represents a type of port common to the East, although the categories are not taken from a preexisting theoretical framework. Existing typologies were too coarse-grained to capture the varieties of commercial organization found in the East, and most describe entire economic systems, rather than focus on foreign trade. My categorization scheme is influenced by Karl Polanyi's well-known typology of reciprocal, redistributive, and market societies (Polanyi 2001: 45–58). Polanyi's use of the term "reciprocal" designated societies in which larger units, moieties or subdivisions, engaged in an interdependent relation of gift exchange— meaning that social or political considerations had equal or greater weight than the economic consequences of exchange. I also use "reciprocal" to indicate societies in which gift exchange occurred between individuals. *Royal monopolies* closely resemble redistributive organization, in which goods are collected by a central authority figure. For Polanyi, the market economy signifies a system dominated by individual exchange in the pursuit of profit. For him, actors' motivation definitively distinguishes markets from what he characterized as "earlier" forms of economic organization. The definitions used here revolve instead around the patterns of interaction produced by market exchange, though the possibility of anonymous exchange remains important.

J. C. Van Leur also used a three-category scheme: agrarian, city, and *oikos*, the last meaning production in and for the household (Van Leur 1955: 56). In this case, the production-based distinction between agrarian and *oikos* is unhelpful. Another useful but ultimately unsatisfactory scheme is the division between échelles and entrepôts. The distinction between échelles, cities placed so as to collect goods from a hinterland of agricultural producers, and entrepôts, cities that collect goods from and serve as transshipment areas for foreign trade, plays into the political economy of ports, but does not entirely determine the state's role in foreign trade. The distinction therefore insufficiently represented the differences between many ports.

In describing the ports and placing them into the different categories, I drew on contemporary historical research as well as sources written during or close to the period of interest. These sources include a number of almanacs, calendars, travelogues, and catalogues of East Indian ports published in the eighteenth and nineteenth centuries to assist the influx of free English traders (Fryer 1698, Barbosa 1918, Barlow and Lubbock [1703] 1934, Blakeney 1841, Dodwell 1773, Hamilton and Foster [1732] 1930, Herbert and Dunn 1791, Horsburgh 1841, Milburne 1813, Milburn and Thornton 1825, Pires 1944, Tennent 1860, Staunton 1797, Stevens 1775, Wright and Gilbert 1804). Other sources not referenced in the descriptions, but used in identifying and categorizing the full set of ports include *Encyclopedia Iranica* (Yarshater 1990), the *Cyclopedia of India and of Eastern and Southern Asia* (Balfour 1895), *Malaysia: A Country Study* (Bunge 1984), *Shipwrecks and Disasters at Sea* (Anon., 1812), *Asiatic Journal and Monthly Miscellany* (East India Company 1843), *The Philippine Islands* (Foreman 1890), and "An Alternative Vietnam? The Nguyen Kingdom in the Seventeenth and Eighteenth Centuries" (Tana 1998). The online *Atlas of Mutual Heritage* (Don et al. 2012) was an invaluable resource. Information on the number of ships at port is drawn from the *Catalogue of East India Company Ships' Journals and Logs* (Farrington 1999b).[1]

In some of the ports opportunities existed that stimulated the expansion of the English private trade. In others, similar opportunities did not exist or were forcibly closed. The result was that durable trade relationships were formed in some ports, while in others the English trade died out. The English Company thrived in ports with open participation in overseas trade *and* commercial sophistication. In each case, the history of engagement shows that decentralization and commercial sophistication sustained the private trade. Commercially sophisticated Asian ports with decentralized access to overseas markets were jointly responsible for the novel organizational structure of the English East India Company, and therefore are indirectly responsible for its success and the effects on English society and foreign policy.

## Madras: Market Society

Madras was perhaps the most successful site of English trade in the East. In all, 2,262 East India Company ships docked at Madras in a steady, uninterrupted stream that lasted over 192 years. The trade between England and Madras continued beyond 1833, but by that time the British government had revoked the Company's trading privileges and its function became that of colonial administrator rather than trader. This was all part of a long process through which the British government took full control over Company operations and assumed territorial control over India. This outcome however was not to come to pass until after the conclusion of almost two centuries of steady, profitable exchange between Indian and English merchants. The regular trade of the English Company with Madras was not the longest in Company history, but its harbor did receive more English ships any other Eastern port.

Its advantages may not have been entirely visible to the untrained eye prior to settlement. Before the arrival of the English, Madras was a small, barren strip of land on the Coromandel Coast of India. Coromandel is roughly the lower third of the east coast of India. At that time, it was a rich textile-producing region with a large and extremely mobile class of skilled weavers. Madras, however, did not have an exceptional harbor and was not well positioned to receive goods from the thriving productive regions clustered over and around the rest of Coromandel. It sat near an established Portuguese port, San Thome.

Coromandel had a somewhat unique political history, when compared to other areas of the subcontinent. When Madras was established, it had not yet been incorporated into the Mughal Empire. The Mughal Empire began its conquest of the Indian Peninsula from the Sind (the area now known as Pakistan) in the mid-sixteenth century. By the late seventeenth century, most of the Indian Subcontinent had fallen under their control. Coromandel resisted the expansion and had remained an independent kingdom. It was a one of the last remnants of the Vijayanagara Empire, a Hindu dynasty that had controlled a large portion of the subcontinent prior to the Mughal incursion. Fragmented government and the continued threat of Mughal invasion consigned the area to political instability (Mukund 1999: 56).

In 1641, the English leased the site of Madras from the Rajah of Chan-
dragiri. Less than a decade later the land was seized from the Rajah by the
reputedly more extortionate Sultan of Golkanda. Soon after, the region
was finally overtaken by the Mughals. The English weathered all storms
by renegotiating leases, redirecting rents, and welcoming in new officials—
though new officials tended to increase taxes as they assumed their new
positions. The Court of Directors in London repeatedly questioned the
wisdom of settling in such a politically volatile area. Through thick and thin
the resident English defended their commitment to Madras by claiming
it was easily fortified to withstand land attacks. It was not so well fortified
however as to prevent the French from taking Madras from 1746 to 1749.

While still under Mughal control in the mid-seventeenth century, the
English Company leased Madras from a *zamindar.* Zamindar was the official title for the gentry-class landholders who served as tax collectors under
the Mughal system. In 1688, the middlemen were done away with and
the English Company was formally assimilated into the Mughal political
system as zamindar of Madras. This transition brought some long-desired
stability to the settlement. It was also indicative of a broad pattern of political accommodation in India.

Much like under the feudal system in Europe, local conflicts were often
resolved by accommodation. Threatening elites were offered relative sovereignty in exchange for performing tax collection duties. This system allowed the English to avoid the costly expenses of military aggression while
establishing effective political control. In addition, the English were given
the right to import the British system of law, although they did so selectively. The complexity caused by the interactions of several groups of foreign merchants, each with different ways of handling late deliveries, fluctuating prices, dips in supply, and the hundreds of other negotiable exigencies
of foreign trade could cause tremendous confusion. Add to this multiple
codes of conduct, different ways to settle disputes, and different standards
of justice, and the advantage of acting as the ultimate arbiter of conflict must
have both reduced the complexity of negotiating between several different
legal regimes and given the English a significant commercial advantage.

Under the direction of the English, and with the encouragement of
their trade, the port flourished and grew. Alexander Hamilton estimated
that the previously desolate spot had grown to house some eighty thousand
inhabitants by the early eighteenth century (Hamilton and Foster [1732]
1930: 203). The historian Ashin Das Gupta has argued that British ports
flourished because of Mughal decline (Das Gupta 1998: 46). It is therefore
important to note that Madras was in the process of becoming a vibrant
trading hub even as it was incorporated into the Mughal Empire.

The success of Madras was built on the regional characteristics of the
Coromandel Coast. Because it was located within this productive region,

Madras soon attracted a large local population of weavers and merchants. Arvind Sinha asserts that the zenith of commercial activity in Coromandel was during the years of Vijayanagar rule, which ended in 1565 (Sinha 2002: 176). (He is referring to the region of Coromandel, not the city of Madras, which had not yet been founded.) The region had a thriving internal trade. Salt, raw cotton, finished cotton, betelnut, pessaloo curry, tobacco, pepper, silk, other spices, benjamin (also known as spicebush), threads, blankets, raw silk, many kinds of cotton cloth, dates, almonds, mailtuta (a dentifrice), and dyes constituted only a small selection of the goods locally available. The legendary European jeweler Jean-Baptiste Tavernier (who may have been prone to exaggeration) reported seeing a caravan of forty thousand oxen laden with goods traveling through that area (Sinha 2002: 33). The famously skilled weavers in the region produced high-quality textiles including calicos, percallas, chintzes, ginghams, pintados, and sailcoth (Babu 1995: 262–63). The English mainly traded silver for these fine-quality cotton goods along with the basic necessities, such as wheat, rice, and firewood.

Trade and production were organized from the bottom up, through social and ethnic cleavages. Weavers were organized into castes around different products. For example, the *Devanga* caste wove dark blue cloth and the *Salewars* made plain white neck clothes. Several castes served as merchants for different types of goods and different regional markets. For example, *Banjaras* handled inland trade and *Coorchivas* handled trade to coastal regions from farther inland. A series of regular festivals and weekly markets also circulated through the region. The presence of festivals drew in *dubashes* and *gomastahs*. Dubashes and gomastahs were local intermediaries who negotiated contracts, served as translators, and saw to most of the details of the English trade. Dubashes independently contracted with the English Company, and gomastahs were hired into the organization.

One important result of this continuous commercial activity was a well-developed capital market and a network of financial institutions that lent support to both Company and individual enterprise. Small-time moneylenders and larger banking families populated the region. The moneylenders were usually bulk dealers in export goods, the largest, most prosperous merchants in the area (Mukund 1999: 62). They worked primarily through bills of exchange carried by agents operating across Coromandel (Sinha 2002: 44).

Madras itself had a distinctive social organization. It was populated by two competing merchant groups, the *Balijas* and *Beri Chettis*. These groups belonged to different castes, the right- and left-hand castes. The city was divided into different streets for different castes. Antagonism between these groups was the basis for both violence and commercial stratagems (Mukund 1999: 67–68). In negotiating this complex world, the Company relied heavily upon a series of prominent merchants (whom the historian

Kanakalatha Mukund refers to as merchant capitalists), who held effective if not nominal control of Chennapatnam, which was called "Black Town" by the English (Sharma 1998: 263).

Mukund argues that elite merchants in the Madras area formed a well-defined, self-conscious class that predated the European presence (Mukund 1999: xi, 61). Elite resident merchants were crucial intermediaries managing Europeans affairs, not only linking them to network of production, but also handling negotiations with state authorities (Sharma 1998: 265, Mukund 1999: 61). It is very clear that the English, as well as other Europeans, relied heavily upon resident merchants. They linked the English to the economy of the hinterland by establishing annual advance contracts between the English and the different castes of weavers. The weavers were paid upfront and found their own supplies. The English attempted to assume the role of supplier to the weavers, but this move was resisted.

Four particularly prominent figures in the early history of Madras include Seshadri Nayak and Koneri Chietti in the 1650s, Beri Timmanna in the 1660s (Mukund 1999: 70), and Kasi Viranna in the 1670s (Sharma 1998: 265). Despite some evidence of socializing and friendship between select English factors and the elite merchants of Madras (Sharma 1998: 283, Mukund 1999: 10), relations were not always amicable. Timmanna and Viranna, for example, were arrested by the English in 1665 (Sharma 1998: 271, Mukund 1999: 71). Company officials repeatedly accused different merchants of embezzlement and fraud.

By the 1670s the Company was regularly dealing with a group of twenty-six chief merchants, who also oversaw a larger number of lesser merchants (Mukund 1999: 105). Once Madras was established, another cosmopolitan community of Portuguese, Muslim, and Armenian merchants moved in and began to invest heavily in the overseas trade to Persia, China, Ganjam, Orissa (Odisha), Surat, Bengal, and Diu. It is worth noting that the Portuguese were central to the community of experienced overseas merchants who turned Madras into a thriving commercial center. As this demonstrates, the proximity of a Portuguese settlement in the long run made the site more attractive as Portuguese merchants could be lured to Madras.

To summarize, political instability did not drive out the English, and the presence of other Europeans encouraged, rather than discouraged, the success of the settlement. The most important factors, however, were flexible political accommodations, large-scale productive capacity, widespread financial sophistication, and developed markets. The existence of a large body of capable and skilled merchants allowed plentiful opportunities for English enterprise across all levels of Company operation. Not only were the larger Company interests served by the environment in Madras, but the employees (operating at lower levels of capital investment) were also well satisfied with their commercial prospects. Trade was decentralized and commercial sophistication high. The result was a very successful permanent establishment.

## BANTAM: OPEN CITY

Madras barely existed before the English entered the East. Its development was an outgrowth of the joint efforts of English and local merchants. The East also contained numerous commercial hubs of astonishing prosperity predating European involvements by hundreds, if not thousands, of years. Trade was literally the lifeblood of these city-states: import-export tax was the main source of government revenue. Thus, the government had a tremendous incentive to encourage foreign trade by reducing barriers to entry. The result was a decentralized market. When successful, they attracted experienced overseas traders from around the world, pushing the average level of commercial sophistication up. The combination was irresistible to the English. Bantam was one of the most prosperous of these trading hubs.

Bantam sits near the western tip of Java. Long before the European companies were formed, the city played host to a richly developed world of sophisticated commerce and served as a transshipment area for merchants hailing from Western India to the far northern ports of China. It was a well-connected, opulent city-state that relied on foreign commerce for its tax base. Situated between two straits, one separating Java and Sumatra and the other the Indonesian Archipelago from the Malay Peninsula, it straddled the regional economies of the Near and Far East. A constant stream of traders crowded the bazaars and city streets. Having long played host to an extremely diverse group of international merchants, Bantam was well equipped with the institutional and commercial mechanisms necessary to manage the various needs of the English officers, crew, and factors.

The Company landed at Bantam in its very first voyages and returned regularly for the next fifty years. This spell of trade ended because of Dutch pressure on the port. The Dutch had made Indonesia their territorial base. Over the course of the seventeenth century, they expanded throughout Java, often taking indirect political control as a means to establish a commercial monopoly over the rich supply of spices produced on the island. They interfered with foreign trade policies by exerting pressure—backed by the threat of military force—on the Sultan of Bantam and his council. The delicate balance the Sultan had maintained between different factions of foreign traders, all seeking political influence and special trading privileges, was destroyed by the Dutch interference. By the end of the seventeenth century, the Dutch had succeeded in pushing the international trade of Java to their headquarters in Batavia, causing trade in Bantam to dry up (Chaudhuri 1978: 16–17). In 1682 the Dutch took Bantam and evicted the English from their factory, banning further settlements (Farrington 2002a: 111). A tipping point was reached and the English and other overseas merchants deserted the once humming metropolis. Over the course of the entire eighteenth century, the English returned to Bantam less than a dozen times.

At its commercial height, Bantam mainly operated as a transshipment center. The major goods included pepper from the island, Chinese silk, tea, porcelain, zinc, copper, ivory, opium, and cotton goods from India. More exotic items included dragon's blood (a bright scarlet resin), elephant's teeth, turmeric, arrack, camphor, aloes, ebony, rare and coveted sugar candy, sapanwood, vermilion, quicksilver, and European odds and ends including beer, cheese, claret, assorted perfumes, musical instruments, and toys. The port was a hub for foreign merchants of all kinds. As quoted by Van Leur, the account of the first Dutch to land in Bantam reported, "There came such a multitude of Javanese and other nations as Turks, Chinese, Bengalis, Arabs, Persians, Gujarati, and others that one could hardly move" (Van Leur 1955: 1).

The Sultan relied on foreign trade to support a lavish lifestyle of conspicuous consumption. The mythology surrounding the Bantenese ruler based his authority on the successful union with the Goddess of the South Seas, *Kanjeng Ratu Kidul*. The success of this union was a token of the divine grace of the ruler; it formed the basis of his legitimate claim to political power. Being otherworldly in nature, the marriage itself was difficult to observe. Instead, the court and people assessed the union by evaluating the Sultan's desirability as a consort. The basis of his legitimacy was appearing in the eyes of the court as a consort worthy of a goddess. "If his visible glory were below standard, if his treasury were inadequate, or if he were unable to deal with persistent rebellions, it would seem most unlikely that this man could be the protégé of the Goddess of the Southern Ocean" (Ricklefs 1974: 25).

Visible glory is costly.[2] The Sultan depended upon his ability to delicately balance relations with foreign merchants in order to maximize trade to the port—and thereby government revenues. The importance of the merchants was so great, the Sultan directly involved them in the administration of the government. The most prestigious and successful of the foreign traders sat on the Sultan's council. The highest office of the port, the *syahbandar* and *laksamana*, could also be occupied by foreign merchants. In the early seventeenth century, a Coromandel merchant took the office of syahbandar and sat on the royal council. Roughly fifty years later a Chinese merchant named Abdul Gafur occupied the same position (Kathirithamby-Wells 1990: 110–13). The opportunities open to foreign merchants were unparalleled in the Western world.

The government policy in support of free trade produced multiple opportunities for the firm and English private traders. Despite the religious/mythological trappings, the commercial sophistication of the government, as well as foreign and resident merchants, was extremely high. The English Company regularly traded with Bantam until the Dutch destroyed the foundations of its commercial prosperity.

## St. Augustine's Bay: Regulated Reciprocity

The society of St. Augustine's Bay was less commercially sophisticated but more regulated than those of Madras and Bantam. St. Augustine's Bay lies on the western coast of Madagascar. It was not commercially developed in the seventeenth century. One consequence of this was the absence of a strict boundary dividing elite and local commercial activities. At one point, itinerant Islamic merchants had controlled overseas trade, but the local ruling elite replaced them before European contact (Kent 1968: 528). Interactions with traveling merchants were deeply embedded in religious beliefs and rituals, but these rites effectively smoothed transactions with strangers. The ruling class dominated trade, but local markets were growing in size and complexity during the sixteenth century and a nascent merchant class was emerging from the inland territories.

The first port visited in the Indian Ocean by English Company ships—the *Susan*, the *Dragon*, the *Hector*, and the *Ascension*—was St. Augustine's Bay. For the next century, the English made sporadic appearances in the area, including a failed attempt to establish a colony. In 1644, 140 settlers led by John Smart and acting apart from the Company landed in St. Augustine's Bay and promptly died in large numbers—destroying hopes for further colonization and causing great distress for the twelve survivors. Another regular spell of trade was not initiated until the eighteenth century. Beginning in 1718, Company ships landed regularly in St. Augustine's for over eighty years. Over the course of those eighty years 110 English Company ships had engaged in some kind of trade at the port.

Slaves were Madagascar's largest export. Other traded items included cattle, yams, coconuts, bananas, sheep, poultry, hogs, milk, salt, potatoes, fish, lances, wax, loincloths, matting, cowry shells, maize, ambergris, and cassis shell. Prior to the European entrance into the Indian Ocean, the Malagasy used these goods to purchase silk, cotton, muskets, flint, gunpowder, glass, jewelry, salt, and ostrich eggs from the *Silamo*. The Silamo were Arab or Muslim merchants that traditionally handled trade with the western coast of Madagascar (Campbell 1993: 130). These Muslim traders linked the northwestern coast of Madagascar to the larger Indian Ocean network by way of Malindi and Mombasa. Though they dealt in other goods, their primary interest was in the slave trade.

Observers have characterized early Madagascar as politically fragmented because the island contained several different political units. However

Europeans had a tendency to underestimate the size of the island, which covers 587,040 square kilometers—making it considerably larger than most European countries. By 1710 most of the western side of the island had been conquered by the Sakalava (Kent 1968: 544). The English crews recognized various levels of aristocracy among the Sakalava and were suitably impressed by their royal stature.

The history of the Sakalava elite's involvement in overseas trade is slightly murky. There is evidence that the Sakalava chief, or king, had taken control of the slave trade from the foreign Islamic merchants at just the moment when the Islamic merchants' larger, international trade network was being threatened by the Portuguese. This timing indicates that the Malagasy elite were directly involved in foreign trade by the sixteenth century. Gwyn Campbell claims the Malagasy ruling class developed international trade at a much earlier stage, but in order to make this argument she treats kidnapping and cattle raiding (on large scales) as forms of long-distance commerce (Campbell 1993: 122).

English trade on the island followed a standard protocol. After reaching an agreement with the chief in authority at the port, the traders usually erected a small warehouse (a factory). The shiplogs contain detailed records of these encounters. There was inevitably a long period in which the travelers waited for the arrival of the rulers, as the people refused to trade until the king or queen arrived and granted permission. When the king and queen arrived, a ritual ceremony was performed in which gifts between the traders and elite were exchanged. In the anthropological literature, this is called a prestation ceremony. The successful conclusion of this ceremony signaled the opening of trade. At this point, the entire community was free to participate, although there were continuing restrictions concerning the type of goods traded.[3] Slaves were a product of warfare and seemed to have been controlled by the king and queen. Trade in local produce, poultry, and meat was conducted with the larger population (East India Company 1752). Prices were determined by advance contract, but the English found that the frequent application of gifts to the rulers was necessary to smooth over continuing transactions. This necessity made final costs hard to predict.

These rules of trade applied to the coastal trade of the Sakalava. Inland trade was a different story. To venture into the interior of the island foreign traders needed a blood bond with the local chief or ruling party of that area. The *fatidra*, as the bond was called, blurred the identities of the two initiates (Campbell 1993: 137). For example, the bonded pair was expected to share wives. Because the accepted stranger was given, or lent, the identity of the chief, the people of the community were expected to treat the stranger as they would the chief. Specifically they were obligated to supply the stranger with provisions and lodging, thus enabling trade. The fatidra was a social innovation that used existing customs to create a well-defined and officially protected social position for merchants.

By the end of the seventeenth century, a new class of agents and translators of European and Malagasy descent began to play a more important role in overseas trade. In 1643, a French colony had been established on the opposite side of the island from St. Augustine's. There were also the infamous pirate settlements such as Cape St. Mary, a sheltered port at the southern tip, home to the Great Pirate Roberts (Nutting 1978: 205). Pirate settlements were wiped out by the 1720s, but they left a legacy behind them. The Malagasy were willing to marry or marry off their daughters—or simply to engage sexual relations with foreigners—as a sign of hospitality (Campbell 1993: 136). Survivors of the French and pirate settlements must have often intermarried with the local population because the women, the wives of Europeans, and their sons and daughters served as agents and translators essential to the European trade.

By the late eighteenth century, indigenous merchant groups spearheaded a veritable market revolution. The salt trade was handled by the *Ampanira Antankarana* or *Belo Sakalava*, who established a temporally located market in the internal region of Imerina. Hemp, wood, cotton, and silk markets sprang up, tied to specific locations, usually in the island's interior. Gwyn Campbell dates the beginnings of market system to the mid-seventeenth century. By the eighteenth a regional system of interlocking markets and fairs had been established (Campbell 1993: 147–48).

Although growing, trade in Madagascar was not well developed compared to that in cities such as Bantam or Coromandel. The society could not be characterized as segmented and interdependent, two basic characteristics of a market society. Capital markets, mints, and courts were absent. But the foundations of a market society were emerging. There was even the essential Marxist precondition for economic development: labor for hire. Europeans used workers, called *maromita*, as porters (Campbell 1993: 135). Trade and commerce had not been entirely confined to elite sections of the society, and reciprocal exchange was common. As time passed and these institutions developed commercial sophistication increased, and the English found it increasingly profitable to make repeated calls at port.

## Canton: Regulated Market

Chinese society was both more centralized and more commercially sophisticated than Malagasy society. The Chinese Empire was arguably the most powerful political unit on the planet and oversaw an immense complex, interdependent, and commercially prosperous society. Although both were sophisticated and wealthy, the Chinese and Bantanese Empires had very different relationships to foreign trade. In Bantam, the survival of the government depended entirely upon foreign trade revenues. In China, the tax on foreign trade played a relatively minor role in government finances. Although customs were a welcome addition to government revenue, foreign trade could not compete with the enormous sums collected from the vast rural hinterlands of the Chinese Empire. At times, the Chinese government suspended all overseas trade and closed their ports to foreign traffic. Even after 1684, when ports were reopened after a hiatus, the Qing dynasty persistently attempted to limit Chinese contact with foreigners. To this end, they constructed an elaborate regulatory system that forced the English Company into several unusual accommodations.

The English Company originally attempted to initiate trade with China through Amoy and Taiwan, but Beijing wanted to isolate the impact of foreigners and worked to draw all overseas trade to Canton (Van Dyke 2005: 6–7). The English Company ships first arrived at Whampoa, port to Canton, in 1689 and returned regularly until the end of the Company's monopoly. During the course of that trade 1,453 Company ships docked at Whampoa. Trade with China increased over these years, but not steadily. From 1690 to 1748 roughly three or four English Company ships docked for trade each year. In 1748, the frequency increased to nine or ten and grew steadily to twenty over the next thirty years. From 1775 to 1786 there was a lull. From 1786 until the demise of the organization over twenty ships arrived annually.

Canton was located up a long and shallow inland river. To reach it the European ships first had to hire native pilots at or near Macao. These pilots navigated the journey to upriver, usually stopping at Bocca Tigris to take on "tidewaiters": Chinese officials brought aboard to monitor the upriver passage and discourage smuggling (Van Dyke 2005: 21–22). At Whampoa the large ships were docked, and goods were floated up the final leg to Canton on shallow crafts called "chop boats" or "lighters." These boats passed through a gauntlet of tollhouses on their way to Canton and were required to stop at each one, every time paying a fee (Van Dyke 2005: 22). The final leg of the journey kept the large ships too far from Canton to threaten it with cannon fire, and the entire tortuous route meant ships were unable to depart without the permission of Chinese authorities.

No European settlements or factories were allowed in China beyond Macao. Permanent residence in Chinese habitations was discouraged. It was not until the 1770s that the English were able to obtain permission for the extended residence of a small group of elite Company merchants, the supercargoes. As a rule, while Europeans stayed in Canton to conduct business, they were largely confined to official quarters and cut off from the general population. All secondary work generated by the exchange, for example, loading and unloading goods, was handled by laborers designated by port officials. The English had to use specially designated boats to load and unload goods, official translators to interact with merchants, official *compradors* (guides) to handle domestic necessities such as food and lodging, and officially chosen linguists to handle translation and communication (Van Dyke 2005: 53, 74, 77–79).

Despite these restrictions, the English were simply one of many European companies to frequent this major port. Chinese trade partners included the French, Danish, Dutch, Ostend, Portuguese, Spanish, Swedish, North Americans, Siamese, and Tonkinese, as well as traders from Cochin China, Japan, Batavia, and others. The English were interested in several commodities. In 1813, a list of goods traded at Canton in *Oriental Commerce* (1825) included tea, silk, chinaware, candy, silk goods, lacquered ware, rhubarb, sugar, nutmeg, silk thread, cloth, agate, alum, jewels, anise, copper, gold, ink, jet, musk, jewels, exotics, and more. The English imported *reals*, silver coins minted in Spanish America (Pond 1941), and mechanical trinkets called sing-songs, and later in the trade Indian cottons. Private traders dealt mainly in opium in the later years.

In order to trade, ships needed the permission of the *hoppo*, the officially appointed port and customs superintendent. Once in port, they were allowed to trade only with merchants chosen by the hoppo (Van Dyke 2005: 11). The merchants in charge of foreign trade were known as the Hong. They were often of Fujian descent and originally had been itinerant merchants involved in the junk trade (Cheong 1997: 33). Their orientation shifted as the European trade grew in importance. The English Company conducted most of their trade with one or two merchants. From 1703 to 1710 Linqua and Anqua supplied most goods, and in the 1720s, Suqua became the dominant figure (Van Dyke 2005: 11). However, the English Company—as well as other European companies—resented the idea of restricting their trade to a small number of officially chosen merchants. This tension haunted the China trade for the duration of the eighteenth century.

The Hong merchants wanted to enforce trade restrictions and at times entered into formal agreements in order to collectively set prices and pool money for potential losses. The hoppo was however more concerned with expanding foreign trade to meet Beijing's customs revenue requirement and increase their own income, and so those occupying the office of hoppo moved to disband these organizations relatively quickly after European complaints (Van Dyke 2005: 10, 20). In any case, formal restrictions seemed to have only a limited impact on the English Company, who frequently circumvented restrictions designating with whom they were to trade (Cheong 1997: 61, 94–96, 110). In fact, the Hong merchants themselves were usually recruited from the ranks of merchants illicitly engaging in foreign trade (Cheong 1997: 92, 97).

In order to accommodate the restrictive regulations in Canton, the English Company had to alter their standard operating procedure. Instead of establishing a factory—which was not allowed—the Company employed "supercargoes." The position of supercargo was a very prestigious title within the Company. They handled all commercial transactions associated with ships' cargo while in Canton. In other ports, factors performed similar duties. In the early stages of the China trade, the English were not allowed to reside in Canton, so supercargoes oversaw one ship at a time. Over time, the Council of Supercargoes was formed, so that one English ship would not undercut another. These councils were groups of three or four supercargoes that arrived on board different ships at the same time. Gradually, and when permitted by Chinese authorities, supercargoes took up residence in Canton—sometimes banished to Macao—and formed a permanent group overseeing all Anglo-Sino trade. After 1770, this group was formally constituted as twelve resident English merchants who oversaw all the Company's commercial interactions (Cheong 1997: 109).

Despite the unusual amount of centralization on the part of the Chinese and English, the private trade flourished. There were ample smuggling opportunities along the long passage to Canton, to which authorities were very willing to turn a blind eye with proper remuneration (Van Dyke 2005: 117–40). Opium was banned from the English Company trade at the request of the Chinese authorities and fell almost entirely into the hands of the English private traders. The early historian of the English trade in Canton, Morse, recorded that the Company allowed generous private trade privileges on early voyages, as part of an incentive to negotiate the difficulties of breaking into the protected markets of Canton (Morse 1926: 73). Morse also found documentation that the captain of the *Lynn* had a cargo of private trade in Canton valued at £3,744 in 1729 (Morse 1926: 74). The employee private trade did not diminish and probably increased in importance over time, as it became an important source of capital for both the Company and the Hong merchants (Cheong 1979: 9).

In Canton, the English faced a stable environment after the 1683 opening of trade. Despite many political shocks in the mainland, the steady expansion of trade in Canton ground on through the eighteenth century (Cranmer-Byng and Wills 2011: 222). Other Europeans were present, but the powerful Chinese government regulated any potential for conflict. A tremendous variety of quality goods were available, and tea was exclusive to China. Commercial sophistication was extremely high, but the strict government regulation of foreign trade was easily the most salient characteristic of Canton for the English. Strict regulation, however, was surrounded by and perhaps supported by informal and illicit activities. Regulations seem to have been routinely flouted by both the Chinese and English merchants. As a result, trade in Canton was centralized in name only. In actual fact, ample opportunities for private trade seemed to grow over time. The historian W. E. Cheong believed that by the 1790s the English Company was actively participating in the appointment of new Hong merchants that had been private trade partners of their employees in the past—exactly because they could handle the demands of both the Company and private trade (Cheong 1997: 92). Despite outward appearances, it was a robust environment for the English Company's hybrid mode of trade.

BATTICALOA: ROYAL MONOPOLY

Batticaloa was similar to Canton. Overseas trade was centralized and entirely in the control of the elite; however it lacked many of the other advantages of China. As a result, the English had little incentive to accommodate the needs of the port by restructuring its organization. The mismatch between the Company and port eventually caused trade relations to fail.

Batticaloa sits very near the center of the east coast of Ceylon. In the eyes of the English Company directors, prospects for trade with Batticaloa were initially bright. The Company attempted to initiate trade with Ceylon for good reason: it was an abundant natural setting rich in resources with a long history of overseas trade (Bastiampillai 1995: 79–95). Europeans, who frequently complained about the noxious fumes and evil airs of the majority of East Indies ports, considered the island a paradise. Elephants filled the jungle and were in high demand in the court circles of India. Sapinwood, rice, honey, wax, areca, shells, rubies, pearls, shells, cat's-eye, topaz, tourmaline, and sapphires were naturally plentiful. The cinnamon produced there was known as the highest quality available in the world. In the history of Asian trade, Ceylon occupied a central position in a thriving commercial network linking Persia, Gujarat, Malabar, Coromandel, Bengal, and Siam. However, foreign merchants handled this trade. Muslim merchants from India traveled to Ceylon in order to bring goods back to the mainland (Arasaratnam 1967: 110–11, Schrikker 2007: 18). These foreign merchants bought goods directly from the king. A royal monopoly on trade included cinnamon (Schrikker 2007: 18), elephants, areca, and pearls (Pieris and Naish 1920: 29–31, 171, 186)—by far the largest exports produced by the island. Products were gathered, prepared, and transferred to the king's warehouses in Colombo. A system of royal villages produced necessities and goods for the king and court society. The economic organization closely approximated an ideal-typical redistributive economy.

Since the state appropriated surplus revenue, indigenous merchants were not needed to circulate goods. The island was organized by caste and predominantly Hindu, although state elites later converted to Buddhism. There were fisherman who engaged in some coastal trade (Arasaratnam

1985: 44), but no dedicated merchant caste (Loten 1935: 27–31). Different castes were assigned to produce different goods for royal export. For example, the *Chalia* caste prepared cinnamon by scraping it from the bark of a small plant. Families were allotted *pangu*, parcels of land. Each plot was a mixture of several types of land (high, low, and waste), arranged so that the families could produce a variety of goods in order to supply their own needs. No standing army existed. Instead, certain plots of land were attached to the responsibility to serve as soldier. Individuals who lived or farmed on that land did so with the understanding that they would serve if called (Pieris and Naish 1920: 37). Despite caste differentiation, specialization was low.

Without exchange relations across communities, there was little social infrastructure in place to guide and regulate relationships between strangers—such as those that occur in foreign trade. Justice was administered locally, by village elders—but only the king had the power of life or death. A common punishment was to force the offender to sit on the ground, draw a circle around them, and forbid them to cross the line (Pieris and Naish 1920: 187)—an inadequate means of dealing with foreign trade disputes. Most ports had a complex of rules and regulations in place to deal with the problems specific to foreign trade and cross-cultural exchange. Sinhalese society largely lacked such rules. Although elites were equipped to do overseas business, most of Sinhalese society lacked the experience, habits, or customs necessary for regular trade (Arasaratnam 1985: 44). It is worth noting, however, that this lack of institutional infrastructure did not stop other Europeans from establishing permanent bases.

When the English landed as traders in 1716, the Portuguese had already come and gone. The Portuguese arrived in Ceylon in 1510. Many individual Portuguese stayed on the island making money as mercenaries for different elite factions in a constant stream of succession battles over the kingship (Pieris and Naish 1920: 38–63). By 1597 they began in earnest to take territorial possession of the island. The Portuguese won a large victory when they were able to appoint a soldier to a large Sinhalese kingship. Dom Jeronymo de Azavedo assumed the title "The King of Ceilam," and quickly assumed the privileges and ritual status of the late Sinhalese King Dharmapala: "He was saluted with prostrations, and the White Shield and Parasol of Sovereignty accompanied him on his progress through the country" (Pieris and Naish 1920: 140). This kingdom did not initially include the East of Ceylon, which is where Batticaloa is located, though the Portuguese did eventually establish a small fort there near the year 1602.

By 1658 the Dutch had ousted the Portuguese, taking over where they had left off, exacting taxes and jealously guarding the royal monopoly. Some of the lasting contributions of the Dutch and Portuguese were to introduce Christianity to the island and make life and trade difficult for Muslim merchants. The Dutch considered this harassment an integral part of a policy intended to encourage the growth of their colonies (Van Goens 1932: 8). By chasing other traders off the island, either through monopoly practices, strict regulations, or some unstable combination of the two, most historians specializing in the area agree that they made prosperity a distant goal for their own struggling merchants by damaging Ceylon's position in the wider East Indian trade network (Arasaratnam 1985: 51, 1967: 110, Schrikker 2007: 34–35).

By the mid-eighteenth century, when the English attempted trade with Batticaloa, the Dutch had taken over much of Ceylon, but had yet to extend their dominion to the eastern coasts. Batticaloa was located in what was known as a wild area of Ceylon inhabited by smugglers and *mocquas*. Dutch relations with the mocquas were strained (Van Goens 1932: 44). The land had formally reverted to the king of Kandy, a powerful inland sovereign, after the expulsion of the Portuguese. It was not until 1766, after the English had already departed, that the Dutch were able to force the king of Kandy's hand and take possession of the Eastern coastal areas. Still Dutch activities across the island affected Batticaloa. Muslim merchants had retained a small presence in Batticaloa, but they were subject to increased duties and petty restrictions intended to harass and discourage their commercial endeavors (Arasaratnam 1985: 51).

There are very few records surrounding the establishment of the English factory at Batticaloa. Farrington's *Catalogue of East India Company Ships' Journals and Logs* reports that Company ships docked at the port in 1716 and 1749. It is unclear which trip was the basis for the establishment of the factory. Foreign trade had been controlled by the ruling elite and handled by itinerant merchants. Local markets and merchants were absent on a large scale. The English factory eventually failed. Commercial sophistication was low. There was an abundance of goods; however, no brokers were available to handle exchange between the English traders and village farms. This lack was itself the product of the political economy of the port. The Sinhalese economic system had a redistributive form. Foreign trade was centralized, first by Sinhalese elites, then by the Portuguese, and then by the Dutch. Not until the English Company reorganized along colonial lines was it able to effectively channel goods out of the area. In the meantime, encounters between the decentralized English and centralized Sinhalese caused frustration for both sides.

## NEW GUINEA: UNREGULATED RECIPROCITY

In the ports described above, decentralization figures prominently in the fortunes of the English East India Company and its private traders. The relative autonomy of merchants in Madras and Bantam greatly encouraged the private trading of the English. In Madagascar, the centralization of control over foreign trade decreased over time, encouraging the presence of the English Company. In Canton, centralized government control excluded private traders, but informal and even illegal markets sprang up to fill the void. In Batticaloa, centralization led to the failed trade relations. New Guinea illustrates a different sort of problem for the English Company. In New Guinea there was a tremendous amount of decentralization; however there was also a lack of commercial sophistication and no evidence of the financial institutions that formed the bases of the thriving commercial societies in China, Java, and across the Indian Subcontinent.

In January of 1760, Captain Thomas Baddison piloted his ship, the *Princess Augustus*, into the straits of New Guinea. He anchored near land and sent boats ashore for firewood. On Saturday, January 7, the purser recorded the following passage:

> At 4pm a prow came aboard. In it were some Malay people who called themselves Janas. They had nothing with them but three or four hundred rotting nutmegs. They told us they came from a town to the northwest of us and going away promised to return again and bring some hogs and turtles with them. They were fearful of coming on board at first, enquiring much if we were Dutch or Spaniards and were much rejoiced when they understood we were English. (East India Company 1760)

On February 9, at the same port of call, the purser again recorded the activities of the day:

> At 3pm four prows came on board. They were Papuas. They brought a large turtle weighing 300. . . . They had nothing else but cajan matts and bows and arrows which they would sell. They set a great value on these things and would sell very dear. They wanted us much to go with the ship to their town, where they said they would bring plenty of hogs and turtles. They said there was good anchoring ground, twenty fathoms, and no shoal or rocks. . . . One of them mistook us so far on enquiring for hogs, he went onshore and brought six dogs. (East India Company 1760)

These passages offer a wealth of information hidden between the lines. They portray a stereotypical encounter between civilized Westerners and primitive locals. This superficial trope obscures less readily apparent evidence in the passage of considerable sophistication on the part of the Papuans. First, we might consider that the Papuans met the boat. They were out trolling for the English with their goods. They spoke English. It would be impossible to mistake hogs for dogs if they did not. They were surprisingly knowledgeable about the anchoring requirements for European ships and measured depth in fathoms. However the English simply passed through without returning. This time it was the English who were dissatisfied with the prospects for trade.

Given the effort and knowledge of the Papuans, why did trade fail? Unfortunately, the logs of the voyage do not record exactly where in New Guinea the *Princess Augustus* laid anchor, and so it is difficult to discuss the social organization of the group they encountered. Most research on New Guinea focuses on the highland areas and the Eastern littoral, home to the Kula Ring. If Malaysians were present, there must have been overseas trade—although it did not figure prominently in any larger overseas network (to China, for example). Despite its relative isolation, communities in New Guinea have been commercially active, entrepreneurial, and known for their skill in trade and negotiation for centuries; however trade was always subordinate to a larger system of status and prestige. Strict rules of reciprocity made gift exchange into the basis of a highly organized stratification system that based social status on participation in exchange rituals (Malinowski 1984, Strathern 1971, Schieffelin 1981). Goods were valued according to internal rules of exchange and traded as part of efforts to enhance local prestige.

The purser made special note of the fact that he believed the Papuans sold much too dear. Because exchange was not oriented toward the accumulation of material wealth, but rather in order to regulate social status, goods were not priced through markets but instead had a ritual value. The accumulation of prestige drove exchange, so the items were often jewels, headdresses, and pieces of adornment valued disproportionately to their use. This pricing scheme was a major barrier to trade: the two sides were not able to settle. The coordination between status-based and market pricing systems was a serious problem—thus the failure to reach a mutually agreeable price.

This bargaining failure could have resolved itself over time if a second condition had been fulfilled. The purser also records being distinctly unimpressed by both the amount and quality of the goods. Because goods were produced for ritual exchange, which had circumscribed limits, there was little reason to produce a surplus of the particular goods the English found valuable. There simply were not enough goods available to make it worth the English Company's time.

Perhaps if New Guinea had not been politically fragmented, a big man, as men of influence within the tribes were called, would have been able to mobilize enough of the population to produce the surplus required to attract the English—but it may not have solved the barriers to trade created by the subordination of commerce to social organization. New Guinea had one of the essential ingredients for a lasting relationship with the Company and its private trading employees—multiple opportunities to trade.

However, it was too decentralized. Individuals were willing to trade, but there was no large-scale market for goods. Merchants and traders did not exist as a separate class. Exchange was so well integrated into the internal dynamics of these societies, there was no external market. Therefore production of goods was limited to the subsistence needs of the villagers and the ceremonies of ritual exchange. There simply was not a sufficient quantity of goods to satisfy the large-scale interests of the Company itself. There was a lack of institutions to deal with the special needs of traveling merchants, and the negotiation of prices posed endless difficulties across cultural boundaries. In the end, the demands of intercontinental trade simply could not be sustained. The English Company departed despite the best efforts of the Papuans.

### GOA: PORTUGUESE COLONY

Contrary to accounts of animosity between the great European companies trading in the East, the English found plentiful opportunities to trade with other Europeans. The Portuguese were no exception. Goa was an extremely cosmopolitan city before and after Portuguese occupation. It sat in the center of a tremendously productive region of India and had long been a hub in the system of trade crisscrossing the Indian Ocean and reaching at its extremes to the shores of the Mediterranean and China. Commercial sophistication was high and there was a thriving class of independent merchants available for trade. It should be no surprise then that the English found it very profitable to visit Goa with frequency.

Goa had long been known as a city of beauty and wealth. It sits on the Deccan Coast of the Indian Subcontinent. The reputation it now has for an exotic luxury resort has been passed down through the centuries. In 1512 Tome Pires wrote of the many travelers who visited Goa to relax in its orchards and chew the locally grown betel leaves (a mild stimulant), which he claimed were the finest in the world. He also noted the presence of beautiful women and fine dancing (Pires 1944: 57). Goa was considered more temperate than most of India, and therefore more pleasant. Strong walls circled the city, which was filled with lush gardens amply supplied with sweet-tasting water. However the arrival of large contingents of unemployed and poor Portuguese soldiers made it into a dangerous city over the course of the sixteenth century (Pearson 1996: 26–27).

The Portuguese strategy in the East had been to capture key ports from which they could control the overseas trade of the Indian Ocean by sheer force. To this end they took and held Columbo, Malacca, Hormuz, Diu, and Goa. Goa was the centerpiece of this string of ports, the shining jewel of the Crown, and the capital of Portuguese colonial possessions in the

East. Well before the Portuguese arrived it was a prominent transshipment area, mediating trade between the interior of the Indian Subcontinent and the coastal regions of Africa, and the Middle East. The buying and selling of Arabian horses, a crucial military commodity, was considered to be the most important market. One could also find areca, calico, fine muslin, betel (of course), rice, and the many spices of the East Indies.

The sheltered island had been fought over by many different empires over the centuries. The population was a diverse religious mixture of Hindus, Muslims, Jews, Parsis, and Christians (even before the Portuguese arrived), and many different nationalities, including Turks, Persians, Abyssinians, and Kurds. Foreign trade revenues and anchorage fees were traditional sources of government revenue. Under the command of Afonso de Albuquerque, the Portuguese took the port in 1510 with high hopes of maintaining its privileged position in the larger Indian Ocean trade network.

The Portuguese maintained their hold over Goa, but their entry was a blow to the trade of the port. As a general rule they established royal monopolies at all their ports. Goa was no exception until faltering finances around the 1570s led the Estado to experiment with various degrees of private participation in trade. The monopoly guarding the spice trade between Goa and Lisbon was leased out to various parties beginning in 1576, and the incorporated Portuguese Company arrived in port after 1628. Neither had much effect on Goa's commercial decline.

The Portuguese both interfered with and relied upon the existing commercial and financial structures of the port. As part of their attempt to convert all inhabitants to Christianity, the Portuguese banished Hindus from the port in 1653 (Scammel 1988: 477–78). Just as in Antwerp, this religious intolerance had a devastating effect on the financial life of the city. The Portuguese backpedaled by making numerous exceptions in order to retain the skilled workers that kept the economy of the port alive as well as the wealthier Hindu merchants who were now keeping the colony afloat with their loans to the local Portuguese government. Such halfhearted interference was typical as the Portuguese depended entirely upon the existing population for financing, trade, production, as well as for men to man their ships and armies (Scammel 1988: 477–78).

The English Company first approached Goa in 1635 and established amicable relations between the Company and the Portuguese Estado. Entrepreneurial English captains disembarked at Goa, en route for an English factory, in order to quickly unload arrack as part of a private commercial scheme. As the Estado waned in the seventeenth century, Goa's fortunes diminished as well. Overseas trade had mostly died out by 1670 (Scammel 1988: 477). And the English stopped coming as well. When it was still a viable port, the English had been very happy to frequent Goa—almost exclusively in order to engage in the private trade. The Portuguese did not repel the English. Far from it. They were a ready market for European goods, which was surprisingly difficult to find in the East. However, when the money ran out, due to Portuguese policies, no one found much use for the trade prospects in the once bustling city.

## BATAVIA: DUTCH COLONY

Batavia was a large Dutch port located on the northwest coast of Java. As with Goa, sporadic hostilities between the European sea powers did not prevent the English from frequenting the harbors of Batavia. The private trade of the English flourished there, despite the best efforts of Dutch officials—in their official capacity. Unofficially, Dutch Company officials, Dutch free men, and Batavian citizens of all kinds participated in a flourishing illicit market in Eastern goods and financial services, which included the English Company servants. In many ways the external appearance of Batavian society was far removed from the daily realities of the port.

Batavia was founded on the site of a once prosperous trade city, Sunda Kalapa. In the early sixteenth century, the powerful Sultan of Bantam took the city by force and renamed it Jayakarta, meaning "great victory." Under the subordination of Bantam, Jayakarta's prosperity diminished. In 1610 the Prince of Jayakarta made an ill-considered decision to collaborate with the Dutch as part of an attempt to split from the Sultan. By March 1619, the Dutch had managed to take possession of the port and renamed it Batavia in honor of their homeland.

Many would attribute this success to the genius of Jan Pieterszoon Coen, the first governor-general of Batavia. His life captures some of the contradictions and complexities of the Dutch commercial empire in the East and life in Batavia. On the one hand, he engineered an innovative multilateral commercial strategy for the Dutch East India Company; on the other he presided over the slaughter of over fifteen thousand Bandanese in an attempt to install a strict monopoly over the Spice Islands. From Europe, the Dutch East India Company seemed like a modern marvel, the first joint-stock, limited-liability corporation. In the East, it had the aspect of a tyrannical and violent despot. This second face was not reserved for Asian communities, but bore down upon company employees and the Dutch citizens of Batavia. By all accounts, the company ruled with an iron fist and little regard for due process or personal rights, despite the outward semblance of Dutch democratic institutions (Blussé 1986: 5).

The Dutch community in Batavia was known for taking the excesses of conspicuous consumption to new levels of fastidious observation. Sumptuary laws regulated details of dress down to the type of shoe buckle to be worn at by men at different levels of employment, and only Christians could wear shoes. The wives of Dutch merchants, often Portuguese-speaking Christians of Indian descent, paraded around town under parasols attended by a clutch of slaves with the object of publicly signaling wealth and status (Abeyasekere 1937: 37).

Outside the townhouses a virulent environment had been created within the city walls. When taken from the Prince of Jayakarta, Batavia was rebuilt in the Dutch model, with sixteen canals and high townhouses framing the waterways. By 1730 this arrangement had created an exceptionally pestilent environment. The canals became stagnant breeding grounds for mosquitoes. High-standing residences blocked fresh air and winds. These conditions led to Batavia's reputation as a diseased city. Travelers complained of insalubrious conditions, "low, hanging poisonous mists," and "killing vapors." The hospital was known as *De Moordkuil*, or the death pit (Blussé 1986: 29).

It is perhaps unsurprising then that the Company had difficulty attracting a small number of free Dutch small businessmen to provide services for the Company employees. These men seem to have been mostly occupied with bartending, brewing, and tavern keeping. The Company had a love-hate relationship with these men. They desired a prosperous Dutch commercial class in Batavia, but hated giving them the means to prosper—specifically unrestricted access to engage in overseas trade. Many of the men responded to these conditions by participating in corrupt practices and the extensive informal trade of the city (Blussé 1986: 20, 95). This trade was another manifestation of the dual nature of the city. Although bound by strict regulations, the rules in this case seem to have been made to be broken. Company servants and residents alike engaged in private trade that directly violated the rules of the Dutch Company (Kathirithamby-Wells 1977: 8).

The illegitimate trade of the Dutch employees acted as a strong draw for the English. A central problem in premodern trade was transferring large amounts of money over long distances. The East India Companies were the only large organizations truly capable of remitting large amounts of money from Asia to Europe. This meant that private traders had to rely upon the companies to get their profits back to Europe. For the Dutch employees—strictly prohibited from engaging in any kind of private trade—this was a serious obstacle. For the English it proved to be a golden opportunity. For a large fee, they would happily facilitate the transfer of funds through their own East India Company, which did not prohibit the pursuit and accumulation of profits through the private trade. Thus the English played an important if dubious role in the economy of Batavia (Adams 1996: 23–24).

A large Chinese community in Batavia was the only part of the population legally allowed to engage in overseas trade outside of the auspices of the Dutch Company. Ironically, this one concession in the end contributed directly to the downfall of Batavia and the Company itself. In the seventeenth century, Europeans had difficulty establishing direct trade with China. As described in the section on Canton, the Chinese strongly discouraged contact with foreign barbarians, which they understood the Europeans to be. Initially then, the large Chinese community in Batavia was a great boon to the port. The expatriate Chinese were deeply embedded in the south China trade network. Their boats, the junk fleets, brought difficult-to-obtain Chinese goods, such as silks, sugar, porcelain, iron pans, nails, needles, umbrellas (in high demand in Batavia), paper, fruit, and textiles, into the port at a very low cost. In fact, the Dutch profited from the variety of fees charged to incoming ships, including anchorage fees, safe conduct passes (a trick from the Portuguese notebook), import and export fees, gifts for the harbormaster, gifts for the revenue collector, gifts for the secretaries, and gifts for the cashier as well. By the eighteenth century, the China trade had become hugely important to all the European East Indies companies. Unfortunately for the Dutch, relations with the Chinese community in Batavia deteriorated over the years. In 1740 the Chinese population in Batavia revolted against the Dutch government. This revolution was put down with characteristic brutality and most of the Chinese population was either killed or expelled from the island of Java. Although the community eventually rebuilt itself, Dutch participation in the Chinese trade was gravely diminished in the meantime (Blussé 1986: 115).The Chinese massacre was only one more tragic debacle in a history of decline for Batavia. The port, however, was a center of trade. Chinese and Dutch merchants brought a high level of commercial sophistication. The trade in remittances, which at that time was a relatively complex commercial transaction, helped bring the English participation into the economy of the port. Although the Dutch Company attempted to regulate the commercial activities of its employees and achieve a complete centralization of overseas trade, they failed to achieve this goal. Instead there was rampant private trade and illicit commercial activity. This de facto decentralization drew the English into many repeated visits to Batavia over the course of the seventeenth and eighteenth centuries.


## CONCLUSION

The growth of the English Company's trade in Asia was not simply British expansion; it was the integration of the English and several Asian economic and social systems. The failure of trade in Batticaloa demonstrates the necessity of looking at both sides of the story. The English were decentralized, the Sinhalese were not. If the English Company had been more hierarchical, it would have been more successful at ports like Batticaloa. Other European companies, such as the Dutch and Portuguese, were in fact much more successful in Ceylon. Conversely, if a class of merchants willing to work with the English had been present in Batticaloa, they should have been able to provide the English with points of access into local production networks.

While at port, factors and captains managed the Company's trade as well as their own, while the officers and crew looked after their own interests. All levels of the organizational hierarchy sought commercial partnership. However, trade is two-sided. For English Company employees to engage in profitable transactions, they needed potential partners. In the example of the Batticaloans, we see that the local community lacked the set of customary practices, religious rituals, or commercial experience that would have allowed them to easily create market relationships with external groups. It is therefore unsurprising that the English did not remain. No merchant class existed in Batticaloa to serve as partners for both the principals and the agents of the English trade.

The Company sent their East Indiaman ships to 264 ports in the East Indies. If all Eastern ports had resembled Batticaloa, the Company would have had to either curb its employees' private trading activities or withdraw from the trade. Because the private trade of the employees was important to the long-term success of the Company, the first path would have spelled eventual failure as well. Without the private traders, the Company would have lost vital local knowledge and the initiative to explore new port and tradable goods. England's sustained expansion into Eastern markets and subsequent commercial and political hegemony might have never occurred without this early fit between firm operations and the structure of opportunity in Eastern ports. The institutions and ports of the East helped to shape the organization of the East India Company itself.

*Chapter 7*

# EASTERN INSTITUTIONS
# AND THE ENGLISH TRADE

The contribution of Eastern ports to the nature of the English trade in the East becomes clear when the entire set of ports included in the Company trade is considered. In this chapter, I categorize the 264 ports recorded in the logs of the English East India Company ships into the types described in the previous chapter to uncover regular patterns of English interactions with the Eastern ports. Looking across these larger patterns reveals that the English were consistently drawn to commercially sophisticated societies with decentralized market institutions. As in Batticaloa, centralized trade in ports blocked off avenues of opportunity to private traders through formal prohibitions. New Guinea simply lacked adequate market institutions. The ports that were both commercially sophisticated and decentralized sustained the English private trade. The decentralized ports of the East reinforced the decentralization of the firm. Their contribution was indispensable to the rapid and sustained expansion of the English trade network.

## A BRIEF TOUR OF THE EAST INDIES

The categories explored in the previous chapter capture the main types of trading cities in the East; however there was a great deal of variation even within these types. Here I explore the variation within categories, provide more descriptive material about the different ports, and record in abbreviated form the basis for port assignments into the different institutional categories: that is, market, royal monopoly, regulated market, and so on. Each of the 264 ports was evaluated on a region-by-region or, as necessary, a port-by-port basis. Some regions had considerably more heterogeneity than others. For example, the Indonesian Archipelago had a unique mixture of entrepôts, échelles, principalities, dependencies, and European colonies. In areas with greater heterogeneity, I considered the ports and kingdoms that constituted this complex of distinct societies. If a regional description is accurate, I consider it sufficient. For example, China was a cohesive political unit. In this case, there is no reason to further explore this categorization beyond the description of Canton.

A number of ports do not vary significantly from the institutional structure described in the ideal-typical accounts given in the case histories. Zanzibar and Pemba resembled Ceylon. These islands were part of a system of Swahili city-states that dotted the coastal areas of East Africa. Swahili elites were often in conflict with the Portuguese and were eventually replaced by Omani elites.[1] Trade resided in the hands of these shifting ruling classes and had left most of the population untouched. If anything, the lower classes were even further removed from commercial life than in Ceylon, although the role of the lower classes in production (rather than trade) is unclear (Gilbert 2002: 20). Most evidence indicates that elite traders made profits off of transshipped goods and by participating in a carrying trade; their activities were limited to importing goods from one place, often the African coast and interior, and shipping them to another, the Middle East or Indian Subcontinent. This sort of intermediate trade made links between elites and resident populations unnecessary for commerce since extensive production of goods was not part of the equation. Similarly, a vast peasantry was excluded from foreign trade in the kingdom of Ayutthaya (now Thailand) (Evers 1987: 757, 764). In Sulu, a fascinating system has been documented by Francis Warren. Elites used the profits and weapons derived from an exclusive foreign trade to extend their political base, while employing extortionate practices that dampened internal trade (Warren 1981: 37, 41). These societies had the same redistributive structure and centralized control of trade as Batticaloa. They were *royal monopolies*.

Persia transitioned from a royal monopoly, under Shah Abbas I (1587–1629), to an open trade policy under Shah Safi (r. 1629–42) (Ferrier 1973: 41). After the accession of Shah Safi, Persian ports had a high incidence of developed commercial institutions and readily available autonomous brokers, traders, bankers, and moneylenders, many of whom were Armenian. Much of India had similar institutions and policies. Ports in these areas are classified as *market societies*. Gujurat and Bengal, conquered by the Mughals in 1573 and 1576, were perhaps the most commercially developed areas of India. Bengal exported indigo, hemp, minerals, lac, opium, cotton goods, saltpeter, silk, sugar, various provisions, and other goods. By at least the eighteenth century, various regions in Bengal specialized in one or more goods and were linked together into a larger economy through a system of interlocking markets (Marshall 1987: 13). Gujaratis and *Baniyas* (or *banyans* as they were known to the English) were renowned traders who operated in these areas. Baniyas were known for internal rifts and competition rather than the organized political front presented by other merchant groups (for example the Armenians) (Barendse 1998: 179). They acted as brokers, overseas merchants, moneylenders (small capital), and bankers (big capital) in ports and cities across the northwest and east of the Indian Subcontinent.

Brokers did not arise as a class to service the needs of Europeans—who rarely mastered local languages. They were absolutely necessary to the European trade in India, serving as an essential link to local producers and distributors, but their existence as a group far predated the European presence in the East. They worked with both seaman and captains by linking them to networks of producers and moneylenders. Factors complained that banyans were ruining young recruits by haunting the harbors, waiting to ensnare naive Englishmen in risky ventures, high-interest loans, and luxurious living the moment they stepped off the boat (Barlow and Lubbock [1703] 1934: 186).

There were many other types of merchants involved in commerce across India. As should be expected, overseas traders were a cosmopolitan group. Most ports in the area played home to the familiar Muslim merchants, as well as Hindu *Vaniyas*, Tamil and Teluga *Chettis*, Jews, Turks, Armenians, and recent Christian converts (Subrahmanyam 1995: 755). Below Gujarat, dense settlements littered the Konkan. The English frequented Dabhol, Karwar, and Rajapur, among others. In these areas, indigenous communities of Saraswat-brahmin and coastal fisherman participated in overseas trade (Barendse 1998: 327–30).

Farther south the situation became patchier. A number of small independent kingdoms on the coast differed from the Mughal and Vijayanagar systems. Large empires tended to depend on land revenues and rural agricultural production. Small coastal kingdoms often relied on commercial revenues and therefore created open cities for merchants. Others formed close political ties with one merchant group, often Muslims, erecting barriers to entry for others. I will discuss this situation as a variant of the royal monopoly form.

Sumatra was another varied and complex region, portions of which were Dutch colonial, royal monopolies, and others had an underdeveloped market structure that was vulnerable to disruption. Three major groups composed the layered social organization of the island. The first layer, a sultanate, was superimposed over a preexisting Malay social structure. The sultan demanded rents from the village leaders (*peroatin*). The villages, the second layer, had an egalitarian structure and loose organization. Villagers were not accustomed to landlords or direct taxation. The majority of the inhabitants were rice or pepper producers. In these groups, control over surplus goods was tied to village status, a situation that complicated English attempts to interact directly with village leaders (Kathirithamby-Wells 1977: 32). Essentially, interference at this level—in the form of trade or extortion—threatened the basis of legitimate authority within the group. Subsequent breakdowns in social order had adverse consequences for external trade as well as negative internal consequences for Sumatran communities. Coastal villages also hosted the third major Sumatran social group: Islamic immigrants of Riau Malay, Javanese, or Bugi descent. These were residents of the island, not traveling merchants. They engaged in small crafts production, fished, and acted as merchants. They were literate, skilled, and well-integrated traders available as intermediaries for the English.

That is, until the English attempted to cut out the middlemen and radically centralize market operations in Sumatra. In making this decision, the English appeared to be aping the Dutch method of monopolistic control used in nearby Batavia or following the pattern established by the Acehnese (Kathirithamby-Wells 1969). In any case, they did not find success in this manner. In their West Sumatran settlements, the English uncharacteristically established themselves as colonial rulers, then used their power to implement a system of forced cultivation.[2] Part of their plan was to require every household in the villages under their control to plant two thousand pepper vines (Bastin 1965: xv). Unsurprisingly, the English did not have the military power to sustain this sort of operation. In March 1719 the Sumatrans forced them off the island. They were eventually let back into their settlements; however the port never achieved much success. Conditions in these ports did not conform to the situation in which the English Company thrived. Instead, this misguided attempt at centralization created conflict on two fronts. Eliminating the middlemen led to widespread local resentment and a destabilization of the existing village power structure. And second, attempting to regulate and control all commercial transactions infringed on employee interests. The monopoly conditions the Company attempted to create in Sumatra left few private trading options. The result was one of the most openly corrupt English factories in the East (Bastin 1961: 154–55, Kathirithamby-Wells 1977: 152).

The English were more successful in the prosperous set of *open cities* that closely resembled Bantam. A few of these cities were independent kingdoms in their own right, Calicut for example. The ruling *Zamorins* had turned that port into a major transshipment area. Merchants dealt in pepper, cinnamon, ginger, coconuts, timber, sugar, rice, areca, textiles, opium, and ambergris. The majority of royal revenues came from customs on overseas trade in these goods. Other similarly structured commercial hubs of the East were Aceh (politically and economically distinct from, though related to, the majority of other Sumatran settlements), Aden, Bandar Abbas, Basra, Hormuz, Johore, Kedah, Malacca, Muscat, Mokha, Jiddah, Quang Nam, Quilon (Kollam), and Banjarmassin.

A number of these open cities fell under the rule of the Ottoman and Safavid Empires. The Ottoman dynasty ruled over a slightly larger area than what we now know of as Turkey. The Safavid Empire was once better known as Persia. Both the Safavid and Ottoman empires depended largely on trade to fill government coffers. They had abundant resources to draw on as they commanded the overland route between Asia and Europe as well as many of the key Asian ports listed above.

Japan remains the best-known case of outright hostility to foreign traders. The commercial organization of external trade resembled that of China. It was a *regulated market*. The isolationism of the Japanese has become part of popular myth. It is less well known that the Japanese continued to trade with the Dutch at Hirado from 1609 to 1641 and at Nagasaki from 1641 until the end of the eighteenth century (Glamann 1981: 168), although all trade was conducted under brutally enforced regulations. In the early sixteenth century a group of Jesuits had visited Japan and succeeded in converting a small proportion of the population to Christianity. The Japanese shogun perceived their success as a threat.[3] In response, he ordered the crucifixion of twenty-six men, many of whom were Jesuits, for the crime of proselytizing.

The shogun's suspicions extended to all Christians, fearing they would attempt similar conversion efforts. European merchants were therefore subject to strict surveillance and cordoned off from the local population. The Dutch persisted under these difficult, and at times threatening, conditions in order to procure a steady stream of Japanese silver. In all likelihood the military organization of the Dutch Company better prepared them to maintain this strict separation. Shogun Tokugawa Iemitsu excluded the English from Japan in 1623 (Van Leur 1955: 172). The strict regulation of the market, which centralized trade in the hands of the few in order to reduce contact with Europeans, made it an incompatible site for the English, despite the abundant silver available at this source.

The greatest variations within one type occurred within the category of the *royal monopoly*. Many royal monopolies came into being when elites wrested control of an already profitable foreign trade from existing merchants groups. One exception to this was the Banda Islands. These islands were the sole home of the nutmeg tree, and therefore the one source of nutmeg and mace. They had long been ruled by a merchant oligarchy called the *orang kaya*. These men exercised strict control over a system of enforced cultivation. "Farmers could approach foreign buyers directly only in great secrecy" (Reid 1993: 34). In this case, state control seems to have emerged out of efforts by traders to monopolize the profits from foreign commerce (Villiers 1990: 83–106). The islands pose a fascinating case of a different evolutionary path to state construction, but displayed a similar institutional configuration as other ports with more mundane patterns of development: high centralization and moderate sophistication.

The term "royal monopoly" also describes ports where elites did not directly engage in trade, but delegated these rights to a single merchant group. For example, Safavid royals were influenced by Armenian merchants, who interacted with the empire as a well-organized merchant lobby. The merchant representative held the formal role of mayor, or *qalantar*, of Julfa. The qalantar sat at court and negotiated on behalf of the community (Barendse 1998: 64). The Armenians used this position to involve themselves in the exclusive royal trade of the Safavids for first part of the seventeenth century, effectively wielding their political power to create a merchant monopoly. However, the Dutch and English were fortunate in that, when they arrived in Persia, Armenian merchants were in the process of expanding their business networks in Northern Europe (Ferrier 1973: 44). This fact, combined with the profits that could be made from the dependent Europeans, led the Armenians to give up their monopoly in most major ports and welcome the Dutch and English into the trade (Ferrier 1973: 45). They entered into commercial partnerships with the English and Dutch, guiding their transactions and profiting as brokers and translators. The result was that open conditions were maintained for the English and Dutch at most major ports of the Safavid Empire.

A coalition of merchants from Madras was more successful in guarding their monopoly over the trade of Natal and Tapanuli Bay in Northern Sumatra. As noted in chapter 6, Madras itself was decentralized. In Natal and Tapanuli Bay, a different context with different incentives, the merchants changed their operations. As a group of foreign overseas traders barely linked into the system of production, the Madras merchants actively discouraged competition. Because they had the political support of the Sultan of Aceh and were able to centralize control of trade within their own coalition, they acted as a *royal monopoly* (Kathirithamby-Wells 1977: 156).[4] It is interesting to note that the Dutch often sought a similar position, that is, a powerful and politically embedded merchant group, as a precursor to colonial occupation. For example, their presence followed this trajectory in Jambi and Palembang, where the Dutch initially used their influence to procure a monopoly on trade in the seventeenth century.

Eastern organized merchant communities could hinder the English Company trade depending on the following conditions: their social organization, the point at which they were linked into the production of goods, and their political power. If one merchants group possessed significant political power, the first two characteristics could lead them to either restrict the Company's access to sophisticated commercial practices (i.e., those that existed within the merchant group) or exclude them (and others) from trade.

If a merchant group practiced social closure, meaning they restricted entry into or relations with the group, they made it more difficult for anyone outside of the group to enter into trade. Merchants create inward-looking coalitions for many reasons. They may form a coalition to gain monopoly power and increase profits, as was the Dutch strategy in the East Indies. They may also exclusively trade with one another in order to build trusting, durable relationships—of great value in the high-risk arena of foreign trade (Greif 1989, 1993, 1994, 2006a, 2006b). In either case, high internal cohesion inevitably discourages competition. If the English encountered highly cohesive coalition-based merchants, it decreased their ability to participate in the trade of the port. Closed merchant communities of overseas traders were not potential partners so much as threatening competitors.

The effects of cohesion, however, are mediated by the location of a group in the production chain. If merchants were located or were able to locate themselves higher up in the production chain, so that goods flowed through them on the way to English traders, the English presence brought a welcome increase in demand. For example, in the Arabian Sea only a small group of pilots had the geographic knowledge crucial to successfully pilot ships through coastal waters. Election into this group was hereditary (Barendse 1998: 12).[5] These pilots profited from increased demand for their services, so new overseas merchants were always welcome.

The position of a commercial group in the production chain often reflected the degree to which they were integrated into a host society. Transient Muslim merchant communities in Madagascar and Ceylon, as opposed to Arabian Sea pilots, were of little help to the English because their commercial activities were limited to imports and exports—which competed with English interests rather than complemented them.

When merchant groups were both organized into closed communities and closely linked to distribution rather than production, they often attempted to use political and economic connections to exclude other merchants from trade. The wealthy Gujarati trader Malik Gopinath was known for "tyrannizing the local Muslim population by using his access to the state machinery" (Subrahmanyam 1995: 765). The Gujaratis were both motivated to exclude other overseas traders and able to manipulate local politics to their advantage. These crucial characteristics, social organization and degree of political influence, depended to a large extent on underlying factors of the land-labor system and geography analyzed by J. Kathirithamby-Wells and John Villiers in Southeast Asia (1990) and by Arthur Stinchcombe (1995) in the West Indies.

Political barriers to foreign trade are closely related to two characteristics of government: the source of revenue and the degree of bureaucratic centralization. If the government has an extensive agricultural base to draw from, it is less likely to tolerate foreign merchants. If revenues are exclusively drawn from foreign commerce, officials are much more likely to extend themselves in order to draw in those merchants. This distinction rests on the difference between coastal and interior kingdoms as well as the navigability of interior waterways (or échelles versus entrepôts). In coastal polities that lack interior waterways, tax rates often go down and legal protection for merchants increases. However, groups may shift priorities over time. If the government begins to engage in the profitable overseas trade, the situation for foreign merchants may deteriorate. Conversely, state organization may arise from the aggrandizement of wealth by merchants plying their trade, as in the Banda Islands and their ruling class of merchant oligarchs, the orang kaya, meaning *rich men* (Villiers 1990: 83–106). In either case, royal monopolies can produce a thriving trade, but close off opportunities to newcomers.

In the context of the Indonesian Archipelago, productive regions often went through different cycles of elite and merchant control, varying with the territorial fortunes of rajahs and sultans, but also through the normal course of the tug-of-war found in all competitive political situations. In a large feudalistic empire, foreign merchants operate below the radar of the emperor, but well within sight of local governors. If power is decentralized, the local governor decides how to extract the highest rents, so that they may take a cut before passing along trade revenues to higher-ranking officials, producing barriers to trade. These characteristics are manifested in greater or lesser degrees of centralization in foreign trade. When overseas trade is concentrated in the hands of one elite-sanctioned merchant group, this port is classified as a royal monopoly. A full list of ports and types is presented in the appendix.

## RATES OF CONTACT

Given this quickly drawn institutional map of the East Indies, the relevant question is where the English had the greatest success. If a long-term English presence is randomly scattered across these many types, the ports themselves must have had little impact on English Company operations. If successful English factories cluster in one or two types, it indicates that those institutional configurations were better suited to the particular trade of the Englis.. Evaluating the similarities and differences across favored and unfavored ports builds a more complete picture of the kind of institutions that were amenable to the English system of decentralized organization. Table 5 presents a tabulation of visits across types produced by categorizing ports into the different institutional configurations.

If decentralization and commercial sophistication significantly affected the ability of the English to establish regular trade, the rate at which they traveled to market societies and open cities should be higher than the rate of contact with royal monopolies. There should also be less trade with

Table 5. Descriptive Statistics: Port Visits by Type

| Type | Visits |
| --- | --- |
| Market | 10,624 |
| Regulated market | 2,819 |
| Colonial, non-English | 1,704 |
| Open city | 817 |
| Regulated reciprocity | 596 |
| Royal monopoly | 346 |
| Unregulated reciprocity | 66 |
| Uninhabited | 12 |

regulated reciprocities, unregulated reciprocities, and regulated markets. These associations can be detected with a count model.[6] The data do not satisfy the strict assumptions necessary for using a Poisson model. Instead a negative binomial, which allows for overdispersion, provides a significantly better fit and has been used here. Covariates would of course be preferable, however the data available for a large proportion of these ports are extremely limited. In many cases all that was available were brief observations made in travel logs, which either stood alone (for example, if the port was uninhabited) or were supplemented with information contained in regional studies. It was not possible to locate all ports in the historical record, so I limit the analysis to the 260 ports for which I was able find information.[7] Period effects are included as controls as well as an offset variable, which controls for the total traffic within periods.[8]

Many ports transitioned between institutional types, most frequently becoming colonial ports at some point in the period under consideration. Visits are categorized by the institutional type of the port at the time of the visit, so one port may contribute visits to different categories. For example, Mauritius contributes to the count of three different incident rates. One when the island was largely uninhabited, one during the Dutch and French colonial periods, and another after the island fell into English hands. Trips to the port in the first period are counted as uninhabited, visits in the second period are counted toward the colonial category, and visits in the final period contribute to counts of the market type. Although Mauritius was an English colony in the final period, the colonial category is meant to capture interactions between the English and other European centers of control. It is also true that although trade within the Company was becoming more restricted during this later period of Mauritian history, private trade outside of the Company was encouraged. So, external conditions in Mauritius as an English colony were closer to market than monopoly conditions. The

Table 6. Market Types and Port Visits

| Type | Estimate | Z value |
| --- | --- | --- |
| Intercept | 6.909*** | 44.678 |
| Market | 1.691*** | 8.499 |
| Regulated markets | 0.2 | 1.003 |
| Open city | −0.432*** | −2.167 |
| Regulated reciprocity | −1.001*** | −5.044 |
| Royal monopoly | −1.336*** | −6.683 |
| Unregulated reciprocity | −3.36*** | −16.289 |
| Uninhabited | −4.981*** | −21.538 |
| Exploratory period | −1.358*** | 0.13 |
| Private trade period | −0.751*** | −6.213 |

*$p < .10$. **$p < .05$. ***$p < .01$.

statistical model captures the association between port type and the number of trips to port made by the ships of the East India Company and is meant to be descriptive.

It should also be noted that only those ports with which the English Company actually attempted to initiate trade are included in the model. There is reason to believe this would produce a biased sample since it is likely that the Company would have tried to initiate trade only with those ports that seemed as though they would make profitable trade partners. This bias could produce artificially high incident rates. However, the goal here is not to estimate the rate of contact at all ports—rather, it is to identify any variation that exists in the amount of time the English spent at different types of ports in the East. A bias that artificially pushes up estimates should not obscure the differences between different types of ports. The sample of ports may be considered to represent the set of known ports that the English considered candidates for potential trade.[9]

Because port types are categorical variables, one must be used as a comparison with which to build up the other estimates. In this case, colonial ports serve as the baseline for port types and the colonial period serves as a baseline for period types. This means that positive estimates indicate a higher rate of contact than experienced by colonial ports, and negative estimates indicate a rate of contact lower than that experienced by colonial ports. Table 6 presents the results in descending order of coefficient strength. As expected, the strongest positive relationship exists between market organization and trips to port. Market ports were clearly more likely to receive visits by Company ships than other port types. Regulated markets are not significant, indicating that they are not significantly different from colonial ports. Open cities are negative and significant, but at lower rates than regulated reciprocities, royal monopolies, and unregulated reciprocities, and uninhabited ports—all of which are both negative and significant.

## TRADE PARTNERS

A second way of approaching Company relations with ports is by identifying patterns of regular exchange with different ports. Some ports may have experienced short bursts of traffic, but proved to be relatively inhospitable over the long run. This pattern could produce high counts without accurately capturing durable trade relations. Therefore it is also advisable to consider whether the English Company was able to form sustained commercial relationships with ports.

In this analysis, the average time elapsed between trips of the East Indiamen to each of the ports serves as a baseline to identify abnormally long lapses between visits that would signify a break in regular trade. The median of the average time between repeat visits for each port was roughly four years.[10] Four years is also a natural cutoff point for regular trade relations with a port as it captures two shipping seasons. In this scheme, a ship may skip a port one voyage, return to it the next, and the interaction would still fit into one spell of trade. The advantage of this measure is that it incorporates considerations of both the frequency and length of trade relations. If four years pass and no East Indiamen stop at a port, the spell of regular exchange is considered complete. Another period of sustained exchange may occur with that port at a later date. Any one port may have several spells over the years of the English Company's existence as a trade organization.

Of the set of 264 ports visited by the English East Indiamen, 143 received repeat visits, or entered into spells of regular trade with the English Company.[11] The average spell is thirty-five years long. The longest span of regular contact with a port is just over two hundred years, with Johanna, an island off the east coast of Africa. Many ports experienced more than one spell. A total of ten ports engaged in three separate spells of trade with the Company. Fifty-one have more than one. This reflects a reality of early modern trade: it was erratic. Ports tended to drop in and out of larger networks as domestic conditions changed. This movement underscores the importance of identifying spells of trade within the timeline of a port's history with the English Company.

Table 7 reports the percentage of ports, by type, with which the English Company established one or more period of regular exchange. The categories of social organization are arranged in decreasing order by the success

Table 7. Regular Trade Spells by Port Type

| Port type | No spells | Experienced regular trade | Total ports |
|---|---|---|---|
| Open city | 19% (3) | 81% (13) | 16 |
| Market | 46% (48) | 54% (57) | 105 |
| Colonial, non-English | 47% (25) | 53% (28) | 53 |
| Regulated market | 56% (15) | 44% (12) | 27 |
| Royal monopoly | 57% (32) | 43% (24) | 56 |
| Regulated reciprocity | 66% (8) | 33% (4) | 12 |
| Uninhabited | 73% (8) | 27% (3) | 11 |
| Unregulated reciprocity | 72% (13) | 21% (5) | 18 |
| Total | 152 | 146 | 298 |

experienced by the English in creating at least one sustained bout of trade with ports of that type. The total number of cases exceeds 264 in this table because, as noted earlier, several ports transitioned between types. In these cases, the port contributes more than one observation.

Table 7 shows that the successful establishment of sustained trade occurred at much higher rates for open cities, market societies, and non-English colonial ports. Behind these were commercially sophisticated ports with strict regulations on overseas trade, the regulated markets. Another advantage of approaching the data this way is to get a sense of not only the count of trips to ports, but also the options that were available to the Company. For example, table 7 shows that the English Company attempted to initiate trade at many royal monopolies, which was a prevalent port type in Asia. Royal monopolies have the second highest number of ports visited by the Company ships: fifty-six ports with royal monopolies entered the English network at some point in the organizational history. Despite these high numbers, the English Company was less successful in establishing regular trade relations at these sites. The Company experienced regular bouts of trade with only 43 percent of these ports. Lower on the list are sites with generalized exchange systems and uninhabited islands.

Table 8 reports the average number of spells, the total number of years spent in regular exchange, and the average duration of those spells across ports types. The list is ordered by the average duration of periods of regular exchange, again in decreasing order. Market societies surpass the others on all dimensions other than average number of periods of regular exchange. This average is low because the Company rarely ended their trade at these venues. There are more ports of this type in the English network and spells of regular exchange with these ports last longer.

Table 8. Average Number of Spells, Years, and Total Years over Port Types

| Port type | Average number of spells | Total years in regular trade | Average duration of trade spells[a] |
|---|---|---|---|
| Market | 0.67 | 3,410 | 28.23 |
| Open city | 1.63 | 836.58 | 27.41 |
| Regulated reciprocity | 0.58 | 441.25 | 25.37 |
| Regulated market | 0.52 | 528 | 18.65 |
| Colonial, non-English | 0.98 | 1,620.92 | 16.17 |
| Royal monopoly | 0.55 | 476.5 | 6.65 |
| Uninhabited | 0.45 | 74.83 | 3.86 |
| Unregulated reciprocity | 0.28 | 57.58 | 3.2 |
| Total | 0.7 | 7,445.66 | 18.24 |

a. Weighted by port.

This table also reveals that although trade spells were initiated more frequently at ports with royal monopolies or those controlled by other co-lonial powers, the Company was able to form more durable relations with the comparatively unsophisticated regulated reciprocities. Market societies were not necessarily the epitome of commercial sophistication. Royal monopolies, open cities, the regulated markets of China, and colonial cities all lay claim to similar commercial practices. The key to sustaining trade with the Company, which may have come down to simply avoiding out-right conflict in many cases, lay in an institutional structure that provided some degree of equal access to markets for nonelites. The importance of the open market organization of foreign trade was the pattern of opportunity it provided for the Company and its employees.

## SOCIAL ORGANIZATION AND DECENTRALIZED TRADE

The unique success of the English Company came from the unusually strong participation in trade at all levels of the firm hierarchy. In order for lower-level actors within the Company to trade, they needed allies outside of the organization. The Company and its employees were foreign traders, so the organization of trade in their host society, the ports of the East, de-termined the availability of these allies. In a number of ports in Asia, elites controlled foreign trade. In these ports, elites traded with a select few offi-cers from the upper levels of the hierarchy, satisfying status considerations and social definitions (i.e., foreign trade is an elite activity) and ensuring their continued control over trade. Opportunities did not exist for those lower on the organizational hierarchy to engage in profitable exchange. In order to sustain the private trading interests of the employees, the key decentralizing element of the firm's organizational structure, the English needed nonelite trade partners in their host societies.

However, the needs of the agents did not entirely supersede the needs of the principal. English ships were large by the standards of the day. It took hundreds of tons of goods to fill the hold. For the Company trade to succeed, large quantities of goods had to be available for sale. Only ports with a large producing class could create the necessary amount. If the production of goods was entirely distributed, the English had neither the time nor the knowledge to collect those goods. For this, they relied on intermediate merchants with several points of access into inland systems of production.

The ready availability of sophisticated financial instruments, such as bills of exchange, and institutions, such as mints, contributed a tremendous amount to the viability of the English trade, and financial markets were essential. Both the employees and the Company often relied on capital advances from local merchants in order to conduct their business. According to William Monson, a young Company employee in Madras, "it is credit with them [Indian merchants] that enables many people to carry on the trade they do" (Mentz 2005: 209). Even Company headquarters acknowledged that "without the aid of the Capital and great Armenian merchants of Julpha [trade] is impossible" (Ferrier 1973: 55). Just like the Medici and the Fuggers, these Eastern merchants used their own vast credit networks and bills of exchange to supply the necessary capital and guarantee English loans. Their financial networks depended in turn upon their access to large-scale production processes. Typically the English deplored this situation, rather than realizing that their success depended upon it.

Lying beneath the inductive categories, the twin dimensions of decentralization and commercial sophistication drove the success or failure of English trade across the East. The eight categories vary in the way in which they combine the open or restricted market access and commercial sophistication. Ports classified as reciprocities rank low on internal economic development, but high on decentralization. Non-English European colonies formally regulated commerce, but had difficulty enforcing regulations in practice, putting them in the middle range of decentralization and mid to high on commercial sophistication. Royal monopolies often had moderate levels of commercial sophistication, but substantial variation existed within the category. Regulated markets, open cities, and markets rank high on commercial sophistication. Open cities and markets also ranked high on decentralization. Regulated markets in contrast were subject to greater centralized control of foreign trade. The variation is represented in figure 13.

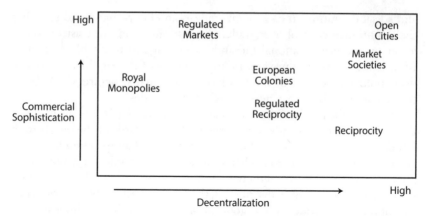

**FIGURE 13**. Port types ordered by commercial sophistication and decentralization of access to foreign trade.

## THE ENGLISH AND THE OTHER COMPANIES

Given the importance of the private trade, it makes sense that the English Company would flourish in decentralized, cosmopolitan ports, but it does not fit with the mythologized process of European expansion into unchartered territories that populated the history books for so long. More interestingly, it was not necessarily what the English Company had desired. The English Company was the only chartered European organization in the East to adopt what we would now consider to be a very reasonable strategy of pursuing largely commercial, rather than colonial, relations with populated ports. But even in the English case, this strategy was the product of organizational weakness—lack of the necessary military strength to forcibly take ports and an inability to control employees. Together, through cooperation and partnership, the English Company and the many ports it visited created a new, and very successful, type of organization.

In comparison, the Portuguese engaged in commerce, but only in order to pursue political aims. The Dutch also pursued a strategy of violent aggression in order to achieve a commercial monopoly. Both the Portuguese and Dutch Companies had rigid hierarchical organizations with strong military overtones. In contrast, in the period covered by this book, the English Company had a strained relationship with the state, low militarization, and loose control over employees' activities.[12]

The different organizational characteristics led the European companies to settle in different types of ports—ultimately creating different types of trade networks. The Portuguese did not establish new ports; they conquered existing centers of commerce. They targeted commercial hubs and used military force to turn these into territorial bases from which to tax the existing trade. The result was that their trade network consisted of a thin chain of strategically located settlements.[13] The Dutch also had a strict hierarchical, militaristic operation (Glamann 1981: 7). The center-piece of their trade strategy was coerced cultivation of goods produced for a militarily enforced monopoly. To this end, they established a strong military and colonial presence in a central hub, Batavia, from which they could oversee the production and distribution of goods within their sphere of influence. This strategy produced a star or spoke-like network of trade, in which country trade voyages radiated out from the center of power in Batavia. The network could efficiently distribute information, but was extremely vulnerable to disruption or control efforts at its center.

The English operated differently. The English Company settlements were concentrated in India. Until the late seventeenth century, these settlements were granted by local rulers—not taken by military force. They located operations in the center of thriving commercial areas, often linked by several competing merchants groups to different regional economies. Trade was usually conducted through local intermediaries who were considered partners or employees of the English Company.[14] Through the private trade of the captains, country trading networks were interwoven with the formal trade of the Company, creating new links between many different established English factories. The result was a malleable and robust decentralized network of multilateral commercial relations stretching across the East Indies.

The root of these network forms lay in structural affinities between the European companies and the ports in which they chose to settle. The Portuguese conquered cosmopolitan city-states in order to gain control of the revenues from foreign trade—in many cases already being appropriated by other elites in those same cities. The Dutch replaced agricultural empires profiting from monopsonistic control over local production—meaning they made themselves the sole buyer of goods in order to increase their power. The English sought market societies that could accommodate the needs of entrepreneurial agents with different levels of capital and commercial aptitude.

## A EUROPEAN THEATER OF WAR?

My emphasis on the decentralized organizational structure of the Company as a driving force behind the settlement patterns runs contrary to another theory of English expansion in the East. It has been argued that the English trade was structured by the attempt to avoid other Europeans. Specifically, the fear of the Dutch and Portuguese is used to account for the large number of English settlements established in the Indian Subcontinent (Bassett 1998: 3–4). In this telling, European trade in the East reflected military tensions that had their origin in the West. The structure of European trade in Asia therefore would not have relied upon conditions in Asia, but instead reflected political realities in the West, and the East was merely a stage upon which the European balance of power was fought.

Two theories exist to explain the role of violence in the English Company trade. One school of thought ignores the Asian context. Militarized trade was important because the English Company needed to defend itself against other hostile European companies. In this view, the expansion of European trade into the East consisted of a series of territorial battles among the Portuguese, Dutch, English, and French nations. English success depended on English naval power (Dodwell 1920: xii, Roberts 1938: 28–34, 91–128), or in a more nuanced fashion, English success depended upon the existence and outcomes of European politics and rivalries (Sinha 2002: 30). A second school of thought puts more emphasis on the importance of Asian institutions and states. The relative weakness of the English Company when compared to other European organizations drove them to arm their ships and to establish trade in areas with strong government. D. K. Bassett hypothesized that the English relied on these governments to protect them from the aggressive Portuguese and Dutch companies (Bassett 1998: 3–4). Both of these theories imply to some extent that the English did not trade or cooperate with other Europeans. Evaluating the overlap of English trade with the presence of other European companies in the 264 ports visited by the English Company does not support these hypotheses.

The data above, in tables 5, 6, 7, and 8, already reveal evidence that European conflict does not seem to have been a dominant concern for trade patterns. Although conflict between European nations may have interrupted trade, non-English European colonial ports were popular destinations for the English Company in both relative and absolute terms. Company ships did not avoid other European settlements; rather, the English Company was more likely to establish factories in ports with other Europeans present than at ports without them.

Of sixteen ports formally occupied by the Estado, the English had spells of regular trade with nine. The total time spent by the English Company engaged in regular exchange with Portuguese ports, tallied over all ports, amounts to 420 years. A similar pattern held with the Dutch, despite the recurrence of Anglo-Dutch conflict over the centuries of Company trade in the East. Of thirty Dutch colonial ports, seventeen entertained regular bouts of trade with the English. Batavia, the political center of Dutch

Indonesia, welcomed 498 English East Indiamen into its harbor during a spell of regular trade that lasted over a century.

As reported in table 8, 1,620 years of regular trade were spread across the colonial ports held by other European powers—this total is second only to the time spent in market ports. Other European companies may have avoided contact with each other—for example, the Dutch may have avoided trade with the Portuguese—but the English bridged these gaps. The presence of other Europeans helped rather than hindered English trade. This finding is consistent with historical documentation of cooperation in the East (e.g., Ray 1999: 112–20, Adams 1996: 23–24). At Surat, it has been recorded that different European nationals dined together, attended each other's funerals, acted as godfathers for each other, and often drank together (Barendse 1998: 102–3).

This cooperation reflects two underlying circumstances. On the one hand, other Europeans were also drawn to ports with open policies designed to encourage foreign trade. On the other, the Dutch Compagnie and Estado da Índia were colonial organizations. They also targeted ports with dual economic organizations consisting of peasant cultivators and merchant elites. Many of these states already operated within the trading world as royal monopolies. In such cases, the Dutch East India Company and Estado simply replaced the the previous elites, took over the existing system of appropriation, and continued to act as monopolists. It was however impossible not to import European commercial practices along with the large body of administrators necessary to regulating colonial life. These Dutch and Portuguese employees made ready commercial partners, already linked in to the system of production from the top down through systems of rent collection and land revenues. In the end, other Europeans produced a three-way interaction that was favorable to the English. Their presence overcame underlying social factors in ports that would have otherwise discouraged the English pattern of trade.

## CONCLUSION

If a general sense of the abundant trade and commerce in Asia in the premodern period has been reestablished by authors such as Janet Abu-Lughod (1989) and Andre Gunder Frank (1998), the variety of institutional settings in the East and the way in which these settings interacted with European forms of commercial organization deserve more attention. Domestic institutions matter a great deal for the development of foreign trade. Confronted with an array of institutional settings, the English had to make strategic decisions about where to concentrate their resources.

Understanding their strategy and success requires evaluating the complex institutional diversity of the trading environment they encountered.[15]

The employees of the English Company took a crucial step when they crossed outside of the hierarchical boundaries of the firm to pursue their own trade. Their transformative opportunism could never have been sustained without local institutions to support the entrepreneurial ambitions of the crew, captain, and officers—as well as the Company itself. In truth, autonomy cannot be created simply through the imposition of a new set of rules and regulations. Employee autonomy can be circumscribed but not entirely created by a central organizational authority. Real autonomy instead depends upon some external basis for control—most likely in the form of access to resources outside of the organization. Employees' relationship to the societies and opportunities outside of their organization are therefore an important basis for any increased autonomy. The East Indies ports provided access to significant commercial resources. The result was a complex and adaptive organization that encouraged sustained innovations centuries before the modern age of networks.

Unfortunately, the English did not seem to realize their dependence upon the preexisting commercial structure of the East, and the positive aspects of these cross-cultural commercial partnerships should not be overemphasized. Even as the English relied upon resident merchants as both individuals and Company agents, racist discourse emerged in colonial ports like Madras and tension and the threat of violence were a frequent presence, even in the relatively peaceful English trade (Subrahmanyam 1990a: 280–81). Cooperation with merchants also did not necessarily extend to the rest of the population. Prasannan Parthasarathi has convincingly argued that weavers and laborers in the south of the Indian Peninsula were subject to increasingly coercive measures as English influence grew in the eighteenth century. In fact, Parthasarathi suggests that this may be one reason why coastal merchants partnered with the English—to better control the weavers (Parthasarathi 2001: 6). There is every reason to believe that the increasing employment of coercive and discriminatory tactics that accompanied the expansion of British imperial power in Asia undermined the foundation of the English Company's own commercial expansion and may well have retarded economic growth in Europe as well as Asia.

*Chapter 8*

# CONCLUSION

_____

Before the founding of the East India Company, Europe was a relative, if rapidly developing, backwater. England was a rural country with a largely agricultural economy, soon to find itself scrambling to emerge out from under the shadow of the Dutch in their golden age. By the time of the Company's dissolution, India was a colony of Britain, which had become the preeminent global political power. The Industrial Revolution had transformed Britain into "the workshop of the world," while the City played home to the most dynamic financial sector the world had yet seen. State capacity had increased dramatically. Economics was playing an increasingly influential role in politics. And inequality between nations had increased dramatically. Not only had England's position in the world changed, the world itself was transformed.

The English East India Company played an important role in these events. Its success generated a tremendous amount of wealth, handed the British government the foundation of a global empire, and permanently altered the trade and economies of Britain and Asia. It will always serve as an example of the importance of overseas trade. In these chapters I have argued that a key component of the Company's ability to successfully expand its operations for nearly two centuries depended upon the local knowledge and adaptive capacity introduced into firm operations through the entrepreneurialism and communication networks of the private traders. Chapter 3 highlighted the distinctiveness of the English Company's relationship to private trade. Chapter 4 showed that increasing employee autonomy by granting private trade privileges was associated with increased transfer of information between ships through social networks via the mechanisms of rational imitation, conditional choice, trust, timing, and information diffusion. The increased information flow also acted to bring new ports into the regular trade network. Chapter 5 demonstrated that private trade pursuits led employees to explore new ports while weaving a cohesive network of trade between ports, creating a robust and efficient communication network for the firm. The process involved a concatenation of mechanisms including the cultivation of a profit-maximizing ethos in Company employees, lack of organizational control leading to nonroutine behavior, small-world effects in which randomness increased network connectivity, and, once again, information diffusion. Chapters 4 and 5 illustrated that the autonomy of firm employees encouraged the exploration of new ports and goods. The networks of decentralized communication that sprang up in this period of autonomy allowed those new goods and markets to be incorporated into the larger system of trade. The result was continued innovation and expansion until the restructuring of the Company in the colonial period.

The title of the book, *Between Monopoly and Free Trade*, indicates my belief that the private trade practices of employees were so widespread and well integrated into Company operations that they effectively altered the organizational structure of the firm. I have argued that it was not truly a monopoly as is commonly held. In the strictest sense, this is not quite accurate. Increasing the trade allowances of employees may have expanded the pool of privileged traders, but it did not actually threaten the monopoly privileges of the Company. It is within the rights of a monopolistic company to license their privileges to others, as was the case with regulated companies of the time. However, the theory of monopoly, where profits are based in exclusive access to markets, does not adequately describe the basis for the East India Company's long-term success. The private trade of its employees was not a pittance, nor did it merely appease employees. A conservative estimate of the size of the private trade, counting only private freight aboard Company ships, is 11 percent of the value of Company goods (Mentz 2005: 129); other more generous estimates value it at equal to or greater than the trade of the Company by the early eighteenth century (Krishna 1924: 125). Monopoly is an attempt to centralize market access, but the responsiveness and innovations found in the East India Company were tied to the opposite principle, increasing access to markets within a controlled framework.

On the flip side of the same token, the Company framework, monopoly privileges included, also benefited the private traders. The trade of the captains suffered tremendously after the 1813 and 1833 Parliamentary Acts stripping the Company of monopoly rights (Sutton 2010: 267–74). It was the Company that had borne the costs of defending the trading privileges—that were also extended to its employees—all along through loans to the government and vigorous prosecution of interlopers. Following a favorable court ruling, the Court of Committees of the Company brought charges against twenty-five private shipowners they considered guilty of trade to the East Indies and encouraged the persecution of sixty-five more (Stern 2011: 59). The advantage such efforts achieved was significant. Even interlopers initially preferred to be included in the monopoly rather than abolish the privilege entirely. Evidence of this lies in their attempts to form the New Company, another chartered monopoly.

The factory system, which depended upon the formal Company framework for the large initial outlays necessary to constructing permanent settlements, was essential to the larger flow of timely information between English traders described in chapter 4. The factories acted as multiple hubs, capturing and dispersing information between merchants within the larger decentralized network. In times of political upheaval, English forts, factories, and settlements provided safe havens for English and even Indian merchants (Watson 1980a: 82). Despite claims to the contrary (Jones and Ville 1996a), there is no evidence that small-scale independent ventures, which would not have had the benefits of forts and factories, would have been more successful than the Company trade. Instead there were clear synergies between the private and formal trades.

Although the Company was a monopoly, it did not operate on monopolistic principles. And although the private trade flourished alongside the Company, this does little to indicate that free merchants trading to the East would have survived without the infrastructure created and maintained by the Company. The Company was not operating in a completely competitive marketplace, but it also never achieved a monopoly of any good. It was somewhere between the two.

In the section that follows I use the case of the English East India Company to reflect on existing knowledge about overseas trade expansion, decentralization within organizations, the importance of context in the emergence and interpretation of networks, and the centrality of micro- to macro-level phenomena in historical change.


## HISTORY, NETWORKS, AND ANALYTICAL SOCIOLOGY

### CONTEXT

There is a tendency to think of networked forms of organization as part of a new movement in organizational design or perhaps as part of a new network organization of society. This perspective has been countered by the view that network forms of organization are enduring features of social and organizational life. If we consider social networks as patterns that link micro-behaviors to macro-outcomes, this clearly implies their existence across all of history and society. However, the perspective is also used in a sense that implies that social networks, understood as informal relations, are a constant feature of social life—a necessary counterpoint or glue for formal or market relations (Granovetter 1985). The English East India Company gives a largely unprecedented opportunity to study the use and development of networks over more than two centuries as the firm developed. It therefore provides the chance to develop and ask more specific questions about informal relations, such as if they are more or less prevalent, more or less effective in different contexts. One of the more interesting findings is then perhaps that the impact of informal social networks varied over the life of the firm, decreasing as centralization increased. The structure of the organization itself had a large impact on network use and formation.

Because the East India Company's structure evolved through contact between diverse societies and cultures different from each other and in many ways different from what we would find around the world today, the importance of social and cultural contexts is more immediately apparent than is the case in contemporary settings. For example, the idea of loyal company service was quite different in Stuart England than it is for employees of a large North American firm of today. The difference in the behavior of East India Company employees and IBM employees is correspondingly large. Considering the unfamiliar historical and cultural terrain of premodern firms highlights the effect of context on organizational practices and routines of both firms,[1] which also feed into patterns of informal network use. The advantage is not particular to the case of the East India Company, although I would argue that historical and transnational network research is particularly well suited to increasing our store of knowledge about how social, cultural, and institutional contexts affect network formation and use.

Network research arguably began with the theoretical work of Georg Simmel. Simmel was a Neo-Kantian who developed the idea of a priori social forms, such as the dyad (two linked individuals) and triad (three linked individuals) (Simmel 1971: 6–22). According to Simmel, these a priori social forms had a determinative effect on the thoughts, beliefs, and behaviors of individuals independent of any specific historical or cultural circumstance.

Simmel's theoretical work on social forms inspired an innovative and productive line of network research that focused on the effects of transposable social patterns of relations; however, as network research has grown an increasing number of voices have been raised in criticism of the emphasis on contextless forms, which seem to come at the expense of an explicit consideration of the characteristics of social actors and social environments (DiMaggio 1992, Emirbayer and Goodwin 1994, Pachucki and Breiger 2010). Instead of adopting a purely formalistic approach to social networks, the analytical sociology framework necessarily drives researchers to extensive consideration of both the agent and the agent's operative social and cultural context. Although analytical sociology consistently asks researchers to base explanations in a lower level of observation, which may seem at first to exclude consideration of the larger environment of actors, that advice is aimed at research in the social sciences that relies exclusively on explanations pitched at the level of impersonal macro-historical forces.[2] The analytical strategy is never to contain explanation at the level of the individual social agent—as in a formalistic sociology or psychology—it is instead to enrich the analysis of large-scale social processes with the lived experiences of the individuals participating in them. This is part of the process by which researchers bridge the micro and macro levels of analysis. Thus cultural context and historical context are always in the end essential components of any network-based explanation that fits within the analytical framework.[3]

In the case of the English East India Company, the individual-level transfer of information through peer networks was tied to decentralization, but this occurred within two layered contexts. The first was a hierarchical organization. The organizational setting cannot be separated out from the peer networks because the effect of networks would have played out differently in other sites. For example, since markets are already decentralized, social networks may well dampen innovation and the adoption of novel ideas in such circumstances, even as they increase innovation in hierarchical organizations. This is an important condition for interpreting the analysis and demonstrates the potentially large impact of context; however it is a description of context that can be abstracted from specific social and historical circumstance.

However the development of effective social networks in the East India Company, that is, social networks that effectively channeled useful information within the firm, also relied upon contact with inclusive economic arenas in the East. The peer networks inside the firm were sustained by external circumstances, implying that open societies may be necessary to maintain networked and decentralized firms—that is to say efficient and innovative firms. At first blush this may sound like a generalization that could survive across different contexts; however even if commercially sophisticated, open societies consistently create stable environments for network forms of organization, which are in turn capable of sustained growth, unique historical circumstances will almost inevitably determine whether open societies arise in the first place, as was the case for the environs of the English Company.

## DECENTRALIZATION AND HISTORY

The question of what causes economic growth also plays into larger arguments about the role of top-down versus bottom-up processes of social change. Because the English Company sat at the nexus of several important strands of global history, the creation of new organizational forms, the rise of Britain to world hegemon, the expansion of global markets, and even the birth of economics, its history illuminates larger processes of historical transformation. The historical importance of the East India Company is not under debate, instead the question of concern here is to what extent the private trade affected the process of historical transformation.

I argue that the private trade worked within the organization itself to introduce vitality, local responsiveness, and capacity for adaptation to a large bureaucratic administration that would otherwise have been left behind by a changing market. The continued expansion of the Company was responsible for the British colonization of India, and the expansion of the British private trade was responsible for making the trade to Europe the largest portion of overseas trade in Asia (Steensgaard 1987: 145).[4] Since the English private trade in Asia depended upon Company facilities and privileges (granted by Asian rulers as well as the English monarch), and the entanglements created by private traders helped draw the Company into the colonization of India, these historical developments should not be linked to either the purely formal structures of the Company or the English private trade in isolation. Instead they depend upon the relation between the private trade and Company. The push and pull between the coordinating hierarchical form of the Company and the many loose ends of the different desires and ambitions of enterprising individuals was at the center of this transformation. After the private trade moved out of the auspices of the Company, in the colonial period, the Company began a long period of decline and settled into a typical and unproductive pattern of exploitation. This history has implications for both globalization and processes of social change.

Globalization was first conceived as an irrepressible force, expanding in concentric circles of *doux-commerce* or culturally devastating cycles of creative destruction (Guillén 2001, Hirschman 1997). Research has shown that globalization, the establishment of international commercial and financial ties, is an uneven and ragged process that expands and shrinks (Fligstein 2001, Williamson 2006, Zelizer 2005), clumps together in certain areas, and excludes others (Kim and Shin 2002). The standard explanation for this uneven process attributes it to variations in the factors of land, labor, and capital that make business opportunities more or less desirable in different regions of the world. In other words, firms react to market conditions.

One objection has been to point to the role of institutions in shaping trade. This explanation has been offered by unorthodox economists as well as economic sociologists who emphasize the state's role in constructing international markets. State intervention has negative effects in the form of trade barriers, tariffs, customs, and duties (Becker 1957, MacDougall

1960). There are also positive effects. Overseas trade requires a host of institutions in order to reduce uncertainty to manageable levels and establish rules of exchange (Fligstein 1996, Fligstein and Mara-Drita 1996). States intervene in international commercial exchange in order to create these necessary institutions, thereby channeling the flow of overseas exchange (Gotham 2006, Duina 2005). In this book, I looked at both the institutional environment and the source of those flows, that is, the firm itself. A large part of the story of the English Company's expansion has to do with firm characteristics. The firm was not driven merely by market conditions. The institutional environments of the East made the decentralization of the Company possible, but once installed, the decentralization of control within the firm drove trade into specific patterns that changed when the organizational structure changed.

When employees were granted a high degree of personal autonomy to pursue private commercial opportunities within Asia and a considerable amount of control over Company resources with which to pursue this private trade, social networks were a mechanism for personal exploration that expanded the size of the larger trade network. When the autonomy of the employees decreased, the impact of social networks on trade was significantly reduced. Internal control efforts shaped individual-level decisions, thereby molding the structure of the English trade network and, through this, affecting the larger process of globalization. The struggle for control between various levels of the firms affected the patterns by which the firm expanded—and since it was a large overseas operation, this also impacted the process of global commercial expansion.

Generally, exploitation is a static state. In an exploitative system, those who have power use it to gather resources and strengthen their own position. They have no reason to change or call into question a system from which they are benefiting—at the expense of others. Instead, they have every reason to protect the existing system in order to defend their own privileged place within that system. The oppressed are often too resource-poor to effectively organize any resistance. On the other hand, an entirely self-organized system is unlikely to produce the degree of coordination necessary to effect real change as well. Certainly, there is little evidence the English trade would have prospered as it did without the existence of the English Company.

It is rare to find instances of social organization that are both sufficiently well organized to collectively solve complex tasks *and* designed to distribute rewards (or profits) meritocratically—a strategy that encourages productivity and growth (Udy 1959). It is the tendency for social systems to fall into static rent-seeking states, which makes it important to identify the dynamics at work in moments when goods are distributed slightly more evenly. It is these moments, when rent seeking is somehow temporarily halted, that produce economic growth (Jones 1988). In this case, that decentralization subtly changed the direction of world history by affecting the history of English–East Indies relations.

A confluence of circumstances temporarily created a situation in which the English private traders could act productively within a large, bureaucratic organization. To use the language of Michael Mann (1993), Harrison White (1992), and Richard Lachmann (2000), this transformative moment, a "conjuncture," "interstitial emergence," or "chain of contingencies," reorganized the relationship between the East and West and affected societies on both sides of the divide. Ultimately, the system of exploitation was reasserted in the colonial period (a system that reduced the autonomy of the employees and, to a much greater degree, the colonial subjects), but the rapid expansion fueled by the private trade had left its mark on the global economy. The relationship between the micro level (i.e., the individuals) and the macro level (i.e., the Company form and social context), which can be analyzed through networks, is an important piece of the larger puzzle, which is framed by the relevance of open societies to economic development. To me it suggests a close connection among networks, employee autonomy, profit sharing, and innovation within successful organizations that I hope will continue to be the basis for further research.

## MICRO-MACRO LINKAGES AND HISTORICAL TRANSFORMATION

Since networks are the primary means by which decentralized coordination and communication can take place, it makes sense that marginal actors, who are both excluded from many formal organizations and the most likely to push for social change, would use networks, that is, informal communications, as a means to coordinate activity. This fact suggests that networks, understood as a mechanism of decentralized communication, may be intrinsically tied up in or a likely or recurring factor in social change—given that communication is necessary for coordination. Networks to a large extent are defined by their mutability—this is, in the end, what makes them different from organizations or institutions. They link people together, but are still flexible enough to accommodate change. And in fact, the change networks facilitate may be a result of linking new groups together.

Harrison White, who presciently embraced and popularized the study of social networks in the 1960s, theorized networks as interfaces that create identity through linking mismatched pairs. The reconciliation of two different and disparate things creates a sense of identity and being (White 2008: 1–19). This insight gives a broad theoretical framework for understanding how networks can be creative forces in the world. Building on relationalist theory, John Padgett and Paul McLean have convincingly argued that social transformation is produced by the intersection of new and different networks, showing that the partnership system of commercial organization emerged as an innovation in Renaissance Florence through the transposition of marriage and economic ties. The intersection and subsequent transformation of these two networks invigorated the Florentine economy—mainly through the dramatically increased capacity of the new partnership system—and transformed society, making it more amenable to the rise of civic humanism and republicanism (Padgett and McLean 2006: 1522). Padgett and Powell have recently developed these insights about network and systemic conjunctures into a general theory of institutional emergence (2012).

Networks are essential to the creation of these transformative linkages, exactly because they operate outside of and in the interstices of formal institutions and organizations. They are boundary-spanning devices, and therefore can create revolutionary connections between otherwise distant people. Thus it should be no surprise to those familiar with the history of the English Company that the dynamic networks within the firm depended upon networks of actors outside of the firm and located in Asia. By exploring these relationships in chapters 6 and 7, I hope to have contributed to the large literature emphasizing the importance of both global relations (Braudel 1972, 1977, Wallerstein 1974, 1980, Sassen 1991, Smith and White 1992, Curtin 1994) and the history of Asia (Lach and Kley 1965, Wong 1997, Pomeranz 2000) to the evolution of the modern world.

However, my attempt to contribute to this extremely macro-structural literature is based very much in the micro-level actions of the individuals of that time, and I hope it demonstrates some of the potential that an analytical approach poses for historical research in the social sciences. Analysis of the relations between individuals, whether communication networks or the availability of exchange partners, can shed new light on old historical dilemmas. Network models in particular give researchers a tool with which to model and analyze decentralized coordination. Since power tends to be centralized, for example in states and empires, and existing powers generally desire to retain the status quo that has kept them in power, coordination among loosely affiliated, disenfranchised actors is likely to be an important source of historical transformation—as it is, for example, in revolutions. In the case considered here, decentralized actors, the English Company employees, were not responsible for a social revolution, but they did inject a vitality into the English Company that transformed its position in the world— and by extension transformed global relations between Europe and Asia.

Since the time when the Annales school shifted history away from the study of great men, many historians have worked to illuminate the lives of the large mass of individuals who fall outside of elite circles, but these have necessarily been focused illuminations of specific stories and individuals (e.g., Ginzburg 1992, Davis 1983). Network analysis presents a new method for studying the relationships between large groups of actors. And since it also reveals the causal force that patterns of relations can have, it provides social scientists and historians a new means of understanding how nonelite actors have shaped the course of history—through emergent patterns as well as goal-directed behavior, for example.

For sociologists the approach used in this book offers both a rich conceptual framework and a rigorous method for investigating and measuring specific social mechanisms. It is one of several tools that can be used to reveal how individual lives intersect and cumulate into larger institutional structures and historical patterns.

*Appendix*

# PORTS

---

| Historical name | Current name | Type |
|---|---|---|
| Aceh | Aceh | Open city |
| Aden | Aden | Open city |
| Amboina | Ambon | Colonial, Portuguese/Dutch (1609) |
| Amoy | Xiamen | Regulated market |
| Amsterdam Island | Ile Amsterdam | Uninhabited |
| Andamans | Andaman Islands | Exclusive |
| Anjengo | Anchuthengu | Market |
| Anjer (Sultan of Banten) | Anyer | Royal monopoly (Dutch) |
| Armagaon | Arumugam | Market |
| Assada | Nosy Be | Regulated reciprocity |
| Ayutthaya | Ayutthaya | Royal monopoly |
| Bachian | Bacan | Colonial, Dutch (1609) |
| Bajalar | Bajawar | Market |
| Balambangan | | Royal monopoly |
| Balasore | Baleshwar | Market |
| Bali | Bali | Royal monopoly |
| Ballamboan | Balamban | Colonial, Spanish |
| Banaca | Bangka Island | Royal monopoly/English (1812) |
| Bancoot (Angre) | | Royal monopoly/market (1755) |
| Banda | Banda | Royal monopoly/colonial, Dutch (1621) |
| Bandar Abbas | Bandar-Abbas | Royal monopoly/open city (1628 Shah Safi) |
| Bangkok | Bangkok | Royal monopoly |
| Banjarmassin | Banjermasin | Open city |

| Historical name | Current name | Type |
|---|---|---|
| Bantal | Bantal | Market |
| Bantam | Banten | Open city/colonial, Dutch (1756) |
| Barrabulla (India) | | Market |
| Barrier Islands (Australia) | Barrier Islands | Unregulated reciprocity |
| Basra | Basra | Open city |
| Bassein | Vasai | Colonial, Portuguese/market (1739) |
| Batavia | Jakarta | Market/colonial, Dutch (1619) |
| Batticaloa | Batticaloa | Royal monopoly |
| Bedthar | Unidentified | Undetermined |
| Benkulen | Bengkulu | Market |
| Bertoonan (West Sumatra) | | Market |
| Bimlipatam | Bheemunipatnam | Market |
| Bocca Tigris | Bocca Tigris | Regulated market |
| Boeton | Buton | Royal monopoly (Dutch) |
| Bombay | Mumbai | Colonial, Portuguese/English (market) (1662) |
| Borrum | | Undetermined |
| Bourbon | Reunion | Uninhabited/colonial, French (1638) |
| Bouro | Bouro | Colonial, Dutch (1658) |
| Boyne Habour (Madagascar) | | Regulated reciprocity |
| Brinjoan | | Market |
| Broken Ground | | Market |
| Bushire | Busehr | Royal monopoly/market (1628 Shah Safi) |
| Cagayan Sulu | Mapun | Royal monopoly |
| Calcutta | Kolkata | Market |
| Calderoon Bay (Coromandel) | | Market |
| Calicut | Kozhikode | Open city |
| Calingapatam | Kalingapatam | Market |
| Cannanore | Kannur | Market/colonial, Dutch (1663)/ market(1772)/English(1790) |
| Canton (Whampoa) | Guangzhou | Regulated market |
| Cap Sing Moon | | Regulated market |
| Capshee Bay | | Regulated market |

| Historical name | Current name | Type |
|---|---|---|
| Carnicobar | Car Nicobar | Exclusive |
| Cavite | Cavite | Colonial, Spanish |
| Ceram | Seram | Colonial, Dutch (1650) |
| Chaul | Chaul | Colonial, Portuguese/market (1740) |
| Cheduba | Cheduba Island | Royal monopoly |
| Chittagong | Chittagong | Market |
| Chumpee (China) | | Regulated market |
| Chusan | Zhoushan | Regulated market |
| Cochin | Kochi | Colonial, Portuguese/Dutch (1663–1795) |
| Cockelee | Unidentified | Undetermined |
| Colombo | Colombo | Colonial, Portuguese/Dutch (1656–1796) |
| Connimere (Coromandel) | | Market |
| Copang Bay | Kupang | Colonial, Portuguese/Dutch (1619–1796) |
| Coringa | | Market |
| Covelong | Kovalam | Market |
| Cox's Island | Cox's Bazaar | Royal monopoly/English (1799) |
| Crooe (West Sumatra) | | Market |
| Culpee | Kalpi | Market |
| Cutch | Kutch | Market |
| Dabhol | Dabhol | Market |
| Daman | Daman | Colonial, Portuguese (1535) |
| Dhufar | Dhofar | Royal monopoly |
| Diamond Harbour | | Market |
| Diamond Island | | Royal monopoly |
| Diamond Point (Sumatra) | Diamond Point | Royal monopoly |
| Diego Garcia | Diego Garcia | Uninhabited |
| Diu | Diu | Colonial, Portuguese (1535) |
| Dunderogipore | Dungarpur | Market |
| Eastern Channel | Unidentified | Undetermined |
| First Bar | | Regulated market |
| Fort Dauphin | Taolagnaro | Colonial, French (1643–74)/regulated reciprocity |
| Fort St David/ Cuddalore | Cuddalore | Market |

| Historical name | Current name | Type |
|---|---|---|
| Fultah | | Market |
| Ganges | Ganges | Market |
| Ganjam | Ganjam | Market |
| Geriah (Angre) | | Royal monopoly/market (1756) |
| Goa | Goa | Colonial, Portuguese |
| Gogha | Ghogha | Market |
| Gomez Island (Gamispola, Pulau Gomez, Sumatra) | | Unregulated reciprocity |
| Gressik | Gresik-Djaratan | Royal monopoly |
| Hainan | Hainan | Regulated market |
| Hirado | Hirado | Regulated market |
| Hobart | Hobart | Unregulated reciprocity |
| Hog River (Bengal) | | Market |
| Hong Kong | Hong Kong | Regulated market |
| Hormuz | Hormuz | Colonial, Portuguese/open city (1622) |
| Howrah | Haora | Market |
| Hugli | Hooghly | Colonial, Portuguese/market (1631) |
| Indramayo | Indramayu | Royal monopoly |
| Indrapura (Sumatra) | Indrapura | Royal monopoly (Dutch) |
| Ingeli | | Market |
| Ipoh (Malaysia) | | Market |
| Jaggernaickpuram | Kakinada | Market/colonial, Dutch (1734–95, 1818–25) |
| Jambi | Jambi | Royal monopoly (Dutch) |
| Japara | Japara | Royal monopoly/colonial, Dutch (1746) |
| Jask | Jask | Royal monopoly/market (1628 Shah Safi) |
| java_head | Java Head | Colonial, Dutch (1619) |
| Jiddah | Jeddah | Open city |
| Johanna | Anjouan | Regulated reciprocity |
| Johore | Johor | Open city |
| Kambelu | Serikkembelo | Colonial, Dutch (1608) |
| Kamree Roads | | Royal monopoly |
| Karakaul | Karaikal | Market |
| Karwar | Karwar | Market |
| Kedah | Kedah | Open city |

| Historical name | Current name | Type |
|---|---|---|
| Kedgeree | | Market |
| Khanderi | | Market |
| Kharg | Kharg | Royal monopoly/market (1628 Shah Safi) |
| Kidderpore (Bengal) | Khidirpur | Market |
| Kisnapatam | Krishnapatam | Market |
| Kitow Point | | Regulated market |
| Kowloon | Kowloon | Regulated market |
| Krakatoa | Uninhabited | Unregulated reciprocity |
| Lagundy | Legundi | Market |
| Lampacao | Lampacau | Regulated market |
| Lankeet Flat | Lankeet Island | Regulated market |
| Lantau Island | Lantau Island | Regulated market |
| Laye (Sumatra) | | Market |
| Lintin | Nei Lingding Island | Regulated market |
| Lombok | Lombok | Royal monopoly |
| Macao | Macau | Colonial, Portuguese |
| Macassar | Makassar | Open city/colonial, Dutch (1667) |
| Madapollam | Madapollam | Market |
| Madras | Chennai | Market |
| Madura | Madura | Royal monopoly/colonial, Dutch (1706) |
| Mahe | Mahe | Uninhabited/colonial, French (1742–1812) |
| Mahuwa | Mahuva | Market |
| Makian | Makian | Royal monopoly (Dutch) |
| Malacca | Malacca | Colonial, Portuguese/Dutch (1641–1798) |
| Maldives | Maldives | Royal monopoly |
| Malwa | Malvan | Market |
| Manabulle (Madagascar) | | Regulated reciprocity |
| Mangalore | Mangalore | Colonial, Portuguese/market (1640) |
| Manila | Manila | Colonial, Spanish |
| Manna (West Sumatra) | | Market |
| Masirah | Masirah | Royal monopoly |

| Historical name | Current name | Type |
|---|---|---|
| Massalege (Island of Mokamba, Petit Massaily) | | Regulated reciprocity |
| Masulipatam | Machilipatnam | Market |
| Mauritius | Mauritius | Uninhabited/colonial, Dutch (1638)/ French (1715)/English (1810) |
| Mayapore | Myapur | Market |
| Mew Bay (Java) | | Uninhabited |
| Moco Moco | | Market |
| Moheli | Moheli | Regulated reciprocity |
| Mokha | Mocha | Open city |
| Monsourcottah | | Market |
| Montague Island | Montague Island | Unregulated reciprocity |
| Morandava | Morandava | Regulated reciprocity |
| Morotai | Morotai | Royal monopoly |
| Morungary (Madagascar) | | Regulated reciprocity |
| Mozambique | Mozambique Island | Colonial, Portuguese |
| Muscat | Muscat | Colonial, Portuguese/open city (1650) |
| Nagasaki | Nagasaki | Regulated market |
| Narsipore | Narsapur | Market |
| Natal | Natal | Royal monopoly |
| Negapatam | Nagappattinam | Market/colonial Dutch (1658)/English (1781) |
| Negrais | Cape Negrais | Royal monopoly |
| New Guinea | New Guinea | Unregulated reciprocity |
| New Year Island | New Year Island | Unregulated reciprocity |
| Norfolk Island | Norfolk Island | Unregulated reciprocity |
| North Island (Borneo) | | Royal monopoly |
| Okinawa | Okinawa | Regulated market |
| Onore | Honnavar | Market |
| Onroot (Onrust, Java) | | Colonial, Dutch (1619) |
| Oshima | Oshima | Regulated market |
| Padang | Padang | Colonial, Dutch (1663) |
| Palembang | Palembang | Royal monopoly (Dutch) |
| Pangasinan | Pangasinan | Colonial, Spanish |

| Historical name | Current name | Type |
|---|---|---|
| Parcelar | Jugru | Royal monopoly |
| Pattani | Pattani | Royal monopoly |
| Pemba | Pemba Island | Royal monopoly |
| Penang | Penang | Open city (Kedah, until 1786) |
| Pescadores | Peng-Hu | Regulated market |
| Petapoli | Nizampatnam | Market |
| Pipli | Pipli | Market |
| Pisang | Syahrir | Colonial, Dutch (1621) |
| Point de Galle | Galle | Colonial, Portuguese/Dutch (1640–1796) |
| Pondicherry | Pondicherry | Colonial, French (1674) |
| Port Philip | Port Phillip | Unregulated reciprocity |
| Porto Novo | Parangipettai | Market |
| Prawdar (Madagascar) | | Regulated reciprocity |
| Priaman | Pariaman | Market |
| Prince's Island | | Uninhabited |
| Pring (West Sumatra) | | Market |
| Pulicat | pulicat | Market |
| Pulo Auroe | Pulau Aur | Unregulated reciprocity |
| Pulo bay (Sumatra) | | Market |
| Pulo Condore | Con Dao Islands | Unregulated reciprocity |
| Pulo Laurott | Laut Island | Unregulated reciprocity |
| Pulo Masey | | Royal monopoly |
| Pulo Run | Run | Colonial, Dutch (1620) |
| Pulo Timan | Tioman Island | Unregulated reciprocity |
| Qishm | Qeshm | Royal monopoly/market (1628 Shah Safi) |
| Quang Nam | Quang Nam | Open city |
| Quilon | Kollam | Colonial, Portuguese/Dutch (1661–1795) |
| Rajah Basa | Rajabasa | Royal monopoly |
| Rajapur | Rajapur | Market |
| Rangoon | Yangon | Royal monopoly |
| Rendezvous (Borneo) | | Uninhabited |
| Resolution | Resolution Bay | Unregulated reciprocity |
| Rodrigues | Rodrigues | Uninhabited/colonial, French (1691) |

| Historical name | Current name | Type |
|---|---|---|
| Rogues River (Bengal) | | Market |
| Ruttera | | Market |
| Ryapore | Royapur | Market |
| Ryukyu Islands | Nansei Islands | Regulated market |
| Sajo Island | Unidentified | Undetermined |
| Salloomah (West Sumatra) | | Market |
| Salsette | Salsette Island | Market |
| Samkoke Island (Packlate) | | Royal monopoly |
| Sandwich | Hawaii, Efate, or Cook Islands | Unregulated reciprocity |
| Sao Thome | Sao Tome | Market |
| Sapi Bay | | Unregulated reciprocity |
| Saugor (Sagor Island) | Sagar Island | Market |
| Scindy | Sindh | Market |
| Second Bar | | Regulated market |
| Semarang | | Royal monopoly/colonial (1705)/ English (1811) |
| Severndroog (Angre) | | Royal monopoly/market (1755) |
| Seychelles | Seychelles | Uninhabited |
| Silebar | Silebar | Market |
| Singapore | Singapore | Open city (Johore, until1819) |
| Socotra | Socotra | Royal monopoly |
| Sohar | Sohar | Royal monopoly/market (1628 Shah Safi) |
| St Augustines | Tulear | Regulated reciprocity |
| Sukadana | Sukadana | Royal monopoly |
| Sulu | Sulu | Royal monopoly |
| Sumbawa | Sumbawa | Royal monopoly |
| Surabaya | Surabaya | Royal monopoly/colonial, Dutch (1743) |
| Surat | Surat | Market |
| Sydney | Sydney | Unregulated reciprocity |
| Tahiti | Tahiti | Unregulated reciprocity |
| Taiwan | Taiwan | Regulated market |
| Tamborneo | | Royal monopoly |

| Historical name | Current name | Type |
| --- | --- | --- |
| Tanjayang | Tangerang | Royal monopoly/colonial, Dutch (1746) |
| Tappanooly Bay | Tapanuli Bay | Royal monopoly |
| Taverapatam (India) | | Market |
| Teinchin | Tianjin | Regulated market |
| Tellicherry | Thalassery | Market |
| Ternate | Ternate | Royal monopoly (Dutch) |
| Tidore | Tidore | Royal monopoly (Dutch) |
| Tiku | Tiku | Royal monopoly (Dutch) |
| Tonga | Tonga | Unregulated reciprocity |
| Tonkin | Tonkin | Regulated market |
| Tranquebar | Tharamgambadi | Colonial, Danish (1620) |
| Trengannu | Terengganu | Royal monopoly |
| Trincomalee | Trincomalee | Colonial, Dutch (1639–1795) |
| Tuloa (Madagascar) | | Regulated reciprocity |
| Tumala Punta | Thummalapenta | Market |
| Tuticorin | Thoothukudi | Colonial, Portuguese/Dutch (1658–1825) |
| Urmstons Bay | Urmston Road | Regulated market |
| Vizagapatam | Vishakapatnam | Market |
| Zanzibar | Zanzibar | Colonial, Portuguese (1698)/royal monopoly |

# NOTES

--------

## PREFACE

1. Calculated from Ralph Davis (1962, 300–301).


## CHAPTER 1: INTRODUCTION

1. It was only with the rise of Britain's Eastern Empire and Henry Dundas's model of the "Emporium of Trade of Asia" that the Company, and the British government, became determined to build a true monopoly.

2. English shipping statistics were compiled from Anthony Farrington's *Catalogue of East India Company Ships' Journals and Logs, 1600–1834* (1999b).

3. Glamann also recognizes that the structural preconditions of the Dutch Company's demise were already present during this period, when it appeared most successful. The structural conditions he identified had to do with the shifting patterns of Asian trade, not the Anglo-Dutch Wars. His analysis supports my argument that adaptation and innovation were central to the continued success of the East India Companies in the global market.

4. Child's War was the result of an attempt by the English Company to strong-arm the powerful Mughal emperor Aurangzeb into trade concessions. The Company was ill prepared for a war with the Mughal Empire and was forced into concessions in 1689. The war began in 1686. It is named Child's War because most blame the onset of aggressions on the aggressive tactics of Sir Josiah Child, then the governor of the Company.

5. In fairness, I should make clear that Steensgaard does not consider the Portuguese, since theirs was not a commercial operation integrating protection costs, but instead a militaristic organization integrating economic costs.

6. The comparison between the English Company and its European competitors is further developed in chapter 3.

7. I want to stress that the question of whether the private trade led to British imperial rule in the East is an entirely different question from the one addressed in this book, which considers the relationship of private trading practices to the effectiveness of the English Company's commercial operations.

8. By this they meant that transferability increased the potential pool of owner-managers, thus providing a higher chance of continuing operations beyond the lifetime, interest, and capacity of a small group of initial investors.

9. Readers may note that this point seems to contradict Chaudhuri's earlier emphasis on the centralization of control over Company operations. Chaudhuri was consistent in singling out the logistical capacity and foresight of Company managers, even when this meant creating a multidivisional structure.

10. For relevant critiques of the transaction cost approach, see Granovetter (1985) and Powell (1990).

11. David Stasavage (2003, 2011) makes a similar, more general argument relative to the development of the state, rather than organization, positing that close ties between merchant elites and state offices initially allow for economic expansion, but devolve into stagnation as the same merchant elites close ranks to competition and gradually find and adopt the more stable but less dynamic rent-seeking strategies typical of landed elites.

12. This conceptualization of culture traces back at least to Durkheim, where the collective consciousness functions at times as a supra-social entity that exists outside of but interacts with individuals and has roots as deep as the history of Western philosophy, in which ideal and material realms have often been treated as distinct planes of existence. The question of the relationships between analytical sociology and culture is then a very deep one that depends upon whether one believes that there is a division between the mind and body or material and ideal worlds—or more specifically, whether culture exists inside or outside the minds of individuals.


## CHAPTER 2: MERCHANT CAPITALISM AND THE GREAT TRANSITION

1. These statistics are taken from O'Rourke and Williamson (2002), who gathered and organized them by drawing from a number of different sources. The growth statistics for the first period are taken from Prakash's *European Commercial Expansion in Early Modern Asia* (1997: 106), and the two subsequent periods are from Chaudhuri's *The Trading World of Asia and the English East India Company, 1660–1760* (1978: 508–10). All are measures of exports in pounds sterling.

2. This range of 1760 to 1780 is used as different authors use different years to mark the transition.

3. Bayly has also hedged his description of commercial development in a later article, "South Asia and the 'Great Divergence'" (2000). It should also be noted

that many of these authors are engaging in a related manner regarding the effect of Mughal decline on the economy of the region.

4. It was the absence of any government representation by state creditors in the absolute monarchy of France, Stasavage argues, that led to the failure of John Law's Banque Royale. Law was attempting to expand public debt by creating financial links between the bank and the French East India Company (Stasavage 2003), so the two cases make for a close comparison. The same reluctance to invest in the Companies was also present in the Portuguese context, very likely for similar reasons.

5. There is some controversy over the authorship of "Considerations upon the East India Trade," outlined by Christine MacLeod in "Henry Martin and the Authorship of 'Considerations upon the East India Trade' (1983).

6. I am not here concerned with the debate over the extent to which economic theory discovers truths as opposed to constructs accounts that support the self-interested actions or promote and sustain the expansion of capitalism, although this debate is also concerned with the historical circumstances of economic thinking (Callon 1998, MacKenzie et al. 2007, Fourcade and Babb 2002, Krippner 2011).

7. Although the limited liability company was legalized in Britain in 1855, the practice of limiting the liability of investors and agents through different contractual forms was common outside of England, and evidence presented by Abraham Udovitch indicates that it originated many centuries prior in the Middle East.

## CHAPTER 3: THE EUROPEAN TRADE
## WITH THE EAST INDIES

1. Bruce Carruthers has written an engaging history of the old Company's encounter with the New East India Company in his larger exploration of the relationship among politics, finance, and commerce in seventeenth-century England (Carruthers 1996).

2. Other remittance methods included respondentia loans, the diamond trade, and shipping goods for sale in London.

3. Mentz arrived at this estimate by subtracting Chaudhuri's figures for the total bullion export of the Company from George White's figures on total bullion export to Asia from England. It puts the outlay for private trade at just over a quarter of the Company's outlay.

4. Mentz's figures show that around twenty or so free merchants were resident at Madras in any given year from 1678 to 1742. The number of free merchants would have been significantly higher at Madras than other smaller Company settlements (Mentz 2005: 202).

5. Officers and crew also sold their freight privileges on occasion, but it was a much smaller share.

6. This was particularly true of the sale of offices (Klaveren 2002: 100)

7. The concession also gave the recipients the ability to invest the resources of Portuguese citizens who had died overseas.

8. The private trade in these smaller companies has not been researched as thoroughly as the private trade of the English, which may introduce a bias here.

## CHAPTER 4: SOCIAL NETWORKS
## AND THE EAST INDIAMAN

1. Individuals exited the service of the English Company for many reasons, but the majority simply died while in its employment. In total, 61 percent of those who exited from service died, or roughly 35 percent dead across different cohorts of service (Hejeebu 2005: 508–9).

2. As noted elsewhere, the Company did not build or own its own ships, but leased them in an effort to cut costs and distribute risks. The owners of the ships were called managing owners or ships' husbands. It was a prestigious position, and many were directors and powerful stockholders.

3. I have not found evidence that the managing owners did more than offer advice, suggestions, and perhaps guidelines to the more inexperienced captains.

4. I discuss validity issues in the data section below. To be entirely clear, I am not claiming that the data are 100 percent accurate all of the time. As with all large data sets, there is random error. However, overall these data give a remarkably good picture of shipping movement in the English Company's fleet.

5. This step may seem unnecessary since the Farrington volume is a catalogue of the ships' voyages, but data are often systematically collected for a purpose that does not correspond with the intentions of those who use them. The sample makes it very unlikely that any systematic distortion of the data, as I use them, was introduced through some part of the data collection process.

6. The model was implemented using the lme4 package in R (Bates, Maechler, and Bolker 2013).

7. An alternative model specification is to use port-to-port pair fixed effects rather than the distance between ports and a time-varying control for rates of traffic between ports. Fixed effects for port-to-port dyads take the baseline probability of a tie between ports and estimate deviations from that baseline. In this case the number of fixed effects is extremely large as it equals the number of possible port-to-port pairs. The central advantage in directly incorporating a control for port-to-port traffic rather than directed-dyad fixed effects is a very significant gain in efficiency. The control for traffic also varies by the time the trip is taken, whereas a port-to-port fixed effect is either time-invariant or constrained by periods (if the fixed effect includes a period component). In this case, fixed effects models have also been estimated. The different models produced very similar results, thus the

more efficient model is presented here, i.e., the time-varying controls for traffic between ports rather than the port-to-port time-invariant fixed effects.

8. An important exception would be the lascars often hired in Asia to man return voyages when a ship's crew had been depleted through death and desertion. Lascars would have access to their own local networks of information; however given their subordinate status it is unclear to what extent they would have been allowed to influence or even communicate with the captain of the ship.

9. Captains might also run into other ships at sea, but this would be an unsystematic, chance occurrence.

10. The *natio* system predated a European presence in Asian trade.

11. There was almost no change in results based on three- and five-month storage periods.

12. Richard Mohun was chief factor at Masulipatnam in the late seventeenth century, when it was a central hub for English private trade.

13. In the colonial period, factors were increasingly forced out of private trade. The free merchants who took their place were English, but not engaged with official Company business.

14. The model was also estimated using the 1776 date as a cutoff. The results showed the same pattern, but were slightly weaker, suggesting that 1757 was the real start of organizational change.

15. An anonymous reviewer suggested this framework for conceiving personal experience.

16. This dual movement, transmission and traversing occurs in many real-world networks, e.g., transportation, migration, and trade networks.

17. Directions to captains are often listed in the first pages of ships logs and appear scattered through the paperwork associated with each voyage, bound in separate volumes in the India Office Records division of the British Library in London.

18. This is almost certainly the case because exploratory voyage were prestigious appointments.

19. The war data came from ICPSR studies "Great Power Wars" and "Major-Minor Power Wars" (Levy 1989, Midlarsky and Park 1991).

20. The Courteen Association, formed with the permission of Charles I, was another challenge to the monopoly of the Company; however it was much less successful and is not generally regarded to have constituted any real threat to the old East India Company (Prakash 2002: 2). Therefore it is not included in the analysis.

21. Not all of these ships actually made it to the East. In particular several voyages failed in the 1640s and 1650s.

22. Exploitation in this sense has no moral overtones. It indicates a situation in which firms exploit known resources or specializations, which could be something as harmless as producing only nuts rather than nuts and bolts. It is also worth noting that although Company profits fell in the colonial period. This decline is

generally associated with the costs of war and governance rather than trade decline, although it is very difficult to disentangle the two.

23. Although *experience* and *networks* require a previous voyage, some trips are not associated with any of these types of information. If a first trip to a port is not associated with *formal orders*, then the subsequent trip may be based on *networks*, *experience*, or *formal orders*.

24. These ports include only those visited over ten times.

## CHAPTER 5: DECENTRALIZATION, CORRUPTION, AND MARKET STRUCTURE

1. Although the monopoly was dissolved in 1833, the last voyage sent out prior to its dissolution did not return until 1835.

2. Principal-agent problems model contractual relations, so although one often assumes that firm owners and managers are the principals and employees are the agents, the model may also work in reverse. For example, if an employer does not pay an employee for time worked, the employee is facing a principal-agent problem, in which the employee is the principal and the employer is the agent. In this case, I am using the framework in a conventional sense—the owners and board of directors of the English Company are considered principals and the captain and crew are considered agents.

3. As Jones and Ville (1996a: 912) note, company histories for the English East India, Hudson Bay, Royal African, and Dutch East India Companies, among others, provide "abundant evidence of persistent opportunism" and sustained, but largely unsuccessful, attempts to counter agent abuse of autonomy.

4. Using four-year intervals allows the identification of structural change over time, while retaining a sufficient number of ties connecting ports to reliably measure structural properties. Voyages are dated by departure in order to preserve their integrity—partitions across time would otherwise split voyages into different time periods, losing links that occurred at or near the moment of partition. This means that a ship that began its voyage in 1701 and continued to travel until 1705 is included in the 1700 observation period only. Comparable analyses for two-year windows are available and show results similar to those reported here.

5. Across each panel, some lines appear darker and thicker than others; however lines in these images are not weighted by the number of voyages. The lines appear thicker because of overlapping voyages along the same route. It is an approximate indication of a dense cluster of similar or geographically proximate routes.

6. The privileges referred to here are the officer's allotment of cargo space on English vessels, described above.

7. This measure avoids bias arising from a steady decrease in the duration of trips and variability due to fluctuations in the weather. The decrease in mean voyage

duration over time was driven less by technical innovation than increased control of the Company over trade routes (Menard 1991: 250).

8. The Company did however occasionally let out ships for local freight voyages. For example, in 1702, the *Colchester* was leased to an Armenian merchant (Sarhad Israeli) to take goods to Balasore and Bandar Abbas from Madras; sometime later the *Hester* was leased (by Janardhan Seth, a Hindu merchant) for a similar freighting voyage (Prakash 1994b: chap. 4, 48). To avoid including such trips, voyages containing only cycles of length 2 are excluded—that is, cycles involving only two ports, e.g., A ↔ B. Neither the *Hester* not the *Colchester*, for example, is coded as a private trader. Including only voyages with cycles of greater than 2 also reduces the likelihood that ships held in the East for military duties—such as transporting troops or defending a port—are included in the set of identified private traders. Such activities became more common as the Company entered its colonial period post-1757.

9. The test is conservative because it assumes that inexperienced captains are more likely to make errors that lead to disaster at sea. This assumption is borne out by the data. The following table shows that experienced captains, those with fewer than two previous voyages with the English Company, have significantly higher odds of experiencing an accident.

Table 4. Cross-tabulation of Disaster over Captains' Career Experience

| Captains' experience | Voyage outcomes: No disaster | Disaster | Total |
|---|---|---|---|
| 0–1 prior voyages | 1,003 (0.97) | 85 (1.60) | 1,088 |
| 2+ prior voyages | 3,138 (1.01) | 127 (0.80) | 3,265 |
| Total | 4,141 | 212 | 4,353 |

*Note:* Pearson $\chi^2(1)$ = 27.1046, Pr = 0.000. Disasters include abandoning ship, wrecks, fires, captured by enemy forces, lost at sea, engaged by pirates, and mutiny. Parentheses enclose odds ratios.

10. This naming convention may seem backward at first, but consider that the networks with the legitimate voyages removed still contain the malfeasant voyages. That is why these networks are called the malfeasant trade graphs.

11. The partitions in the *legitimate trade graphs* occur across regions; for example, in 1712 the partition is between India and Indonesia, while in 1720 and 1728 the partition lies between the western and eastern Indian Ocean.

12. If the total network has an integration level of 2, this would mean that every port would have at least two redundant pathways to every other port in the network—i.e., the graph would be a bicomponent. Here extremely high scores characteristic of knotted and cyclic networks are present.

13. Further confirmation of results using simulation methods is available in Erikson and Bearman 2006.

## CHAPTER 6: THE EASTERN PORTS

1. The above list of citations is not a comprehensive record of works consulted nor a list of relevant research; it includes only those works that contained information useful to identifying, locating, describing, or categorizing the larger set of ports.

2. One of the most expensive manifestations of visible glory was the *Taman Sari*. Kathirithamby-Wells describes this fortress/pleasure garden/religious site as a "fantasy of fountains, rock gardens, subterranean channels, tunnels, and artificial lakes" (Kathirithamby-Wells 1986: 337).

3. It is difficult to characterize otherwise, but it is also unfair to think of these rules entirely as restrictions. The rules ordering who traded what gave structure to the Malagasy conduct of trade. It was a system of organization that enabled an increase in trade similar to the way in which a corporation is a system that greatly increases a group's capacity to engage in trade.

## CHAPTER 7: EASTERN INSTITUTIONS AND THE ENGLISH TRADE

1. The Omani originally had a rural base. As elite activities expanded overseas, the balance of power shifted and the state took on mercantilist shades (Sheriff 1987: 18–24).

2. This colonial activity was uncharacteristic of the Company in the first 150 years of commercial expansion. It was later to become more characteristic—after the period of interest of this book.

3. The Japanese shogunate had only recently been consolidated into a unified government after many decades of war and bloodshed. The shogun was protecting his position by excluding potentially disruptive alliances with foreign merchants. Religion, as a cohesive social force, also would have drawn allegiance away from the crown. Japanese exposure to Western religions was at that time limited to the Jesuits, which would have given them an image of a powerful and deeply political religious order.

4. The Madras merchants were led by Gowan Harrop. Overseas trade in Madras was cosmopolitan. It is very likely the coalition consisted of a mixture of Muslim, English, Hindu, and Armenian merchants.

5. To this day sea pilots in the United States retain an exclusive membership, not dissimilar to that of their forebears in the Arabian Sea.

6. A count cannot include negative numbers, which potentially causes distortions of the coefficient estimates if an OLS model is used, which depends upon normal distributions. Count models account for this problem.

7. In some cases this absence of ports seems to be due to idiosyncratic naming conventions employed in particular log books. In other cases it may be the result of misspelling or mistranscription from the log to catalog.

8. The offset converts the dependent variable into a rate of visits over the log of the number of ships out in that period. Traffic increased significantly over time, so this is an important control.

9. This is similar to looking at what is called "the effect of the treatment upon the treated" in epidemiology and econometrics. It is a pragmatic approach.

10. Each port contributes one average; however this weighted average of time between trips showed a significant skew due to a small number of exceptional ports, which is why the median of averages is employed.

11. Duration implies time elapsed between visits. I do not consider spells formed by simultaneous arrivals. Also, since East Indiamen ships sometimes traveled in convoy, I did not consider extremely short durations to indicate repeated visits. Rather they indicate one trip of more than one ship. Therefore spells of less than one year are not included. This time frame is reasonable since ships were often separated and delayed.

12. This is true for the first century and a half of English activity in the East, when commercial expansion took place, but not later.

13. Contemporaries and historians often referred to the Portuguese colonial possessions in the East as a jeweled necklace.

14. Again, this situation describes what occurred during commercial expansion, not the colonial period after the mid-eighteenth century.

15. Sanjay Subrahmanyam makes a similar point by emphasizing the great variety of merchant states—putting to rest simplistic notions of oriental despotism and predatory states (1995).


# CONCLUSION

1. In some ways, the disinterested model of loyalty for modern employees is perhaps stranger than the employee malfeasance found in the English Company (Sennett 1998).

2. This lower level has generally served as a shorthand for individuals, i.e., explaining collective outcomes by virtue of the actions of individuals, but it has also been argued that the relevant social agents for analytical sociology may in fact be interactions (Sawyer 2011).

3. This observation has been made repeatedly by contributors to analytical sociology (Hedström 1998, Rydgren 2009, Goldstein 2009: 162, Manzo 2010: 156, Demeulenaere 2011, Edling 2012). The importance of cultural context to understanding individual behavior has also been explored in great detail outside of analytical sociology (DiMaggio 1992, Martin 2011).

4. Steensgaard estimates that European overseas trade grew to more than Asian overseas trade in the first half of the eighteenth century—when the English private trade was growing exponentially and other companies were either stagnating, i.e., the Dutch, holding steady, or relatively small in comparison.

# BIBLIOGRAPHY

Abeyasekere, Susan. 1987. *Jakarta: A History*. Oxford: Oxford University Press.

Abu-Lughod, Janet L. 1989. *Before European Hegemony: The World System A.D. 1250–1350*. New York: Oxford University Press.

Acemoglu, Daron, and Simon Johnson. 2005. "Unbundling Institutions." *Journal of Political Economy* 113(5): 949–95.

Acemoglu, Daron, Simon Johnson, and James A. Robinson. 2005a. "Institutions as a Fundamental Cause of Long-Run Growth." In *Handbook of Economic Growth*, edited by Philippe Aghion and Steven N. Durlauf. Amsterdam: Elsevier, 385–472.

———. 2005b. "The Rise of Europe: Atlantic Trade, Institutional Change, and Economic Growth." *American Economic Review* 95(3): 546–79.

Adams, Julia. 1994a. "The Familial State: Elite Family Practices and State-Making in the Early Modern Netherlands." *Theory and Society* 23(4): 505–39.

———. 1994b. "Trading States, Trading Places: The Role of Patrimonialism in Early Modern Dutch Development." *Comparative Studies in Society and History* 36 (2): 319–55.

———. 1996. "Principals and Agents, Colonialists and Company Men: The Decay of Colonial Control in the Dutch East India Company." *American Sociological Review* 61: 12–28.

———. 2005. *The Familial State: Ruling Families and Merchant Capitalism in Early Modern Europe*. Ithaca, N.Y.: Cornell University Press.

Allen, Robert C., Jean-Pascal Bassino, Debin Ma, Christine Moll-Murata, and Jan Liuten van Zanden. 2011. "Wages, Prices, and Living Standards in China 1738–1925: In Comparison with Europe, Japan, and India." *Economic History Review* 64(s1): 8–38.

Almeida, Paul, and Anupama Phene. 2004. "Subsidiaries and Knowledge Creation: The Influence of the MNC and Host Country on Innovation." *Strategic Management Journal* 25(8/9): 847–64.

Anderson, Gary M., Robert E. McCormick, and Robert D. Tollison. 1983. "The Economic Organization of the English East India Company." *Journal of Economic Behavior and Organization* 4: 221–38.

Anderson, Gary M., and Robert D. Tollison. 1982. "Adam Smith's Analysis of Joint-Stock Companies." *Journal of Political Economy* 90(6): 1237–56.

Anon. 1812. *Shipwrecks and Disasters at Sea*. Vol. 3 Edinburgh: Archibald Constable.

Appleby, Joyce Oldham. 1978. *Economic Thought and Ideology in Seventeenth Century England*. Princeton, N.J.: Princeton University Press.

Arasaratnam, Sinnappah. 1967. "Dutch Commercial Policy in Ceylon and Its Effect on Indo-Ceylon Trade (1690–1750)." *Indian Economic and Social History Review* 4: 109–30.

———. 1979. "Trade and Political Dominion in South India, 1750–1790: Changing British, Indian Relationships." *Modern Asian Studies* 13(1): 19–40.

———. 1985. "Elements of Social and Economic Change in Dutch Maritime Ceylon (Sri Lanka) 1658–1796." *Indian Economic and Social History Review* 22(1): 35–54.

———. 1986. *Merchants, Companies and Commerce on the Coromandel Coast, 1650–1740*. Delhi: Oxford University Press.

———. 1989. "Coromandel Revisited: Problems and Issues in Indian Maritime History." *Indian Economic and Social History Review* 26: 101–10.

———. 1995. *Maritime Trade, Society and European Influence in South Asia, 1600–1800*. Aldershot: Variorum.

Babu, S. 1995. "Commodity Composition of the English Trade on the Coromandel Coast (1611–1652)." In *Merchants, Mariners, and Oceans: Studies in Maritime History*, edited by K. S. Mathew. New Delhi: Manohar, 261–72.

Bagchi, Amiya Kumar. 1976. "Deindustrialization in India in the Nineteenth Century: Some Theoretical Implications." *Journal of Development Studies* 12(2): 135–64.

Baker, Wayne. 1984. "The Social Structure of a National Securities Market." *American Journal of Sociology* 89: 775–811.

Balfour, Edward. 1885. *Cyclopedia of India and of Eastern and Southern Asia*. 3rd ed. London: Barnard Quaritch.

Barber, William J. 1975. *British Economic Thought and India, 1600–1858: A Study in the History of Development Economics*. Oxford: Clarendon.

Barbosa, Duarte. 1918. *The Book of Duarte Barbosa: An Account of the Indian Ocean and Their Inhabitants, Written by Duarte Barbosa and Completed about the Year 1518*. Translated by Mansel Longworth Dames. London: Hakluyt Society.

Barendse, R. J. 1998. *The Arabian Seas, 1640–1700*. Leiden: Leiden University and International Institute of Asian Studies Leiden.

Barkey, Karen. 1994. *Bandits and Bureaucrats: The Ottoman Route to State Centralization*. Ithaca, N.Y.: Cornell University Press.

———. 2009. "Historical Sociology." In *The Oxford Handbook of Analytical Sociology*, edited by Peter Hedström and Peter Bearman. Oxford: Oxford University Press, 712–33.

Barlow, Edward, and Basil Lubbock. [1703] 1934. *Barlow's Journal of His Life at Sea in King's Ships, East & West Indiamen & Other Merchantmen from 1659 to 1703*. London: Hurst and Blackett.

Barnard, Chester Irving. 1938. *The Functions of the Executive*. Cambridge, Mass.: Harvard University Press.

Bartlett, Christopher A., and Sumantra Ghoshal. 1989. *Managing across Borders: The Transnational Solution*. Boston: Harvard Business School Press.

Bassett, D. K. 1960. "The Trade of the English East India Company in the Far East, 1623–84: Part I: 1623–65." *Journal of the Royal Asiatic Society of Great Britain and Ireland* 1/2: 32–47.

———. 1989. "British 'Country' Trade and Local Trade Networks in the Thai and Malay States, c. 1680–1770." *Modern Asian Studies* 23(4): 625–43.

———. 1998. "Early English Trade and Settlement in Asia, 1602–1690." In *Trade, Finance, and Power*, edited by Patrick J. N. Tuck. London: Routledge, 1–25.

Bastiampillai, Bertram E.S.J. 1995. "Maritime Relations of Sri Lanka (Ceylon) up to the Arrival of the Westerners." In *Mariners, Merchants, and Oceans: Studies in Maritime History*, edited by K. S. Mathew. New Delhi: Manohar, 79–95.

Bastin, John Sturgus. 1961. *Essays on Indonesian and Malayan History*. Singapore: Eastern Universities Press.

———. 1965. *The British in West Sumatra, 1685–1825*. Kuala Lumpur: University of Malaya Press.

Bates, Douglas, Martin Maechler, and Ben Bolker. 2013. "Lme4: Linear Mixed-Effects Models." Version 0.999999–2; published April 15, 2013. http://lme4 .r-forge.r-project.org/.

Bayly, Christopher A. 1983. *Rulers, Townsmen, and Bazaars: North Indian Society in the Age of British Expansion, 1770–1870*. Cambridge: Cambridge University Press.

———. 2000. "South Asia and the 'Great Divergence.'" *Itinerario* 24(3–4): 89–103.

Bearman, Peter S. 1993. *Relations into Rhetorics: Local Elite Social Structure in Norfolk, England, 1540–1640*. New Brunswick, N.J.: Rutgers University Press.

Becker, Gary. 1957. *The Economics of Discrimination*. Chicago: University of Chicago Press.

Benner, M. J., and M. Tushman. 2003. "Exploitation, Exploration, and Process Management: The Productivity Dilemma Revisited." *Academy of Management Journal* 28(2): 238–56.

Bingham, Hiram. 1906. "The Early History of the Scots Darien Company." *Scottish Historical Review* 3(10): 210–17.

Birkinshaw, Julian. 1997. "Entrepreneurship in Multinational Corporations: The Characteristics of Subsidiary Initiatives." *Strategic Management Journal* 18(3): 207–29.

Blakeney, Richard. 1841. *The Journal of an Oriental Voyage in His Majesty's Ship Africaine*. London: Marshall Simpkin.

Blussé, Leonard. 1986. *Strange Company: Chinese Settlers, Mestizo Women and the Dutch in VOC Batavia*. Dordrecht: Foris.

Bonney, Richard. 1995. "The Eighteenth Century. II. The Struggle for Great Power Status and the End of the Old Fiscal Regime." In *Economic Systems and State Finance*, edited by Richard Bonney. Oxford: Oxford University Press, 315–86.

Borsa, Giorgio. 1990. "Recent Trends in Indian Ocean Historiography 1500–1800." In *Trade and Politics in the Indian Ocean: Historical and Contemporary Perspectives*, edited by Giorgio Borsa. New Delhi: Manohar, 3–14.

Bosher, J. F. 1995. "Huguenot Merchants and the Protestant International in the Seventeenth Century." *William and Mary Quarterly*, Third Series 52(1), 77–102.

Boulle, P. H. 1981. "French Mercantilism, Commercial Companies and Colonial Profitability." In *Companies and Trade: Essays on Overseas Trading Companies during the Ancien Régime*, edited by Léonard Blussé and F. S. Gaastra. Leiden: Leiden University Press, 97–117.

Bowen, H. V. 1989. "Investment and Empire in the Later Eighteenth Century: East India Stockholding, 1756–1791." *Economic History Review* 42(2): 186–206.

———. 1996. "The East India Company and Military Recruitment in Britain, 1763–1771." In *The Organization of Interoceanic Trade in European Expansion, 1450–1800*, edited by Pieter Emmer and Femme Gaastra. Aldershot: Variorum/ Ashgate, 351–64.

———. 2002. "'No Longer Mere Traders': Continuities and Change in the Metropolitan Development of the East India Company, 1600–1834." In *The Worlds of the East India Company*, edited by H. V. Bowen, Margarette Lincoln, and Nigel Rigby. Suffolk: Boydell Press, 19–32.

———. 2006. *The Business of Empire: The East India Company and Imperial Britain, 1756–1833*. Cambridge: Cambridge University Press.

Bower, J. L., and C. M. Christensen. 1995. "Disruptive Technologies: Catching the Wave." *Harvard Business Review* 73: 43–53.

Boxer, C. R. 1965. *The Dutch Seaborne Empire, 1600–1800*. London: Hutchinson.

———. 1969. *The Portuguese Seaborne Empire, 1415–1825*. New York: Knopf.

———. 1974. *The Anglo-Dutch Wars of the 17th Century, 1652–1674*. London: HM Stationery Office.

Brass, Daniel J., Joseph Galaskiewicz, Henrich R. Greve, and Wenpin P. Tsai. 2004. "Taking Stock of Networks and Organizations: A Multilevel Perspective." *Academy of Management Journal* 47(6): 795–817.

Braudel, Fernand. 1972. *The Mediterranean and the Mediterranean World in the Age of Philip II*. New York: Harper & Row.

———. 1977. *Afterthoughts on Material Civilization and Capitalism*. Baltimore: Johns Hopkins University Press.

———. 1992a. *The Perspective of the World: Civilization and Capitalism, 15th–18th Century*. Vol. 3. New York: HarperCollins.

———. 1992b. *Structures of Everyday Life: The Limits of the Possible: Civilization and Capitalism, 15th–18th Century*. Vol. 1. New York: HarperCollins.

———. 1992c. *The Wheels of Commerce: Civilization and Capitalism, 15th–18th Century*. Vol. 2. New York: HarperCollins.

Breen, Timothy H. 1985. *Tobacco Culture: The Mentality of the Great Tidewater Planters on the Eve of Revolution*. Princeton, N.J.: Princeton University Press.

Brenner, Robert. 1976. "Agrarian Class Structure and Economic Development in Pre-Industrial Europe." *Past & Present* 70: 30–75.

———. 2003. *Merchants and Revolution Commercial Change, Political Conflict, and London's Overseas Traders, 1550–1653*. London: Verso.

Broadberry, Stephen, and Bishnupriya Gupta. 2006. "The Early Modern Great Divergence: Wages, Prices and Economic Development in Europe and Asia, 1500–1800." *Economic History Review* 59(1): 2–31.

———. 2010. "Indian GDP before 1870: Some Preliminary Estimates and a Comparison with Britain." CEPR Discussion Paper No. DP8007.

Bruijn, Jaap R., and Femme S. Gaastra. 1993. *Ships, Sailors and Spices: East India Companies and Their Shipping in the 16th, 17th and 18th Centuries.* Amsterdam: NEHA.

Bruijn, Jaap R., F. S. Gaastra, and Ivo Schöffer. 1979–87. *Dutch-Asiatic Shipping in the 17th and 18th Centuries.* Vols. 1–3. The Hague: Martinus Nijhoff.

Buchan, P. Bruce. 2003. "The Emergence of the Technostructure: Lessons from the East India Company, 1713–1836." *Management Decision* 41(1): 105–16.

Buckeridge, Nicholas. 1973. *Journal and Letter Book of Nicholas Buckeridge, 1651–1764.* Edited by John R. Jenson. Minneapolis: University of Minnesota Press.

Bunge, Frederica M. 1984. *Malaysia: A Country Study.* Washington, D.C.: Government Printing Office.

Burke, Edmund, and P. J. Marshall. 1981. *The Writings and Speeches of Edmund Burke.* Vols. 5–7. Oxford: Clarendon.

Burt, Ronald S. 2004. "Structural Holes and Good Ideas." *American Journal of Sociology* 110(2): 349–99.

Burt, Ronald S., and Marc Knez. 1995. "Kinds of Third-Party Effects on Trust." *Rationality and Society* 7(3): 255–92.

Cain, P. J., and A. G. Hopkins. 1986. "Gentlemanly Capitalism and British Expansion Overseas I. The Old Colonial System, 1688–1850." *Economic History Review* 39(4): 501–25.

Callon, Michel. 1998. *The Laws of the Markets.* Oxford: Blackwell.

Campbell, Gwyn. 1993. "The Structure of Trade in Madagascar, 1750–1810." *International Journal of African Historical Studies* 26: 111–48.

Carlos, Ann M., and Jamie Brown Kruse. 1996. "The Decline of the Royal African Company: Fringe Firms and the Role of the Charter." *Economic History Review* 49(2): 291–313.

Carlos, Ann M., and Stephen Nicholas. 1988. "'Giants of an Earlier Capitalism': The Chartered Trading Companies as Modern Multinationals." *Business History Review* 62(3): 398–419.

———. 1990. "Agency Problems in Early Chartered Companies: The Case of the Hudson's Bay Company." *Journal of Economic History* 50(4): 853–75.

———. 1996. "Theory and History: Seventeenth-Century Joint-Stock Chartered Trading Companies." *Journal of Economic History* 56: 916–24.

Carruthers, Bruce G. 1996. *City of Capital: Politics and Markets in the English Financial Revolution.* Princeton, N.J.: Princeton University Press.

Cartwright. Charles. 1788? *An Abstract of the Orders and Regulations of the Honourable Court of Directors, and of Other Documents.* London?

Castells, Manuel. 1996. *The Rise of the Network Society*. Cambridge, Mass.: Blackwell.

Chandler, Alfred D., Jr. [1962] 2003. *Strategy and Structure: Chapters in the History of the American Industrial Enterprise*. Washington, D.C.: Beard Books.

Chandra, Satish, ed. 1987. *The Indian Ocean: Explorations in History, Commerce and Politics*. New Delhi: Sage.

Charrad, Mounira A., and Julia Adams. 2011. "Patrimonialism, Past and Present." *Annals of the American Academy of Political and Social Science* 636: 6–15.

Chaudhuri, K. N. 1965. *The English East India Company: The Study of an Early Joint-Stock Company, 1600–1640*. New York: Reprints of Economic Classics.

———. 1978. *The Trading World of Asia and the English East India Company, 1660–1760*. Cambridge: Cambridge University Press.

———. 1981. "The English East India Company in the 17th and 18th Centuries: A Pre-Modern Multinational Organization." In *Companies and Trade: Essays on Overseas Trading Companies during the Ancien Régime*, edited by Léonard Blussé and F. S. Gaastra. Leiden: Leiden University Press, 29–46.

———. 1985. *Trade and Civilization in the Indian Ocean: An Economic History from the Rise of Islam to 1750*. Cambridge: Cambridge University Press.

———. 1986. "The English East India Company and Its Decision-Making." In *East India Company Studies: Papers Presented to Professor Sir Cyril Philips*, edited by Kenneth Ballhatchet and John Harrison. Hong Kong: Asian Studies Monograph Series, 97–121.

———. 1993. "The English East India Company's Shipping (c. 1660–1760)." In *Ships, Sailors, and Spices: East India Companies and Their Shipping in the 16th, 17th, and 18th Centuries*, edited by J. R. Bruijn and F. S. Gaastra. Amsterdam: NEHA, 49–80.

Cheong, W. E. 1979. *Mandarins and Merchants: Jardine, Matheson, & Co., a China Agency of the Early Nineteenth Century*. London: Curzon.

———. 1997. *The Hong Merchants of Canton: Chinese Merchants in Sino-Western Trade*. London: Curzon.

Clark, Gregory. 2001. "The Secret History of the Industrial Revolution." Unpublished manuscript, Department of Economics, University of California, Davis.

Clingingsmith, David, and Jeffrey G. Williamson. 2008. "Deindustrialization in 18th and 19th Century India: Mughal Decline, Climate Shocks and British Industrial Ascent." *Explorations in Economic History* 45(3): 209–34.

Clough, Shepard Bancroft. 1968. *European Economic History: The Economic Development of Western Civilization*. New York: McGraw-Hill.

Cole, Juan R. I. 1987. "Rival Empires of Trade and Imami Shiism in Eastern Arabia, 1300–1800." *International Journal of Middle East Studies* 19(2): 177–203.

Cole, W. A. 1958. "Trends in Eighteenth-Century Smuggling." *Economic History Review*, New Series 10 (3), 395–410.

Coleman, James. 1990. *Foundations of Social Theory*. Cambridge, Mass.: Belknap.

Colombijn, Freek. 2003. "The Volatile State in Southeast Asia: Evidence from Sumatra, 1600–1800." *Journal of Asian Studies* 62(2): 497–529.

Copland, Samuel. 1970. *A History of the Island of Madagascar, Comprising a Political Account of the Island, the Religion, Manners, and Customs of Its Inhabitants, and Its Natural Productions, with an Appendix Containing a History of the Several Attempts to Introduce Christianity into the Island*. Westport, Conn.: Negro Universities Press.

Cortes, Rosario Mendoza. 1974. *Pangasinan, 1572–1800*. Quezon City: University of the Philippines Press.

Cotton, Evan. 1949. *East Indiamen: The East India Company's Maritime Service*. London: Batchworth Press.

Crafts, N.F.R. 1985. *British Economic Growth during the Industrial Revolution*. Oxford: Clarendon.

Cranmer-Byng, John L., and John E. Wills, Jr. 2011. "Trade and Diplomacy with Maritime Europe, 1644–c. 1800." In *China and Maritime Europe, 1500–1800: Trade, Settlement, Diplomacy and Missions*, edited by John E. Wills, Jr. Cambridge: Cambridge University Press.

Curtin, Philip D. 1994. *Cross-Cultural Trade in World History*. Cambridge: Cambridge University Press.

Dale, Stephen F. 1990. "Trade, Conversion and the Growth of the Islamic Community of Kerala, South India." *Studia Islamica* 71: 155–75.

Das Gupta, Ashin. 1979. *Indian Merchants and the Decline of Surat, c. 1700–1750*. Wiesbaden: Franz Steiner.

———. 1998. "Trade and Politics in 18th Century India." In *Trade, Finance, and Power*, edited by Patrick J. N. Tuck. London: Routledge, 46–81.

Das Gupta, Ashin, and M. N. Pearson. 1987. *India and the Indian Ocean, 1500–1800*. Delhi: Oxford University Press.

Datta, K. K., ed. 1958. *Fort William—India House Correspondence and Other Contemporary Papers Relating Thereto (Public Series)*. Delhi: National Archives of India.

Davis, Natalie Zemon. 1983. *The Return of Martin Guerre*. Cambridge, Mass.: Harvard University Press.

Davis, Ralph. 1962. "English Foreign Trade, 1700–1774." *Economic History Review* 15(2): 285–303.

De Vries, Jan. 1976. *The Economy of Europe in an Age of Crisis, 1600–1750*. Cambridge: Cambridge University Press.

Deane, Phyllis, and William Alan Cole. 1967. *British Economic Growth, 1688–1959: Trends and Structure*. London: Cambridge University Press.

Demeulenaere, Pierre, ed. 2011. *Analytical Sociology and Social Mechanisms*. Cambridge: Cambridge University Press.

Deshpande, Anirudh. 1995. "The Bombay Marine: Aspects of Maritime History 1650–1850." *Studies in History* 11(2): 281–301.

Dickson, P.G.M. 1967. *The Financial Revolution in England: A Study in the Development of Public Credit, 1688–1756*. London: St. Martin's.

DiMaggio, Paul. 1992. "Nadel's Paradox Revisited: Relational and Cultural Aspects of Organizational Structure." In *Networks and Organizations: Structure,*

*Form, and Action*, edited by Nitin Nohria and Robert G. Eccles. Boston: Harvard Business School Press, 118–42.

———, ed. 2009. *The Twenty-First-Century Firm: Changing Economic Organization in International Perspective*. Princeton, N.J.: Princeton University Press.

Dincecco, Mark. 2011. *Political Transformations and Public Finances: Europe, 1650–1913*. Cambridge: Cambridge University Press.

Disney, A. R. 1977. "The First Portuguese India Company, 1628–33." *Economic History Review* 30(2): 242–58.

Dodwell, George. 1773. *A Narrative of the Principal Transactions betwixt the Agents, and Officers of the Hon. East India Company, and George Dodwell, Esq. Commander of the Ship Patty; Respecting a Voyage to Sooloo in 1765 and 1766: With an Appendix, Containing the Original Papers*. London.

Dodwell, Henry. 1920. *Dupleix and Clive: The Beginning of Empire*. London: Methuen.

Don, P., G. L. Balk, Matthijs van Otegem, and M. Gosselink. 2012. *Atlas of Mutual Heritage Project*. http://www.atlasofmutualheritage.nl.

Duina, Francesco. 2005. *The Social Construction of Free Trade: The European Union, NAFTA, and MERCOSUR*. Princeton, N.J.: Princeton University Press.

East India Company. 1689. "Instructions to Captain Brown Commander of the Benjamin." Log of the *Benjamin*. India Office Records, British Library. L/MAR/A/XCVII.

———. 1752. Log of the *Dragon*. India Office Records, British Library. L/MAR/B/598D.

———. 1760. Log of the *Princess Augustus*. India Office Records, British Library. L/MAR/B/590C.

———. 1843. *The Asiatic Journal and Monthly Miscellany*. Vol. 17. London: Wm. H. Allen.

East India Company, George Christopher Molesworth Birdwood, and William Foster. 1893. *The Register of Letters, &c., of the Governour and Company of Merchants of London Trading into the East Indies, 1600–1619*. London: B. Quaritch.

Edling, Christopher. 2012. "Analytical Sociology Is a Research Strategy." *Sociologica* 1. http://www.sociologica.mulino.it/journal/article/index/Article/Journal:ARTICLE:544/Item/Journal:ARTICLE:544.

Ekelund, Robert B., Jr., and Robert D. Tollison. 1980. "Mercantilist Origins of the Corporation." *Bell Journal of Economics* 11(2): 715–20.

Emigh, Rebecca Jean. 2004. "[The] Transition(s) to Capitalism(s)? A Review Essay." *Comparative Studies in Society and History* 46(1): 188–98.

———. 2005. "The Great Debates: Transitions to Capitalisms." In *Remaking Modernity: Politics, History, and Sociology*, edited by Julia Adams, Elisabeth S. Clemens, and Ann Shola Orloff. Durham, N.C.: Duke University Press, 355–80.

Emirbayer, Mustafa, and Jeffrey Goodwin. 1994. "Network Analysis, Culture, and the Problem of Agency." *American Journal of Sociology* 99(6): 1411–54.

Emmer, P. C., and Femme Gaastra, eds. 1996. *The Organization of Interoceanic Trade in European Expansion, 1450–1800*. Aldershot: Variorum.

England and Wales, Sovereign (1660–1685: Charles II), and Charles. 1665. "By the King. A Proclamation for the Due Observance of the Charter and Priviledges Lately Granted to the Governour and Company of Merchants Trading to the Canaria-Islands." London: John Bill and Christopher Barker.

Erikson, Emily, and Peter Bearman. 2006. "Malfeasance and the Foundations for Global Trade: The Structure of English Trade in the East Indies, 1601–1833." *American Journal of Sociology* 112: 195–230.

Evers, Hans-Dieter. 1987. "Trade and State Formation: Siam in the Early Bangkok Period." *Modern Asian Studies* 21(4): 751–71.

Fang, Christina, Jeho Lee, and Melissa A. Schilling. 2010. "Balancing Exploration and Exploitation through Structural Design: The Isolation of Subgroups and Organizational Learning." *Organization Science* 21(3): 625–42.

Farrington, Anthony. 1999a. *Biographical Index of East India Company Maritime Service Officers, 1600–1834*. London: British Library.

———. 1999b. *Catalogue of East India Company Ships' Journals and Logs, 1600–1834*. London: British Library.

———. 2002a. "Bengkulu: An Anglo-Chinese Partnership." In *The Worlds of the East India Company*, edited by H. V. Bowen, Margarette Lincoln, and Nigel Rigby. Suffolk: Boydell Press, 111–18.

———. 2002b. *Trading Places: the East India Company and Asia, 1600–1834*. London: British Library.

Faulkner, Robert, and Andy B. Anderson. 1987. "Short-Term Projects and Emergent Careers: Evidence from Hollywood." *American Journal of Sociology* 92(4): 879–909.

Feldbæk, Ole. 1969. *India Trade under the Danish Flag 1772–1808: European Enterprise and Anglo-Indian Remittance and Trade*. Lund: University of Copenhagen.

Ferrier, R. W. 1973. "The Armenians and the East India Company in Persia in the Seventeenth and Early Eighteenth Centuries." *Economic History Review* 26(1): 38–62.

Findlay, Ronald, and Kevin O'Rourke. 2007. *Power and Plenty: Trade, War, and the World Economy in the Second Millennium*. Princeton, N.J.: Princeton University Press.

Finkelstein, Andrea. 2000. *Harmony and the Balance: An Intellectual History of Seventeenth-Century English Economic Thought*. Ann Arbor: University of Michigan Press.

Fitzgerald, Keane. 1777. *A Letter to the Directory of the East India Company*. London: T. Payne.

Fligstein, Neil. 1990. *The Transformation of Corporate Control*. Cambridge, Mass.: Harvard University Press.

———. 1996. "Markets as Politics: A Political-Cultural Approach to Market Institutions." *American Sociological Review* 61(4): 656–73.

———. 2001. *The Architecture of Markets: An Economic Sociology of Twenty-First-Century Capitalist Societies*. Princeton, N.J.: Princeton University Press.

Fligstein, Neil, and Iona Mara-Drita. 1996. "How to Make a Market: Reflections on the Attempt to Create a Single Market in the European Union." *American Journal of Sociology* 102(1): 1–33.

Foreman, John. 1890. *The Philippine Islands: A Historical, Geographical, Ethnographical, Social and Commercial Sketch of the Philippine Archipelago and Its Political Dependencies*. London: S. Low, Marston.

Foster, William, ed. 1899. *The Embassy of Sir Thomas Roe to the Court of the Great Mogul 1615–1619*. London: Hakluyt Society.

———. 1912. "An English Settlement in Madagascar in 1645–6." *English Historical Review* 27(106): 239–50.

Fourcade, Marion, and Sarah L. Babb. 2002. "The Rebirth of the Liberal Creed: Paths to Neoliberalism in Four Countries." *American Journal of Sociology* 108(3): 533–79.

Frank, Andre Gunder. 1998. *ReORIENT: Global Economy in the Asian Age*. Berkeley: University of California Press.

Freese, Jeremy. 2009. "Preferences." In *The Oxford Handbook of Analytical Sociology*, edited by Peter Hedström and Peter Bearman. Oxford: Oxford University Press, 94–114.

Fried, Vance, and Robert Hisrich. 1994. "Toward a Model of Venture Capital Investment Decision Making." *Financial Management* 23(3): 28–37.

Fryer, John. 1698. *A New Account of East-India and Persia, in Eight Letters Being Nine Years Travels Begun 1672 and Finished 1681: Containing Observations Made of the Moral, Natural and Artificial Estate of Those Countries*. London: Chiswell.

Furber, Holden. 1948. *John Company at Work: A Study of European Expansion in India in the Late Eighteenth Century*. Cambridge, Mass.: Harvard University Press.

———. 1965. *Bombay Presidency in the Mid-Eighteenth Century*. New York: Asia Pub. House.

———. 1976. *Rival Empires of Trade in the Orient, 1600–1800*. Minneapolis: University of Minnesota Press.

Furber, Holden, and Rosane Rocher. 1997. *Private Fortunes and Company Profits in the India Trade in the 18th Century*. Brookfield, Vt.: Variorum.

Gaastra, Femme S. 2003. *The Dutch East India Company: Expansion and Decline*. Zutphen: Walburg Pers.

Gambetta, Diego. 1998. "Concatenation of Mechanisms." In *Social Mechanisms: An Analytical Approach to Social Theory*, edited by Peter Hedström and Richard Swedberg. Cambridge: Cambridge University Press, 102–24.

Génaux, Maryvonne. 2002. "Early Modern Corruption in English and French Fields of Vision." In *Political Corruption: Concepts and Contexts*, 3rd ed., edited by Arnold J. Heidenheimer and Michael Johnston. New Brunswick, N.J.: Transaction, 107–22.

Gilbert, Erik. 2002. "Coastal East Africa and the Western Indian Ocean: Long-Distance Trade, Empire, Migration and Regional Unity, 1750–1970." *History Teacher* 36: 7–34.

Ginzburg, Carlo. 1992. *The Cheese and the Worms: The Cosmos of a Sixteenth-Century Miller.* Baltimore: Johns Hopkins University Press.

Glamann, Kristof. 1981. *Dutch-Asiatic Trade, 1620–1740.* Copenhagen: Martinus Nijhoff.

Go, Julian. 2011. *Patterns of Empire: The British and American Empires, 1688 to the Present.* Cambridge: Cambridge University Press.

Goldstein, Daniel G. 2009. "Heuristics." In *The Oxford Handbook of Analytical Sociology,* edited by Peter Hedström and Peter Bearman. Oxford: Oxford University Press, 140–67.

Goldstone, Jack A. 1998. "The Problem of the 'Early Modern' World." *Journal of the Economic and Social History of the Orient* 41(3): 249–84.

———. 2000. "The Rise of the West—or Not? A Revision to Socio-economic History." *Sociological Theory* 18(2): 175–94.

———. 2002. "Efflorescences and Economic Growth in World History: Rethinking the 'Rise of the West' and the Industrial Revolution." *Journal of World History* 13(2): 323–89.

———. 2003. "Europe vs. Asia: Missing Data and Misconceptions." *Science & Society* 67(2): 184–95.

Gorski, Philip S. 2003. *The Disciplinary Revolution: Calvinism and the Rise of the State in Early Modern Europe.* Chicago: University of Chicago Press.

Gotham, Kevin Fox. 2006. "The Secondary Circuit of Capitalism Reconsidered: Globalization and the U.S. Real Estate Sector." *American Journal of Sociology* 112(1): 231–75.

Gould, Roger V. 1995. *Insurgent Identities: Class, Community, and Protest in Paris from 1848 to the Commune.* Chicago: University of Chicago Press.

Granovetter, Mark. 1985. "Economic-Action and Social-Structure: The Problem of Embeddedness." *American Journal of Sociology* 91(3): 481–510.

Greenberg, Michael. 1951. *British Trade and the Opening of China, 1800–42.* Cambridge: Cambridge University Press.

Greif, Avner. 1989. "Reputation and Coalitions in Medieval Trade: Evidence on the Maghribi Traders." *Journal of Economic History* 49: 857–82.

———. 1993. "Contract Enforceability and Economic Institutions in Early Trade: The Maghribi Traders' Coalition." *American Economic Review* 83: 525–48.

———. 1994. "Cultural Beliefs and the Organization of Society: A Historical and Theoretical Reflection on Collective and Individualist Societies." *Journal of Political Economy* 102: 912–50.

———. 2006a. "Institutions, Markets, and Games." In *The Economic Sociology of Capitalism,* edited by Victor Nee and Richard Swedberg. Princeton, N.J.: Princeton University Press, ix–xxxii.

———. 2006b. *Institutions and the Path to the Modern Economy: Lessons from Medieval Trade.* Cambridge: Cambridge University Press.

Grofman, Bernard, and Janet Landa. 1983. "The Development of Trading Networks Among Spatially Separated Traders as a Process of Proto-Coalition Formation: The Kula Trade." *Social Networks* 5: 347–65.

Gross, Neil. 2009. "A Pragmatist Theory of Social Mechanisms." *American Sociological Review* 74: 358–79.

Guillén, Mauro. 2001. "Is Globalization Civilizing, Destructive or Feeble? A Critique of Five Key Debates." *Annual Review of Sociology* 27: 235–60.

Gulati, Ranjay. 1995. "Social Structure and Alliance Formation: A Longitudinal Analysis." *Administrative Science Quarterly* 40: 619–52.

———. 1998. "Alliances and Networks." *Strategic Management Journal* 19(4): 293–317.

Halliday, Terence C., and Bruce G. Carruthers. 2007. "The Recursivity of Law: Global Norm Making and National Lawmaking in the Globalization of Corporate Insolvency Regimes." *American Journal of Sociology* 112(4): 1135–202.

Hamilton, Alexander, and William Foster. [1732] 1930. *A New Account of the East Indies*. London: Argonaut Press.

Hansard, T. C. 1812. *The Parliamentary Debates*. Hansard.

Harris, Ron. 2009. "The Institutional Dynamics of Early Modern Eurasian Trade: The *Commenda* and the Corporation." *Journal of Economic Behavior and Organization* 71(3): 606–22.

Hedström, Peter. 1998. "Rational Imitation." In *Social Mechanisms: An Analytical Approach to Social Theory*, edited by Peter Hedström and Richard Swedberg. Cambridge: Cambridge University Press, 306–27.

———. 2005. *Dissecting the Social: On the Principles of Analytical Sociology*. Cambridge: Cambridge University Press.

Hedström, Peter, and Peter Bearman, eds. 2009. *The Oxford Handbook of Analytical Sociology*. Oxford: Oxford University Press.

Hedström, Peter, and Richard Swedberg, eds. 1998. *Social Mechanisms: An Analytical Approach to Social Theory*. Cambridge: Cambridge University Press.

Hejeebu, Santhi. 2005. "Contract Enforcement in the English East India Company." *Journal of Economic History* 65(2): 496–523.

Herbert, William, and Samuel Dunn. 1791. *A New Directory for the East-Indies: Containing, I. The First Discoveries Made in the East-Indies by European Voyagers VI. Directions for Sailing to and from the East-Indies The Whole Being a Work Originally Begun upon the Plan of the Oriental Neptune, Augmented and Improved by Mr. Will. Herbert, Mr. Will. Nichelson, and Others; and Now Methodised, Corrected, and Further Enlarged*. 6th ed. London: Gilbert and Wright.

Hertz, Gerald B. 1907. "England and the Ostend Company." *English Historical Review* 22(86): 255–79.

Hill, S. C. 1905. *Bengal in 1756–1757*. London: J. Murray.

Hirschman, Albert O. 1997. *The Passions and the Interests: Political Arguments for Capitalism Before Its Triumph*. Princeton, N.J.: Princeton University Press.

Hodacs, Hanna. 2013. "The Scandinavian East India Companies: Company and Private Trade." Unpublished manuscript.

Horsburgh, James. 1841. *The India Directory, or, Directions for Sailing to and from the East Indies, China, Australia, and the Interjacent Ports of Africa and South America*. London: W.H. Allen.

Hunt, Margaret H. 1996. *The Middling Sort: Commerce, Gender, and the Family in England, 1680–1780*. Berkeley: University of California Press.

Irwin, Douglas A. 1991. "Mercantilism as Strategic Trade Policy: The Anglo-Dutch Rivalry for the East India Trade." *Journal of Political Economy* 99: 1296–1314.

———. 1992. "Strategic Trade Policy and Mercantilist Trade Rivalries." *American Economic Review* 82(2): 134–39.

Israel, Jonathan I. 1998. *The Dutch Republic: Its Rise, Greatness and Fall, 1477–1806*. Oxford: Clarendon.

Jackson, R. V. 1990. "Government Expenditure and British Economic Growth in the Eighteenth Century: Some Problems of Measurement." *Economic History Review* 43(2): 217–35.

Johnson, E.A.J. 1937. *Predecessors of Adam Smith: The Growth of British Economic Thought*. New York: Prentice Hall.

Jones, E. L. 1988. *Growth Recurring: Economic Change in World History*. Oxford: Clarendon.

———. 2003. *The European Miracle: Environments, Economies, and Geopolitics in the History of Europe and Asia*. Cambridge: Cambridge University Press.

Jones, S.R.H., and Simon P. Ville. 1996a. "Efficient Transactors or Rent-Seeking Monopolists? The Rationale for Early Chartered Trading Companies." *Journal of Economic History* 56: 898–915.

———. 1996b. "Theory and Evidence: Understanding Chartered Trading Companies." *Journal of Economic History* 56: 925–26.

Kathirithamby-Wells, J. 1969. "Achehnese Control over West Sumatra up to the Treaty of Painan, 1663." *Journal of Southeast Asian History* 10(3): 453–79.

———. 1977. *The British West Sumatran Presidency, 1760–1785: Problems of Early Colonial Enterprise*. Kuala Lumpur: Penerbit Universiti Malaya.

———. 1986. "The Islamic City: Melaka to Jogjakarta, c. 1500–1800." *Modern Asian Studies* 20(2): 333–51.

———. 1990. "Banten: A West Indonesian Port and Polity during the Sixteenth and Seventeenth Century." In *The Southeast Asian Port and Polity: Rise and Demise*, edited by J. Kathirithamby-Wells and John Villiers. Singapore: Singapore University Press, 107–25.

Kathirithamby-Wells, J., and John Villiers. 1990. *The Southeast Asian Port and Polity: Rise and Demise*. Singapore: Singapore University Press.

Kent, R. K. 1968. "Madagascar and Africa: II. The Sakalava, Maroserana, Dady and Tromba before 1700." *Journal of African History* 9: 517–46.

Khan, Shafaat Ahmad. 1975. *The East India Trade in the XVIIth Century in Its Political and Economic Aspects*. New Delhi: S. Chand.

Kieser, Alfred. 1989. "Organizational, Institutional, and Societal Evolution: Medieval Craft Guilds and the Genesis of Formal Organizations." *Administrative Science Quarterly* 34(4): 540–64.

Kim, Sangmoon and Eui-Hang Shin. 2002. "A Longitudinal Analysis of Globalization and Regionalization in International Trade: A Social Network Approach." *Social Forces* 81(2): 445–71.

Kling, Blair B., M. N. Pearson, and Holden Furber. 1979. *The Age of Partnership: Europeans in Asia before Dominion*. Honolulu: University of Hawaii Press.

Knaap, Gerrit. 2003. "Headhunting, Carnage and Armed Peace in Amboina, 1500–1700." *Journal of the Economic and Social History of the Orient* 46(2): 165–92.

Knight, Jack and Itai Sened, eds. 1995. "Introduction." In *Explaining Social Institutions*, edited by Jack Knight and Itai Sened. Ann Arbor: University of Michigan Press, 1–14.

Koninckx, Christian. 1980. *The First and Second Charters of the Swedish East India Company (1731–1756): A Contribution to the Maritime, Economic, and Social History of North-western Europe in Its Relationships with the Far East*. Kortrijk, Belgium: Van Ghemmert.

Körner, Martin. 1995. "Public Credit." In *Economic Systems and State Finance*, edited by Richard Bonney. Oxford: Oxford University Press, 507–32.

Krippner, Greta R. 2011. *Capitalizing on Crisis: The Political Origins of the Rise of Finance*. Cambridge, Mass.: Harvard University Press.

Krishna, Bal. 1924. *Commercial Relations between India and England (1601 to 1757)*. London: Routledge.

Lach, Donald F., and Edwin J. Van Kley. 1965. *Asia in the Making of Europe*. Chicago: University of Chicago Press.

Lachmann, Richard. 2000. *Capitalists in Spite of Themselves: Elite Conflict and Economic Transitions in Early Modern Europe*. New York: Oxford University Press.

Lahiri, Shompa. 2002. "Contested Relations: The East India Company and Lascars in London." In *The Worlds of the East India Company*, edited by H. V. Bowen, Margarette Lincoln, and Nigel Rigby. Suffolk: Boydell Press, 169–81.

Landa, Janet. 1981. "A Theory of the Ethnically Homogeneous Middleman Group: An Institutional Alternative to Contract Law." *Journal of Legal Studies* 10(2): 349–62.

Lane, Frederic Chapin. 1966. *Venice and History*. Baltimore: Johns Hopkins University Press.

———. 1979. *Profits from Power: Readings in Protection Rent and Violence-Controlling Enterprises*. Albany: State University of New York Press.

Lawson, Philip. 1993. *The East India Company: A History*. London: Longman.

Lazarsfeld, Paul, and Robert K. Merton. 1954. "Friendship as a Social Process: A Substantive and Methodological Analysis." In *Freedom and Control in Modern Society*, edited by Morroe Berger, Theodore Abel, and Charles H. Page. New York: Van Nostrand, 18–66.

Lemire, Beverly. 2011. "Revising the Historical Narrative: India, Europe, and the Cotton Trade, c. 1300–1800." *The Spinning World: A Global History of Cotton Textiles, 1200–1850*, edited by Giorgio Riello and Prasannan Parthasarathi. New York, Oxford: Oxford University Press, 205–26.

Letwin, William, Josiah Child, and Thomas Culpeper. 1959. *Sir Josiah Child, Merchant Economist*. Boston: Baker Library.

Levitt, Barbara, and James G. March. 1988. "Organizational Learning." *Annual Review of Sociology* 14: 319–40.

Levy, Jack S. 1989. "Great Power Wars, 1495–1815" [Computer file]. New Brunswick, N.J.: Jack S. Levy and T. Clifton Morgan [producers], 1989. Ann Arbor, Mich.: Inter-university Consortium for Political and Social Research [distributor], 1994.

Lieberman, Victor. 1997. "Transcending East-West Dichotomies: State and Culture Formation in Six Ostensibly Disparate Areas." *Modern Asian Studies* 31(3): 463–546.

Little, Daniel. 2012. "Analytical Sociology and the Rest of Sociology." *Sociologica* 1. http://www.sociologica.mulino.it/doi/10.2383/36894.

Lombard, Denys. 1981. "Questions on the Contact between European Companies and Asian Societies." In *Companies and Trade: Essays on Overseas Trading Companies during the Ancien Régime*, edited by Léonard Blussé and F. S. Gaastra. Leiden: Leiden University Press, 179–87.

Loten, Joan Gideon. 1935. *Selections from the Dutch Records of the Ceylon Government: Memoirs of Joan Gideon Loten*. Translated by E. Reimers. Colombo: Ceylon Government Press.

Luhmann, Niklas. 1995. *Social Systems*. Stanford, Calif.: Stanford University Press.

MacDougall, G.D.A. 1960. "The Benefits and Costs of Private Investment from Abroad: A Theoretical Approach." *Bulletin of the Oxford University Institute of Economics & Statistics* 22(3): 189–211.

Machamer, Peter, Lindley Darden, and Carl F. Craver. 2000. "Thinking about Mechanisms." *Philosophy of Science* 67(1): 1–25.

MacKenzie, Donald A., Fabian Muniesa, and Lucia Siu. 2007. *Do Economists Make Markets? On the Performativity of Economics*. Princeton, N.J.: Princeton University Press.

MacLeod, Christine. 1983. "Henry Martin and the Authorship of 'Considerations upon the East India Trade.'" *Historical Research* 56(134): 222–29.

Mahoney, James. 2010. *Colonialism and Postcolonial Development*. Cambridge: Cambridge University Press.

Malinowski, Bronislaw. 1984. *Argonauts of the Western Pacific: An Account of Native Enterprise and Adventure in the Archipelagoes of Melanisian New Guinea*. Prospect Heights, Ill.: Waveland.

Maneschi, Andrea. 2002. "The Tercentenary of Henry Martyn's Considerations upon the East-India Trade." *Journal of the History of Economic Thought* 24(2): 233–49.

Mann, Michael. 1986. *The Sources of Social Power*. Vol. 1. Cambridge: Cambridge University Press.

———. 1993. *The Sources of Social Power*. Vol. 2. Cambridge: Cambridge University Press.

Manning, Catherine. 1996. *Fortunes à Faire: The French in Asian Trade, 1719–48*. Aldershot: Variorum.

Manzo, Gianluca. 2010. "Analytical Sociology and Its Critics." *European Journal of Sociology*, 51(1): 129–70.

March, James. 1991. "Exploration and Exploitation in Organizational Learning." *Organization Science* 2: 71–87.

Marco, Pilar Nogués, and Camila Vam Malle-Sabouret. 2007. "East India Bonds, 1718–1763: Early Exotic Derivatives and London Market Efficiency." *European Review of Economic History* 11(3): 367–94.

Marshall, P. J. 1965. *The Impeachment of Warren Hastings*. Oxford: Oxford University Press.

———. 1976. *East Indian Fortunes: The British in Bengal in the Eighteenth Century*. Oxford: Clarendon.

———. 1987. *Bengal: The British Bridgehead: Eastern India, 1740–1828*. Cambridge: Cambridge University Press.

———. 1993. *Trade and Conquest: Studies on the Rise of British Dominance in India*. Aldershot: Variorum.

Martin, John Levi. 2011. *The Explanation of Social Action*. New York: Oxford University Press.

Marx, Karl, and Shlomo Avineri. 1969. *Karl Marx on Colonialism and Modernization; His Despatches and Other Writings on China, India, Mexico, the Middle East and North Africa*. Garden City, N.Y.: Doubleday.

Mathew, K. M. 1988. *History of the Portuguese Navigation in India, 1497–1600*. Delhi: Mittal.

McGilvary, George K. 2008. *East India Patronage and the British State: The Scottish Elite and Politics in the Eighteenth Century*. London: Tauris Academic Studies.

McGrath, Charles Ivar, and Chris Fauske, eds. 2008. *Money, Power, and Print: Interdisciplinary Studies on the Financial Revolution in the British Isles*. Newark: University of Delaware Press.

McLean, Paul D. 2007. *The Art of the Network: Strategic Interaction and Patronage in Renaissance Florence*. Durham, N.C. Duke University Press.

McPherson, Kenneth. 1990. "Chulias and Klings: Indigenous Trade Diasporas and European Penetration of the Indian Ocean Littoral." In *Trade and Politics in the Indian Ocean*, edited by Giorgio Borsa. New Delhi: Manohar Press, 33–46.

McPherson, M., L. Smith-Lovin, and J. Cook. 2001. "Birds of a Feather: Homophily in Social Networks." *Annual Review of Sociology* 27: 415–44.

Menard, R. 1991. "Transport Costs and Long-Range Trade, 1300–1800: Was There a European 'Transport Revolution' in the Early Modern Era?" In *Political Economy of Merchant Empires*, edited by James D. Tracy. Cambridge: Cambridge University Press, 228–75.

Mentz, Søren. 2005. *The English Gentleman Merchant at Work*. Copenhagen: Museum of Tusculanum Press.

Midlarsky, Manus I., and Kun Y. Park. 1991. "Major-Minor Power Wars, 1495–1815" [Computer file]. Champaign-Urbana, Ill.: Data Development in International Research [producer], 1991. Ann Arbor, Mich.: Inter-university Consortium for Political and Social Research [distributor], 1994.

Milburn, William. 1813. *Oriental Commerce; Containing a Geographical Description of the Principal Places in the East Indies, China, and Japan, with Their Produce, Manufactures, and Trade*. London: Black Parry.

Milburn, William, and Thomas Thornton. 1825. *Oriental Commerce, or, The East India Trader's Complete Guide Containing a Geographical and Nautical Description of the Maritime Parts of India, China, Japan, and Neighbouring Countrieswith an Account of Their Respective Commerce*. London: Kingsbury Parbury and Allen.

Mische, Ann. 2008. *Partisan Publics: Communication and Contention across Brazilian Youth Activist Networks*. Princeton, N.J.: Princeton University Press.

Mishra, Rupali. 2010. "Merchants, Commerce, and the State: The East India Company in Early Stuart England." Ph.D. diss., Princeton University.

Misselden, Edward. 1622. *Free Trade, or, The Meanes to Make Trade Florish. Wherein, the Causes of the Decay of Trade in This Kingdome Are Discouered and the Remedies Also to Remooue the Same Are Represented*. London: John Legatt for Simon Waterson.

———. 1623. *The Circle of Commerce. Or the Ballance of Trade in Defence of Free Trade: Opposed to Malynes Little Fish and His Great Whale, and Poized Against Them in the Scale. Wherein Also, Exchanges in Generall Are Considered: and Therein the Whole Trade of This Kingdome with Forraine Countries, Is Digested into a Ballance of Trade, for the Benefite of the Publique. Necessary for the Present and Future Times*. London: Iohn Dawson, for Nicholas Bourne.

Modelski, George, and William R. Thompson. 1988. *Seapower in Global Politics, 1494–1993*. Hampshire: Macmillan.

Mokyr, Joel. 1999. "Editor's Introduction: The New Economic History and the Industrial Revolution." In *The British Industrial Revolution: An Economic Perspective*, edited by Joel Mokyr. Boulder, Colo.: Westview, 1–127.

———. 2003. "Industrial Revolution." In *The Oxford Encyclopedia of Economic History*. Oxford: Oxford University Press. http://www.oxford-economichistory.com /entry?entry=t168.e0369.

Moody, James. 2004. "The Structure of a Social Science Collaboration Network: Disciplinary Cohesion from 1963 to 1999." *American Sociological Review* 68: 213–38.

Moody, James, and Douglas R. White. 2003. "Social Cohesion and Embeddedness: A Hierarchical Conception of Social Groups." *American Sociological Review* 68: 103–27.

Moreland, W. H. 1923. *From Akbar to Aurangzeb: A Study in Indian Economic History*. London: Macmillan.

Morse, Hosea Ballou. 1926. *The Chronicles of the East India Company, Trading to China 1635–1834*. Oxford: Clarendon.

Mortimer, Thomas. [1772] 1780. *The Elements of Commerce, Politics and Finances, in Three Treatises on Those Important Subjects*. London: Baldwin.

Muchmore, Lynn. 1970. "A Note of Thomas Mun's 'England's Treasure by Forraign Trade.'" *Economic History Review*, New Series 23(3): 498–503.

Mukund, Kanakalatha. 1999. *The Trading World of the Tamil Merchant*. Himayatnagar: Orient Longman.

———. 2005. *The View from Below: Indigenous Society Temples and the Early Colonial State in Tamilnadu, 1700–1835*. Himayatnagar: Orient Longman.

Neal, Larry. 1977. "Interpreting Power and Profit in Economic History: A Case Study of the Seven Years War." *Journal of Economic History* 37(1): 20–35.

———. 1990. "The Dutch and English East India Companies Compared: Evidence from the Stock and Foreign Exchange Markets." In *The Rise of Merchant Empires: Long-Distance Trade in the Early Modern World, 1350–1750*, edited by James D. Tracy. Cambridge: Cambridge University Press, 195–223.

Nierstrasz, Chris. 2012. *In the Shadow of the Company: The Dutch East India Company and its Servants in the Period of its Decline, 1740–1796*. Leiden: Brill.

Nightingale, Carl H. 2008. "Before Race Mattered: Geographies of the Color Line in Early Colonial Madras and New York." *American Historical Review* 113(1): 48–71.

Nightingale, Pamela. 1985. *Fortune and Integrity: A Study of the Moral Attitudes in the Indian Diary of George Paterson*. Delhi: Oxford University Press.

Nordenflycht, Andrew von. 2002. "The Theory of the Firm Meets the 17th Century: The Case of the Chartered Trading Companies." Working paper, MIT.

North, Douglass C. 1973. *The Rise of the Western World: A New Economic History*. Cambridge: Cambridge University Press.

———. 1981. *Structure and Change in Economic History*. New York: Norton.

———. 1990. *Institutions, Institutional Change, and Economic Performance*. Cambridge: Cambridge University Press.

North, Douglass C., and Robert Paul Thomas. 1973. *The Rise of the Western World: A New Economic History*. Cambridge: Cambridge University Press.

North, Douglass C., John Joseph Wallis, and Barry R. Weingast. 2009. *Violence and Social Orders: A Conceptual Framework for Interpreting Recorded Human History*. Cambridge: Cambridge University Press.

North, Douglass C., and Barry R. Weingast. 1989. "Constitutions and Commitment: The Evolution of Institutions Governing Public Choice in Seventeenth-Century England." *Journal of Economic History* 49(4): 803–32.

Nutting, P. Bradley. 1978. "The Madagascar Connection." *American Journal of Legal History* 22(3): 202–15.

O'Brien, Patrick. 1982. "European Economic Development: The Contribution of the Periphery." *Economic History Review* 35(1): 1–18.

———. 2000. "The Reconstruction, Rehabilitation and Reconfiguration of the British Industrial Revolution as a Conjuncture in Global History." *Itinerario* 24(3–4): 117–34.

O'Brien, Patrick, Trevor Griffiths, and Philip Hunt. 1991. "Political Components of the Industrial Revolution: Parliament and the English Cotton Textile Industry, 1660–1774." *Economic History Review* 44(3): 395–423.

O'Brien, Patrick, and Philip A. Hunt. 1999. "England, 1485–1815." In *The Rise of the Fiscal State in Europe, c.1200–1815*, edited by Richard Bonney. Oxford: Oxford University Press, 53–100.

Ogborn, Miles. 2007. *Indian Ink: Script and Print in the Making of the English East India Company*, Chicago: University of Chicago Press.

Ogilvie, Sheilagh. 2011. *Institutions and European Trade: Merchants Guilds, 1000–1800*. Cambridge: Cambridge University Press.

O'Reilly, C. A., and M. Tushman. 2004. "The Ambidextrous Organization." *Harvard Business Review* 82(2): 74–81.

O'Rourke, Kevin H., and Jeffrey G. Williamson. 2002. "After Columbus: Explaining Europe's Overseas Trade Boom, 1500–1800." *Journal of Economic History* 62(2): 417–56.

———. 2005. "From Malthus to Ohlin: Trade, Industrialisation and Distribution since 1500." *Journal of Economic Growth* 10(1): 5–34.

Ovington, John. [1689] 1976. *India in the Seventeenth Century, Being an Account of the Two Voyages to India by Ovington and Thevenot, to Which Is Added the Indian Travels of Careri*. Edited by J. P. Guha. New Delhi: Associated Pub. House.

Pachucki, Mark, and Ronald Breiger. 2010. "Cultural Holes: Beyond Relationality in Social Networks and Culture." *Annual Review of Sociology* 36: 205–24.

Padgett, John F., and Christopher K. Ansell. 1993. "Robust Action and the Rise of the Medici, 1400–1434." *American Journal of Sociology* 98(6): 1259–319.

Padgett, John F., and Paul McLean. 2006. "Organizational Invention and Elite Transformation: The Birth of Partnership Systems in Renaissance Florence." *American Journal of Sociology* 111(5): 1463–568.

Padgett, John F., and Walter W. Powell. 2012. *The Emergence of Organizations and Markets*. Princeton, N.J.: Princeton University Press.

Parker, Geoffrey. 1991. "Europe and the Wider World." In *Political Economy of Merchant Empires*, edited by James D. Tracy. Cambridge: Cambridge University Press, 161–95.

Parthasarathi, Prasannan. 2001. *The Transition to a Colonial Economy: Weavers, Merchants and Kings in South India, 1720–1800*. Cambridge: Cambridge University Press.

Parthesius, Robert. 2010. *Dutch Ships in Tropical Waters: The Development of the Dutch East India Company (VOC) Shipping Network in Asia 1595–1660*. Amsterdam: Amsterdam University Press.

Pearson, M. N. 1987. *The Portuguese in India*. Cambridge: Cambridge University Press.

———. 1988a. *Before Colonialism: Theories on Asian-European Relations, 1500–1750*. Delhi: Oxford University Press.

———. 1988b. "Brokers in Western Indian Port Cities: Their Role in Servicing Foreign Merchants." *Modern Asian Studies* 22: 455–72.

———. 1996. "The People and the Politics of Portuguese India during the Early Sixteenth and Seventeenth Centuries." In *The Organization of Interoceanic Trade in European Expansion, 1450–1800*, edited by P. C. Emmer and Femme Gaastra. Aldershot: Variorum, 25–29.

Perlin, Frank. 1983. "Proto-industrialization and Pre-colonial South Asia." *Past & Present* 98: 30–95.

Petersen, Trond. 2009. "Opportunities." In *The Oxford Handbook of Analytical Sociology*, edited by Peter Hedström and Peter Bearman. Oxford: Oxford University Press, 115–39.

Philips, C. H. 1937. "The East India Company 'Interest' and the English Government, 1783–4." *Transactions of the Royal Historical Society* 20: 83–101.

———. 1940. "The New East India Board and the Court of Directors, 1784." *English Historical Review* 55(219): 438–46.

———. 1951. *The Correspondence of David Scott, Director and Chairman of the East India Company Relating to Indian Affairs, 1787–1805, Vol. 1*. London: Offices of the Royal Historical Society.

Pieris, P. E., and R. B. Naish. 1920. *Ceylon and the Portuguese, 1505–1658*. Tellippalai: American Ceylon Mission Press.

Pincus, Steven C. A. 1992. "Popery, Trade and Universal Monarchy: The Ideological Context of the Outbreak of the Second Anglo-Dutch War." *English Historical Review* 107(422): 1–29.

———. 1995. "'Coffee Politicians Does Create': Coffeehouses and Restoration Political Culture." *Journal of Modern History* 67(4): 807–34.

Pires, Tome. 1944. *The Suma Oriental of Tome Pires: An Account of the East, from the Red Sea to Japan, Written in Malacca and India in 1512–1515*. London: Hakluyt Society.

Plane, David A., and Peter A. Rogerson. 1994. *The Geographical Analysis of Population with Applications to Planning and Business*. New York: John Wiley.

Platt, Virginia Bever. 1969. "The East India Company and the Madagascar Slave Trade." *William and Mary Quarterly* 26: 548–77.

Polanyi, Karl. 2001. *The Great Transformation: The Political and Economic Origins of Our Time*. Boston: Beacon.

Pomeranz, Kenneth. 2000. *The Great Divergence: China, Europe, and the Making of the Modern World Economy*. Princeton, N.J.: Princeton University Press.

Pond, Shepard. 1941. "The Spanish Dollar: The World's Most Famous Coin." *Bulletin of the Business Historical Society* 15(1): 12–16.

Powell, Walter W. 1990. "Neither Market nor Hierarchy: Network Forms of Organization." *Research in Organizational Behavior* 12: 295–336.

Powell, Walter, Kenneth W. Koput, and Laurel Smith-Doerr. 1996. "Interorganizational Collaboration and the Locus of Innovation: Networks of Learning in Biotechnology." *Administrative Science Quarterly* 41: 116–45.

Prakash, Om. 1976. "Bullion for Goods: International Trade and the Economy of Early Eighteenth Century Bengal." *Indian Economic and Social History Review* 13(2): 159–86.

———. 1979. "Asian Trade and European Impact." In *The Age of Partnership: Europeans in Asia before Dominion*, edited by Blair B. Kling, M. N. Pearson, and Holden Furber. Honolulu: University of Hawaii Press, 43–70.

————. 1985. *The Dutch East India Company and the Economy of Bengal, 1630–1720*. Princeton, N.J.: Princeton University Press.

————. 1991. "European and Asian Merchants in Asian Maritime Trade, 1500–1800: Some Issues of Methodology and Evidence." *Revista de Cultura* 13/14: 131–39.

————. 1994a. "The European Factories in India: A Blessing or a Curse?" In *International Conference on Shipping, Factories, and Colonization*, edited by Everaert J. Parementier. Brussels: Wetenschappelijk Comité voor Maritieme Geschiedenis Koninklijke Academie, 14–20.

————. 1994b. *Precious Metals and Commerce: The Dutch East India Company in the Indian Ocean Trade*. Aldershot: Variorum.

————. 1997. *European Commercial Expansion in Early Modern Asia*. Aldershot: Variorum.

————. 2002. "The English East India Company and India." In *The Worlds of the East India Company*, edited by H. V. Bowen, Margarette Lincoln, and Nigel Rigby. Suffolk: Boydell Press, 1–17.

————. 2005. "The Great Divergence: Evidence from Eighteenth Century India." Paper presented at the Seventh GEHN Conference at Istanbul, September 11–12.

Price, Jacob M. 1989. "What Did Merchants Do? Reflections on British Overseas Trade, 1660–1790." *Journal of Economic History* 49(2): 267–84.

Pritchard, Earl Hampton. 1930. *Anglo-Chinese Relations during the Seventeenth and Eighteenth Centuries*. Urbana: University of Illinois.

————. 1970. *The Crucial Years of Early Anglo-Chinese Relations, 1750–1800*. New York: Octagon Books.

Raub, Werner, and Jeroen Weesie. 1990. "Reputation and Efficiency in Social Interactions: An Example of Network Effects." *American Journal of Sociology* 96(3): 626–54.

Rauch, James E. 1999. "Networks versus Markets in International Trade." *Journal of International Economics* 48(1): 7–35.

Reed, Isaac Ariail. 2012. "Analytical Sociology: Appreciation and Ambivalence." *Sociologica* 1. http://www.sociologica.mulino.it/journal/article/index/Article/Journal:RWARTICLE:36901/Item/Journal:RWARTICLE:36901.

Reid, Anthony. 1993. *Southeast Asia in the Early Modern Era: Trade, Power, and Belief*. Ithaca, N.Y.: Cornell University Press.

Ricklefs, M. C. 1974. *Jogjakarta under Sultan Mangkubumi, 1749–1792: A History of the Division of Java*. Oxford: Oxford University Press.

Roberts, P. E. 1938. *History of British India under the Company and the Crown*. Oxford: Clarendon.

Rodger, Nicholas A. M. 2004. *The Command of the Ocean: A Naval History of Britain, 1649–1815*. London: Allen Lane.

Rolfe, Meredith. 2009. "Conditional Choice." In *The Oxford Handbook of Analytical Sociology*, edited by Peter Hedström and Peter Bearman. Oxford: Oxford University Press, 419–46.

Roover, Raymond de. 1951. "Monopoly Theory Prior to Adam Smith: A Revision." *Quarterly Journal of Economics* 4: 492–524.

Roy, Tirthankar. 2010. "Economic Conditions in Early Modern Bengal: A Contribution to the Divergence Debate." *Journal of Economic History* 70(1): 179–94.

Rydgren, Jens. 2009. "Beliefs." In *The Oxford Handbook of Analytical Sociology*, edited by Peter Hedström and Peter Bearman. Oxford: Oxford University Press, 72–93.

Sainsbury, Ethel Bruce. 1922. *A Calendar of the Court Minutes of the East India Company, 1660–1663*. Oxford: Clarendon.

———. 1925. *A Calendar of the Court Minutes of the East India Company, 1664–1667*. Oxford: Clarendon.

———. 1929. *A Calendar of the Court Minutes of the East India Company, 1668–1670*. Oxford: Clarendon.

———. 1932. *A Calendar of the Court Minutes of the East India Company, 1671–1673*. Oxford: Clarendon.

Sassen, Saskia. 1991. *The Global City: New York, London, Tokyo*. Princeton, N.J.: Princeton University Press.

Sawyer, Keith. 2011. "Conversation as Mechanism: Emergence in Creative Groups." In *Analytical Sociology and Social Mechanisms*, edited by Pierre Demeulenaere. Cambridge: Cambridge University Press, 78–98.

Saxe, Elizabeth Lee. 1979. "Fortune's Tangled Web: Trading Networks of English Entrepreneurs in Eastern India, 1657–1717." Ph.D. diss., Yale University.

Scammel, G. V. 1988. "The Pillars of Empire: Indigenous Assistance and the Survival of the 'Estado da India' c. 1600–1700." *Modern Asian Studies* 22(3): 473–89.

Schieffelin, Edward. 1981. "Evangelical Rhetoric and the Transformation of Traditional Culture in Papua New Guinea." *Comparative Studies in Society and History* 23(1): 150–56.

Schrikker. Alicia. 2007. *Dutch and British Colonial Intervention in Sri Lanka, 1780–1815: Expansion and Reform*. Vol. 7. Leiden: Brill.

Scott, James. 1972. *Comparative Political Corruption*. Englewood Cliffs, NJ: Prentice Hall.

Scott, William Robert. 1910. *The Constitution and Finance of English, Scottish and Irish Joint-Stock Companies to 1720*. Cambridge: Cambridge University Press.

Semmel, Bernard. 1970. *The Rise of Free Trade Imperialism: Classical Political Economy, the Empire of Free Trade and Imperialism 1750–1850*. Cambridge: Cambridge University Press.

Sennett, Richard. 1998. *The Corrosion of Character: The Personal Consequences of Work in the New Capitalism*. New York: Norton.

Sewell, William H., Jr. 2012. "The Irreducibility of Cultural Structures." *Sociologica* 1. http://www.sociologica.mulino.it/journal/article/index/Article/Journal:ARTICLE:540/Item/Journal:ARTICLE:540.

Sharma, Yogev. 1998. "A Life of Many Parts: Kasi Viranna—A Seventeenth Century South Indian Merchant Magnate." *Medieval History Journal* 1(2): 261–90.

Sheriff, Abdul. 1987. *Slaves, Spices & Ivory in Zanzibar: Integration of an East African Commercial Empire into the World Economy, 1770–1873*. London: Ohio University Press.

Sherman, Arnold A. 1976. "Pressure from Leadenhall: The East India Company Lobby, 1660–1678." *Business History Review* 50(3): 329–55.

Silva, Chandra Richard de. 1974. "The Portuguese East India Company 1628–1633." *Luso-Brazilian Review* 11(2): 152–205.

Silver, Morris. 1983. "Karl Polanyi and Markets in the Ancient Near East: The Challenge of the Evidence." *Journal of Economic History* 43(4): 795–829.

Simmel, Georg. 1971. *On Individuality and Social Forms: Selected Writings*. Edited by Donald N. Levine. Chicago: University of Chicago Press.

Simon, Herbert. 1997. *Administrative Behavior*. New York: Free Press.

Sinha, Arvind. 2002. *The Politics of Trade, Anglo-French Commerce on the Coromandel Coast, 1763–1793*. New Delhi: Manohar.

Smith, Adam. [1776] 1999. *The Wealth of Nations*. New York: Penguin.

Smith, David, and Douglas R. White. 1992. "Structure and Dynamics of the Global Economy: Network Analysis of International Trade 1965–1980." *Social Forces* 70(4): 857–93.

Sood, Gagan D. S. 2007. "'Correspondence Is Equal to Half a Meeting': The Composition and Comprehension of Letters in Eighteenth-century Islamic Eurasia." *Journal of the Economic and Social History of the Orient* 50: 172–214.

Sorenson, Olav. 2003. "Social Networks and Industrial Geography." *Journal of Evolutionary Economics*, 13: 513–27.

Sperber, Dan. 2011. "A Naturalistic Ontology for Mechanistic Explanations in the Social Sciences." In *Analytical Sociology and Social Mechanisms*, edited by Pierre Demeulenaere. Cambridge: Cambridge University Press, 64–77.

Stasavage, David. 2003. *Public Debt and the Birth of the Democratic State: France and Great Britain, 1688–1789*. Cambridge: Cambridge University Press.

———. 2011. *States of Credit: Size, Power, and the Development of European Polities*. Princeton, N.J.: Princeton University Press.

Staunton, George Leonhard. 1797. *An Authentic Account of an Embassy from the King of Great Britain to the Emperor of China*. London: G. Nicol.

Steensgaard, Niels. 1974. *The Asian Trade Revolution of the Seventeenth Century: The East India Companies and the Decline of the Caravan Trade*. Chicago: University of Chicago Press.

———. 1981. "The Companies as a Specific Institution in the History of European Expansion." In *Companies and Trade: Essays on Overseas Trading Companies during the Ancien Régime*, edited by Léonard Blussé and F. S. Gaastra. Leiden: Leiden University Press, 245–64.

———. 1987. "The Indian Ocean Network and the Emerging World-Economy, c. 1500–1750." In *The Indian Ocean: Explorations in History, Commerce, and Politics*, edited by Satish Chandra. New Delhi: Sage, 125–50.

———. 1990. "The Growth and Composition of the Long-Distance Trade of England and the Dutch Republic before 1750." In *The Rise of Merchant Empires:*

*Long-Distance Trade in the Early Modern World, 1350–1750*, edited by James D. Tracey. Cambridge: Cambridge University Press, 102–52.

———. 1996. "The Dutch East India Company as an Institutional Innovation." In *The Organization of Interoceanic Trade in European Expansion, 1450–1800*, edited by P. C. Emmer and Femme Gaastra. Aldershot: Variorum, 133–55.

Stein, Burton. 1990. "A Decade of Historical Efflorescence." *South Asia Research* 10(2): 125–38.

Stern, Philip J. 2011. *The Company-State: Corporate Sovereignty and the Early Modern Foundations of the British Empire in India*. Oxford: Oxford University Press.

Steuart, James. [1966] 1759. *Inquiry into the Principles of Political Economy*. Edinburgh: Oliver & Boyd.

Stevens, Robert. 1775. *The New and Complete Guide to the East-India Trade Containing a Table of East-India Interest, Tables to Reduce Rupees into Sterling, Tables of Bombay Maunds By the Late Mr. Robert Stevens*. London: D. Steel, S. Bladon, and S. Hooper.

Stinchcombe, Arthur L. 1995. *Sugar Island Slavery in the Age of Enlightenment: The Political Economy of the Caribbean World*. Princeton, N.J.: Princeton University Press.

Strathern, Andrew. 1971. *The Rope of Moka: Big-men and Ceremonial Exchange in Mount Hagen, New Guinea*. Cambridge: Cambridge University Press.

Studer, Roman. 2008. "India and the Great Divergence: Assessing the Efficiency of Grain Markets in Eighteenth- and Nineteenth-Century India." *Journal of Economic History* 68(2): 393–437.

Subrahmanyam, Sanjay. 1988. "Asian Trade and European Affluence? Coromandel, 1650–1740." *Modern Asian Studies* 22(1): 179–88.

———. 1990a. *The Political Economy of Commerce: Southern India, 1500–1650*. Cambridge: Cambridge University Press.

———. 1990b. "Rural Industry and Commercial Agriculture in Late Seventeenth-Century South-Eastern India." *Past & Present* 126: 76–114.

———. 1995. "Of Imarat and Tijarat: Asian Merchants and State Power in the Western Indian Ocean, 1400 to 1750." *Comparative Studies in Society and History* 37(4): 750–80.

Subramanian, Lakshmi. 1987. "Banias and the British: The Role of Indigenous Credit in the Process of Imperial Expansion in Western India in the Second Half of the Eighteenth Century." *Modern Asian Studies* 21(3): 473–510.

———, ed. 1999. *The French East India Company and the Trade of the Indian Ocean: A Collection of Essays by Indrani Ray*. Calcutta: Munshiram Manoharlal.

Supple, Barry. 1959. *Commercial Crisis and Change in England, 1600–1642: A Study in the Instability of a Mercantile Economy*. Cambridge: Cambridge University Press.

Sutherland, Lucy. 1952. *The East India Company in Eighteenth Century Politics*. London: Oxford University Press.

Sutton, Jean. 1981. *Lords of the East: The East India Company and Its Ships*. London: Conway Maritime Press.

————. 2010. *The East India Company's Maritime Service, 1746–1834: Masters of the Eastern Seas*. Suffolk: Boydell Press.

Tana, Li. 1998. "An Alternative Vietnam? The Nguyen Kingdom in the Seventeenth and Eighteenth Centuries." *Journal of Southeast Asian Studies* 29(1): 111–21.

Tate, H. R. 1944. "A Mediaeval Navigator: Vasco da Gama." *Journal of the Royal African Society* 43(171): 61–65.

Taylor, Jean Gelman. 1983. *The Social World of Batavia: European and Eurasian in Dutch Asia*. Madison: University of Wisconsin Press.

Tennent, James Emerson. 1860. *Ceylon: An Account of the Island, Physical, Historical, and Topographical, with Notices of Its Natural History, Antiquities and Productions*. London: Longman Green Longman and Roberts.

Thévenot, Jean de. [1684] 1976. *India in the Seventeenth Century, Being an Account of the Two Voyages to India by Ovington and Thevenot, to Which Is Added the Indian Travels of Careri*. Edited by J. P. Guha. New Delhi: Associated Pub. House.

Thomas, James H. 1999. *The East India Company and the Provinces in the Eighteenth Century: Portsmouth and the East India Company, 1700–1815*. Lewiston: Edwin Mellen Press.

Tracy, James D. 1990. *The Rise of Merchant Empires: Long-Distance Trade in the Early Modern World, 1350–1750*. Cambridge: Cambridge University Press.

Tripathi, Amales. 1956. *Trade and Finance in the Bengal Presidency, 1793–1833*. Bombay: Orient Longmans.

Udovitch, Abraham L. 1962. "At the Origins of the Western Commenda: Islam, Israel, Byzantium?" *Speculum* 37(2): 198–207.

Udy, Stanley H. 1959. *Organization of Work: A Comparative Analysis of Production among Nonindustrial Peoples*. New Haven, Conn.: HRAF Press.

Van Doosselaere, Quentin. 2009. *Commercial Agreements and Social Dynamics in Medieval Genoa*. Cambridge: Cambridge University Press.

Van Dyke, Paul Arthur. 2005. *The Canton Trade: Life and Enterprise on the China Coast, 1700–1845*. Hong Kong: Hong Kong University Press.

Van Goens, Ryckloff. 1932. *Selections from the Dutch Records of the Ceylon Government: Memoirs of Ryckloff Van Goens, 1752–1757*. Colombo: Ceylon Government Press.

Van Klaveren, Jacob. 2002. "Corruption as a Historical Phenomenon." In *Political Corruption: Concepts and Contexts*, 3rd ed., edited by Arnold J. Heidenheimer and Michael Johnston. New Brunswick, N.J.: Transaction, 83–94.

Van Leur, J. C. 1955. *Indonesian Trade and Society: Essays in Asian Social and Economic History*. The Hague: W. Van Hoeve.

Van Niel, Robert. 1988. "II. Dutch Views and Uses of British Policy in India around 1800." *Itinerario* 12(Special Issue 1): 17–32.

Van Veen, Ernst. 2001. "VOC Strategies in the Far East (1605–1640)." *Bulletin of Portuguese/Japanese Studies* 3: 85–105.

Vaughn, James M. 2009. "The Politics of Empire: Metropolitan Development and the Imperial Transformation of the British East India Company, 1675–1775." Ph.D. diss., University of Chicago, History Department.

Vermeulen, A.C.J. 1996. "The People on Board." In *The Organization of Inter-oceanic Trade in European Expansion, 1450–1800*, edited by P. C. Emmer and Femme Gaastra. Aldershot: Variorum, 321–50.

Villiers, John. 1990. "The Cash-Crop Economy and State Formation in the Spice Islands in the Fifteenth and Sixteenth Centuries." In *The Southeast Asian Port and Polity: Rise and Demise*, edited by J. Kathirithamby-Wells and John Villiers. Singapore: Singapore University Press, 83–105.

Walker, C. E. 1931. "The History of the Joint Stock Company." *Accounting Review* 6(2): 97–105.

Wallerstein, Immanuel Maurice. 1974. "The Rise and Demise of the Capitalist World System: Concepts for Comparative Analysis." *Comparative Studies in Society and History* 16: 387–415.

———. 1976. *The Modern World-System I: Capitalist Agriculture and the Origins of the European World-Economy in the Sixteenth Century*. New York: Academic Press.

———. 1980. *The Modern World-System II: Mercantilism and the Consolidation of the European World-Economy, 1600–1750*. New York: Academic Press.

———. 1983. "European Economic Development: A Comment on O'Brien." *Economic History Review* 36(4): 580–83.

———. 1986. "Incorporation of Indian Subcontinent into Capitalist World-Economy." *Economic and Political Weekly* 21(4): 28–39.

———. [1989] 2011. *The Modern World-System III: The Second Era of Great Expansion of the Capitalist World-Economy, 1730–1840s*. Berkeley, Los Angeles, London: University of California Press.

Warren, James Francis. 1981. *The Sulu Zone, 1768–1898: The Dynamics of External Trade, Slavery, and Ethnicity in the Transformation of a Southeast Asian Maritime State*. Singapore: Singapore University Press.

Washbrook, D. A. 1988. "Progress and Problems: South Asian Economic and Social History c.1720–1860." *Modern Asian Studies* 22(1): 57–96.

Watson, I. Bruce. 1980a. "Fortifications and the 'Idea' of Force in Early English East India Company Relations with India." *Past & Present* 88: 70–87.

———. 1980b. *Foundation for Empire: English Private Trade in India 1659–1760*. New Delhi: Vikas.

Watts, Duncan J. 1999. "Networks, Dynamics, and the Small-World Phenomenon." *American Journal of Sociology* 105(2): 493–527.

Weber, Max. 1978. *Economy and Society: An Outline of Interpretive Sociology*. Berkeley: University of California Press.

———. 1991. *From Max Weber: Essays in Sociology*. Edited by Hans Heinrich Gerth, C. Wright Mills, and Bryan S. Turner. London: Routledge.

Webster, Anthony. 1990. "The Political Economy of Trade Liberalization: The East India Company Charter Act of 1813." *Economic History Review* 43: 404–19.

———. 2007. *The Richest East India Merchant: The Life and Business of John Palmer of Calcutta, 1767–1836*. Suffolk: Boydell Press.

Wellington, Donald C. 2006. *French East India Companies: A Historical Account and Record of Trade*. Lanham, Md.: Hamilton.

White, Douglas, and Frank Harary. 2001. "The Cohesiveness of Blocks in Social Networks: Node Connectivity and Conditional Density." *Sociological Methodology* 31: 305–59.

White, Harrison C. 1992. *Identity and Control: A Structural Theory of Social Action*. Princeton, N.J.: Princeton University Press.

———. 2008. *Identity and Control: How Social Formations Emerge*. Princeton, N.J.: Princeton University Press.

Willan, T. S. 1953. "The Russia Company and Narva, 1558–81." *Slavonic and East European Review* 31(77): 405–19.

Williamson, Jeffrey G. 2006. "Globalization, Convergence, and History." *Journal of Economic History* 56(2): 277–306.

Wills, John E. 1993. "Review: Maritime Asia, 1500–1800: The Interactive Emergence of European Domination." *American Historical Review* 98(1): 83–105.

Wilson, Nicholas Hoover. 2012. "Economies, Moralities, and State Formations in British Colonial India." Ph.D. diss., University of California, Berkeley.

Winius, George D., and Marcus P. M. Vink. 1994. *The Merchant-Warrior Pacified: The VOC (The Dutch East India Company) and Its Changing Political Economy in India*. Delhi: Oxford University Press.

Winship, Christopher. 2009. In *The Oxford Handbook of Analytical Sociology*, edited by Peter Hedström and Peter Bearman. Oxford: Oxford University Press, 498–520.

Wolff, Robert S. 1998. "De Gama's Blundering: Trade Encounters in Africa and Asia during the European 'Age of Discovery,' 1450–1520." *History Teacher* 31: 297–318.

Wong, R. Bin. 1997. *China Transformed: Historical Change and the Limits of European Experience*. Ithaca, N.Y.: Cornell University Press.

Wright, Gabriel, and Herbert W. Gilbert. 1804. *A New Nautical Directory for the East-India and China Navigation*. London: W. Gilbert.

Yapp, M. E. 1986. "'The Brightest Jewel': The Origins of a Phrase." In *East India Company Studies: Papers Presented to Professor Sir Cyril Philips*, edited by Kenneth Ballhatchet and John Harrison. Hong Kong: Asian Research Service, 31–68.

Yarshater, Ehsan, ed. 1990. *Encyclopedia Iranica*. Vol. 4. London: Routledge.

Zelizer, Viviana. 2005. "Circuits within Capitalism." In *The Economic Sociology of Capitalism*, edited by Victor Nee and Richard Swedberg. Princeton, N.J.: Princeton University Press, 289–322.

# INDEX

_____